THE FRENCH
LEGAL SYSTEM

AUSTRALIA
The Law Book Company
Brisbane • Sydney • Melbourne • Perth

CANADA
Carswell
Ottawa • Toronto • Calgary • Montreal • Vancouver

AGENTS:
Steimatzky's Agency Ltd, Tel Aviv;
N.M. Tripathi (Private) Ltd, Bombay;
Eastern Law House (Private) Ltd, Calcutta;
M.P.P. House, Bangalore;
Universal Book Traders, Delhi;
Aditya Books, Delhi;
MacMillan Shuppan KK, Tokyo;
Pakistan Law House, Karachi, Lahore

THE FRENCH LEGAL SYSTEM

Second Edition

By

CHRISTIAN DADOMO
Maitrise en droit, D.E.A. (Strasbourg)
Lecturer in Law, University of the West of England, Bristol

and

SUSAN FARRAN
B.A. (Hons.), LL.B., LL.M. (Natal and Cantab.)
Principal Lecturer in Law, University of the West
of England, Bristol

LONDON • SWEET & MAXWELL • 1996

349.244

First Edition, 1993, by Christian Dadomo & Susan Farran

Published in 1996 by
Sweet & Maxwell Limited of
South Quay Plaza
183 Marsh Wall
London, E14 9FT

Computerset by P.B. Computer Typesetting, Pickering, N. Yorks
Printed in England by Clays Ltd, St Ives plc

No natural forests were destroyed to make this product:
only farmed timber was used and re-planted

ISBN 0 421 53970 4

**A CIP catalogue record for this book is available
from the British Library**

To Sean and Aileen
European citizens of tomorrow

Preface to Second Edition

The purpose of this book is to provide the reader — be they a practitioner, a law student, a litigant, or simply a non-lawyer — with an introduction to the fundamental structures and concepts of the French legal system. It does not seek to provide detailed information on specific areas of law such as contract or company law, nor to provide a step by step guide to following a case through the courts, but rather to familiarise the reader with sources of French law, the structure of the courts and professions, and the characteristics of the legal process, while at the same time indicating some of the main differences between the English legal system and the French.

Although the book is directed at the non-French reader, after much thought, it was decided to retain the French terminology, giving English translations or conceptual summaries either in the text, immediately afterwards, or in the footnotes. The difficulties and dangers of translation — particularly legal translation — were constantly with us. Moreover it is becoming apparent that legal terminology is being increasingly influenced by the shared language of the European Community. In many cases this is more strongly influenced by Civil Law systems than that of the English law. It is appreciated that some readers will be more familiar with the language of the European institutions than others, nevertheless it was decided that where applicable, the terminology used in this book should reflect this linguistic trend. Occasionally, it is not possible to render a French term in English, either because no satisfactory equivalent term or concept exists, or because any translation could be misleading.

We hope that this book will provide a starting point for all of those who would like to understand the French legal system better, and that it provides the necessary foundations for the study of more specific and substantive areas of law.

The absence of a general bibliography is a deliberate omission as most of the sources referred to are in French, and would be of little use to a non-French reader. However, references to French as well as English sources are made in footnotes throughout the book where relevant.

We are extremely grateful to Lord Slynn who graciously agreed to write the Foreword to the first edition of this book.

The second edition presents the law as at May 1 1995, taking into account changes made by the reforms of the Code of Criminal Procedure and, notably, the amendments to the Constitution. A number of changes have been made in terms of style and presentation, and we are most grateful to all of those who have taken the time and trouble to offer us constructive criticism and comment. We alone remain responsible for any errors and omissions which appear in this work.

Susan Farran
Christian Dadomo

May 1, 1995

Foreword

As we need increasingly to apply European Community law so we need increasingly to understand the principles upon which it is based. Many of the concepts and the procedures of European Community Law have been influenced substantially by French law and procedure. It is in consequence of practical value to know something about that law which has equally had a strong influence on the legal systems of some of the other Member States. The subject is also one of intrinsic interest — in its historical origins, its differences with the Common law system, in the structure of its courts, in the trial processes and in the organisation of the legal profession.

The structure both of the laws and of the courts in France seems to the outsider to be complex and there is much that is unfamiliar to a Common lawyer — divisions not just between civil and criminal law but between "ordinary" and "administrative," between the *juridiction de droit commun* and the *juridiction d'exception*. The powerful role of the *Conseil d'Etat*, the task of the *Tribunal des conflits* in ruling on disputes as to jurisdiction, the *Conseil Constitutionnel*, which decides whether legislation is within the constitution, have no equivalent in the United Kingdom. The authors explain all these differences. They show how the difficulties encountered by the French courts in recognising the supremacy of European Community Law, which have only been sorted out in the last few years, are due to the nature and concepts of the French system. It is right to comment that those difficulties are to be contrasted with the ready acceptance of the principle of the supremacy of Community law to be found in the European Communities Act 1973 and in a number of judgments in the House of Lords.

I find of considerable interest the very clear description of the various courts — who sits on the *tribunal d'instance* and the *tribunal de grande d'instance*, the *conseil de prud'hommes*, the social security and lands tribunals and what each of them does: what is the role of the pre-trial investigatory court (*juridiction d'instruction*), the *chambre d'accusation*, the *Parquet*. It is interesting to reflect how the *cour d'assises* differs from our own old Assize courts; how does the volume of cases dealt with by them compare with our work load in this country? What is the *Cour de Cassation* — how different is its jurisdiction from that of a court of appeal? What is the effect of merging the professions of *avocat* and *conseil de juridique*? How different is the *recours pour excès de pouvoir* from judicial review? What happens at a criminal trial and what are the judge's powers on sentencing? All these and many other matters are dealt with.

Apart from structural differences, this book brings out many of the conceptual differences between the Civil law and the Common law systems. It explains the obligation of the judge to decide a case before him, the breach of which is punishable as a criminal offence, the nature of judicial decisions which do not create binding precedents, the notion of "*jurisprudence constante*," the influence of "*la doctrine*" not as a source of law "but rather as an inspiration and influence."

I have recently often heard English lawyers talk of "public law" and "private law" as if the distinction had already been accepted here. There are, or course, now judgements where reference is made to "public law" but before we go too far down this path (abandoning the notion that there is "law" which is applied by one set of courts, even if in different ways, to public and private bodies) we should carefully consider the origins of the distinction in France and the problems which can arise. These are referred to in the introductory chapters of this book.

Our newspapers not infrequently refer to proceedings in the French courts — this book will provide a valuable means of understanding which court is concerned and what its powers are. The authors are right to keep the French names, giving literal translations where reasonably possible. There could be great confusion if the terms were simply translated and no French name given. Thus the *Haute Cour de Justice* has almost nothing to do with the High Court of Justice and simply to use the English expression might be misleading. Some of the phrases would be very difficult to translate and one has to see them in context. Thus "*droit de défense*" and the "*principe du contradictoire*" need to be · remembered as special concepts which are not fully explained by literal translations.

I find this a highly informative book; it is nonetheless very readable despite the considerable detail. Law students and practitioners should certainly read it unless they are absolutely committed to not seing beyond our shores. I believe that many who are not lawyers will also find it a book of considerable interest and usefulness.

Slynn of Hadley

Contents

2. Sources of law—*cont.*

3. The courts' structure   46

4. The legal profession   114

4. The legal profession—*cont.*

5. Judicial proceedings   160

5. Judicial proceedings—*cont.*

Table of Cases

xvii

Table of Statutes

Table of European, International and Foreign Legislation

Table of Codes

Table of Diagrams and Tabular Material

Grateful acknowledgment is made to the following for their permission to reproduce the statistics published in Chapter 3 of this book:—

— Le Rapport public 1991 du Conseil d'Etat — Collection Etudes et Documents — La Documentation Française — Paris 1992.

— Le Rapport 1994 de la Cour de Cassation — La
Documentation Française — Paris 1995.

— L'Annuaire statistique 1988–1992 de la Justice — La
Documentation Française — Paris 1995.

— L'Annuaire statistique 1989-1990 de la Justice — La
Documentation Française — Paris 1992.

Table of Abbreviations

A.J.D.A.	*Actualité Juridique de Droit Administratif*
Cass.	*Cour de Cassation*
Cass. Civ.	*Cour de Cassation, chambre civile*
Cass. Crim.	*Cour de Cassation, chambre criminelle*
C.C.	*Conseil Constitutionnel*
C.Civ.	*Code civil*
C.Com.	*Code de commerce*
C.E.	*Conseil d'Etat*
C.E. Ass.	*Conseil d'Etat, Assemblée plénière*
C.E. Sect.	*Conseil d'Etat, Section du contentieux*
C.G.I.	*Code générale des impôts*
C.Nat.	*Code de la nationalité*
C.O.J.	*Code de l'organisation judiciaire*
C.P.	*Code pénal*
C.P.C.	*Ancien Code de procédure civile*
C.P.P.	*Code de procédure pénale*
CTA	*Code des tribunaux administratifs et des cours administratives d'appel*
C.Trav.	*Code du travail*
D.	*Recueil Dalloz*
D. Chron.	*Recueil Dalloz, chronique*
D.S.	*Recueil Dalloz Sirey*
EDCE	*Etudes et Documents du Conseil d'Etat*
Gaz. Pal.	*Gazette du Palais*
GA	*Grands Arrêts de la jurisprudence administrative* (Long, Weil, Braibant, 9th. ed., 1990)
ICLQ	International and Comparative Law Quarterly
J.C.P.	*La Semaine Juridique (Jurisclasseur Périodique)*

JORF	*Journal Officiel de la République Française*
La.L.R.	Lousiana Law Review
Mich. L.R.	Michigan Law Review
M.L.R.	Modern Law Review
N.C.P.C.	*Nouveau Code de procédure civile*
Ord.	*Ordonnance*
R.D.C.C.	*Recueil des décisions du Conseil Constitutionnel*
R.D.P.	*Revue de Droit Public et de Science Politique*
Rec. Lebon	*Recueil Lebon (du Conseil d'Etat)*
R.F.D.A.	*Revue Française de Droit Administratif*
Rev. Prat. Dr. Soc.	*Revue Pratique de Droit Social*
R.S.	*Recueil Sirey*
T.A.	*Tribunal administratif*
T.C.	*Tribunal des conflits*

Chapter One
Introduction

1. HISTORICAL BACKGROUND

EARLY LEGAL INFLUENCE

One of the most important identifying features of French law, and one that distinguishes it most obviously from Common law, is that it is a Civil law system, historically influenced — to a greater or lesser extent depending on the subject area — in its structure and form by Roman law.

There were two phases of Roman law which were of significance for the development of French law: the original law of the Roman Empire, and the Roman law which was revived by intellectual legal study during the twelfth and subsequent centuries.

As part of the Roman Empire, France (Gaul) fell under the *jus gentium*.[1] For the greater part this body of law related to public and administrative law matters and private law issues were left to be determined by local laws. Nevertheless Roman law influenced French law in two ways. First, it became part of the local law and was absorbed into the national law, particularly in the South of France. Secondly, it was adopted either in preference to local law or because there was no local law (this was particularly so in the North, where German customary law prevented the wholesale reception of Roman law)[2].

The early Roman influence: the Corpus Juris Civilis of Justinian

By A.D. 476 the Western Roman Empire had collapsed and the most important Roman law influences emanated from the Eastern

---

[1] This was the law applicable to non-Roman citizens and applied throughout the Empire, while *jus civilis* was reserved for Roman citizens.
[2] Three-fifths of the country north of a line drawn parallel with the Loire, from the Gironde to Lake Geneva, was largely ruled by customary law (*droit coutumier*), the southern half by written law (*droit écrit*).

1

Roman Empire during the period of the Dominate (A.D. 285–565) with its centre at Byzantium. Foremost among these were the legal authorities compiled under the guidance of the Emperor Justinian between A.D. 527 and 560.[3] Justinian's compilations, were collectively known as the *Corpus Juris Civilis*,[4] and consisted of a collection of imperial legislation; the *Codex* (A.D. 534); a collection of the writings of "jurists"; the *Digest* (A.D. 533); a legal textbook; the *Institutes*;[5] and the *Novella*, which were collections of updated enactments compiled after A.D. 534. Justinian's work brought together in a concise form a number of different sources of Roman law and organised them in an accessible structure. For example, the compilation of the *Codex* provided an opportunity to exclude obsolete or contradictory legislation of previous emperors, while the Digest reflected the contemporary body of Roman law (*jus*), as developed by the edicts and statements of the *praetors*, and the writings and opinions of eminent jurists (*juris prudentes*/*juris consulti*).[6]

The importance of this achievement for French law, and indeed all Civil law systems, was that the *Corpus Juris Civilis* survived the Dark Ages between the seventh and tenth centuries, and emerged, via legal research in the universities of Italy, during the first half of the eleventh century (during the second phase of Roman law influence).

The laws of the Barbarians

The Eastern Roman Empire did not long survive Justinian. The infiltration of Germanic barbarian tribes such as the Visigoths, Ostrogoths and Lombards, first as legionaries and then as settlers,

---

[3] Roman law consisted of two major parts: *jus* which was the settled body of law developed during the classical period of jurisprudence under the Principate (27 B.C.–A.D. 285); and *leges* which was the legislation of the Emperors, who had the power to pass laws since the middle of the 2nd Century A.D.

[4] Originally known as the *Codex Repetiae Praelictionis*, the title *Corpus Juris Civilis* was coined in the 16th Century.

[5] Entitled the *Imperatoris Justiniani Institutiones*, this was modelled on the *Institutes* of Gaius, and was given the force of law.

[6] *e.g.* Gaius, Salvius Julianus, Papinian, Paul, Ulpian and Modestinus. It should be noted that there had been codes before Justinian, *e.g.* the *Codex Gregorianus* A.D. 291; *Codex Hermogenianus* A.D. 295; and the *Codex Theodosianus* A.D. 439.

had started in the fourth and fifth centuries A.D.[7] Just as the Romans had done, the invading barbarians adopted the idea of the "personality of laws", allowing people to be governed by their own private laws. Thus for a while Romans continued to live according to Roman law.[8] Nevertheless, there was a general deterioration in the administration of justice from the fifth century onwards as the Empire disintegrated. Attempts were made by various leaders to compile codes combining both Roman and barbarian laws.[9] The process was gradual but it led to a certain degree of Romanisation of customary laws, partly because Roman law was more sophisticated in terms of its scope and organisation, and also because it had been committed to writing and was therefore more ascertainable.[10] One of the effects of the barbarian codes was to replace the emphasis on national origin with that of regional or territorial origin, each territory striving to establish a common law.[11] This process came to a halt during the ninth and tenth centuries when economic depression and political disintegration occasioned by threatened invasions from a new wave of barbarians[12] plunged Europe into the Dark Ages, stifling commerce, legal development and learning.

It was not until the emergence of Otto the Great in A.D. 962 and the establishment of the Holy Roman Empire and the Carolingian Empire in France, together with the centralisation of

---

[7] e.g. S.W. Gaul and Spain had been overrun by the Visigoths in A.D. 412, N. Africa by the Vandals in A.D. 429, E. Gaul by the Burgundians in A.D. 413 and N. Gaul by the Franks. By A.D. 520 the whole of Gaul was under Frankish rule. See K.W. Ryan, *An Introduction to the Civil Law* (The Law Book Company of Australia, 1962), p. 5.

[8] In many respects there was no choice as barbarian law was rudimentary, and anyway the barbarians had no desire to destroy the Roman heritage, simply to gain a share of the benefits.

[9] The most important of these were the *Lex Romana Burgundiorum* (A.D. 500) passed by King Gundobad for the Romans, the *Edictum Theodorici* passed by Theodoric the Great, King of the Ostrogoths, for the Romans and the Ostrogoths, and the *Lex Romana Visigothorum/Breviarium Alaricianum* of Alaric II, King of the Visigoths, for the Roman population of S.W. Gaul and Spain, in A.D. 506.

[10] The Romanisation of law seems to have been strongest in the Visigothic and Burgundian Codes, and weakest in the Salic and Ripuarian Codes.

[11] For example the *Leges Visigothorum* (A.D. 654) applied to all the subjects of the King of the Visigoths whether they were of Roman or Germanic origin. Similarly the imperial statutes of the Carolingian Emperors — the *Capitularies* — applied to all subjects from about A.D. 800 onwards.

[12] These were the Norsemen, Saracens, Slavs and Magyars.

the Government of the Church in Rome, that order was once more restored and the barbarian invaders driven back.

The second phase of Roman law influence

The legal renaissance started in Italy, where trade with northern Europe and the East developed the commerce, industry and prosperity of the northern Italian towns which formed the politically powerful and influential Lombard League.[13] Schools for studying the native Lombard law[14] were established in Pavia, Mantua and Verona in the first half of the eleventh century. Then at the end of the century new schools arose focusing their study on Roman law and its use to improve native law. Called the *moderni*, these schools were established in Ravenna and Bologna, and their main texts were those of Justinian.

This revival of interest in Roman law rekindled the idea of law as a science. The method of study and exposition was the gloss,[15] whereby the works of Justinian were studied and annotated in order to present a clear, complete and comprehensible statement of Roman law.[16]

During the twelfth century the academic study of law moved to France, particularly to the universities of Montpellier and Toulouse, and it was from France that the next major school of juristic thinking had its origin. Known as the "Commentators",[17] these jurists sought to apply and adapt Roman law as explained by the Glossators, to the needs and conditions of medieval life, particularly with a view to establishing a unified system of law from the mixture of customary law, canon law, municipal law

---

[13] In 1176 the League defeated the Emperor, and much of the interest in law was fuelled by the political controversy between Popes and Emperors, both sides seeking legal justification for domination.

[14] This was the dominant law, Italy having been overrun by the Ostrogoths in A.D. 476 and in A.D. 489. It was briefly recaptured for Rome in A.D. 536, but then taken by the Lombards in A.D. 568.

[15] The method had been used at Pavia with Lombard law.

[16] Known as the "Glossators", these jurists used interlinear and marginal glosses, explanatory notes, commentaries, written analysis and internal comparisons to try and arrive at the true meaning and significance of Justinian's law. The main school was at Bologna between 1100 and 1250 and included among its ranks, Irnerius and Accursius — whose own gloss the *Glossa Ordinaria* became itself the main subject of study of latter glossators.

[17] The most famous of these were Cinus, Baldus and Bartolus. The latter's commentaries, written during the first half of the 12th Century, were the most influential.

and the law of the Empire.[18] This school was influential between 1200 and 1500.

The *Pays de droit coutumier* and the *Pays de droit écrit*

Customary law provided diversity in regional laws and in some areas of law resistance to the infiltration of Roman law. Although originally unwritten and ascertained only by way of a local public enquiry, customary law was gradually reduced to writing, first under the authority of local *seigneurs*,[19] and later under royal ordinance, for example the *Ordonnance de Montils-les-Tours* of Charles VII in 1453. It became an important source of written law with considerable influence later on the content of certain parts of the Napoleonic Code. Not only did customary law gradually form a body of written law, it also gave rise to written commentaries in the same way as the *Corpus Juris Civilis* had done, and this in turn enhanced its authority and reputation.[20]

France was divided into two legal areas, the *Pays du droit écrit* in the South, where Roman law had the greatest influence, and the *Pays du droit coutumier* in the North. In fact the distinction was not clear cut, largely because during the thirteenth century collections of customs were reduced to writing under the influence of Roman and canon law.[21] This process was not without its problems as the certainty of oral, customary law had to be established by an *enquête par turbe* (an oral investigation) among the local people.

---

[18] Italian law was extremely fragmented. There were remnants of the original Roman law, customary law with Germanic origins, and customary law with Italian feudal origins, ecclesiastical law, and a mixture of statutes and decrees. The aim was to create a synthesis of non-Roman and glossed-Roman law.

[19] These were known as *chartes des coutumes*.

[20] Commentaries on customary law were written by Du Moulin (1500–66), Domat (1625–1695), Loysel (1536–1617), Coquille (1523–1603), and Pothier (1699–1772) who gave a complete picture of private law — particularly obligations — at the time, providing valuable material for incorporation into the Code. The work of these commentaries created a common body of general principles of French customary law, despite differences in detail and regional diversification.

[21] This was also partly a result of the fragmentation of Frankish law following the replacement of the Carolingian Empire with that of the Capetians during the late 10th and 11th Centuries. Early compilations of customs were the *Livre de Justice et de Plet* of Orléans, the *Coutumes de Beauvaisis*, and the *Grand Coutumier de la Normandie* — which forms the basis of Channel Island law.

Gradually, however, much customary law became written law. Diversity of customary laws had given rise to conflicts of laws, a problem which was addressed by the *Coutume de Paris* which was published in 1510 under the influence of the *Parlement de Paris*, which had wide jurisdiction in the region of the *droit coutumier*.[22]

The effect of this was to strengthen customary law against Roman law, so that in France there was no wholesale reception of Roman law, but rather a gradual infiltration.

Ecclesiastical law

Ecclesiastical or canon law consisted initially of rules relating to the government and regulation of the established Church which were themselves based on the teachings of the Apostles as manifested in various writings.[23] Gradually collections of such writings were made and compiled together with the canons of various Church councils, papal decretals, commentaries on the scriptures, and rules relating to Church discipline. The twelfth century renaissance of legal learning included not only Roman law but also canon law, the latter being inspired by a need to modernise canon law to provide for a developing Church and also to reconcile conflicting and inconsistent canons. Indeed, the *Decretum Discordantium* — or *Concordia Canonum* — written in 1151 by Gratian, a Bolognese monk, became for canon lawyers the equivalent of the *Corpus Juris* of Justinian. The process continued under later Popes, culminating in the *Corpus Juris Canonici* created by Pope Gregory XIII in 1151. During the early Middle Ages canon law also infiltrated civil law and secured jurisdiction over certain persons and matters, either exclusively or concurrently with civil law, and this jurisdiction continued until the Revolution of 1789.

Other influences

Two subsidiary sources of French law which were to have an influence on its development were royal ordinances and judicial decisions. The most influential of the former were those

---

[22] With the exception of Normandy and Brittany.
[23] *e.g.* the Doctrine of the Twelve Apostles at the end of A.D. 1, and the Apostolic Constitutions which were influential between A.D. 260–325.

emanating from Louis XIV, from the seventeenth century onwards, concerned with commercial, procedural, and administrative law. Indeed, a number of the royal ordinances of the seventeenth and eighteenth centuries were to provide useful material for the process of codification, for example the 1667 *Ordonnance Civile*, the 1670 *Ordonnance Criminelle* and the 1731 *Ordonnance sur les Donations*.

As regards the latter source of law, the regional courts — *Parlements* — could issue *arrêts de règlements* which were binding on everyone within their jurisdiction. Judicial decisions either ruling on disputes concerning customs, or issued as decisions of a legislative nature, became for a time an important source of law, particularly those of the *Parlement de Paris*. Indeed, the strength of the *Parlements* was one of the aspects of the *Ancien Régime* that the Revolution sought to abolish.

CODIFICATION

The movement towards codification and the early codes

The principle that the complete body of law could be found in a code had been evident in the *Corpus Juris Civilis*, the barbarian codes, and the codes of customary law. During the sixteenth century there was strong support in favour of developing a common private law contained in a code for political and judicial purposes.[24] The *Coutume de Paris* had been reissued in 1580 and a number of commentaries supporting the idea of generally applicable and universal principles of law for the whole of France were produced during the sixteenth, seventeenth and eighteenth centuries.[25] The process of centralisation was also fostered by the more frequent use of royal ordinances.[26]

---

[24] Just as William the Conqueror had done in England, the French kings, assisted by powerful practising lawyers, were interested in the centralisation of justice in the royal courts and the development of a national "common" law.

[25] e.g. in 1689 Domat's *Les loix civiles dans leur ordre naturel*, and in 1720 Bourjon's *Le droit commun de la France et la coutume de Paris réduit en principes*.

[26] Originally these had been concerned with aspects relating to feudalism, the organisation of the courts and procedure. Important among these were: the 1566 *Ordonnance de Moulins*, the 1673 *Ordonnance du Commerce*, the 1681 *Code de la Marine* and the 1731 *Ordonnance des Donations*.

Besides practical considerations, codification was favoured by legal philosophers of the natural law school who maintained a belief in the existence of independent and autonomous principles of nature from which could be inferred a system of legal rules.

The *Droit Intermédiaire* and the background to the *Code Napoléon*

The period of the *Droit Intermédiaire* was between the first session of the *Assemblée Constituante* in 1789 and Napoleon's assumption of power in 1799. Contemptuous of both Roman law and customary law, the first thing that the revolutionary government did was to abolish all the institutions of the *Ancien Régime*; for example the absolute powers of monarchy, the *noblesse de robe* — *i.e.* the nobility, the clergy and the judiciary, and all the incidents of feudalism — the territorial division of land into provinces, the system of landholding, the court structure and the fiscal system.[27] In 1791 all feudal servitudes, all privileges of primogeniture and all distinctions relating to succession of property based on age or sex were abolished. In order to achieve equality in the distribution of estates, freedom of testation and donation were also abolished. The aim of the *Assemblée Constituante* was to establish a code of civil law which would be common to all.

In 1793 the *Convention Nationale* replaced the *Assemblée Constituante* but the philosophy of equality persisted. The power of the father (*patria potestas*) which had existed in the *Pays de droit écrit* was abolished, as were restraints on marriage and the differential status of legitimate and illegitimate children. Marriage became a civil contract with the possibility of divorce recognised.

In 1793 Cambacéres drafted the first national code of articles. When this was rejected because it was too complicated, he drafted the second in 1794. This was also rejected. In 1796 he laid the third draft before the legislative body of the *Directorat*, the *Conseil des Cinq-Cents*.

---

[27] The political philosophy of the Revolution, influenced by thinkers such as Diderot, Voltaire and Rousseau, was that all individuals should have equal rights, freedom of conscience, belief and economic activity.

In 1799 Napoleon Bonaparte took power. Originally appointed as the first *Consul* of a three-member *Consulat*, which had the power to propose legislation,[28] he became first *Consul* for life in 1802.

On July 13, 1800 (24 *thermidor an* VII) the *Consulat* had appointed a commission to draft a code.[29] The first draft was completed in four months, having been submitted to the Court of Appeal and the Court of Cassation, and was laid before the *Conseil d'Etat* — which Napoleon chaired — for discussion prior to going before the legislative body for acceptance or rejection.[30] Originally the idea had been to divide the code into sections and submit these for discussion by the *Tribunat*. However, Napoleon withdrew the whole project from the *Tribunat*'s scrutiny after it had rejected the first section. He then purged the membership of the *Tribunat* and recommended the procedure in 1803. Legislation was consolidated on March 21, 1804 and the *Code civil des Français* was promulgated.[31]

The impact of the Napoleonic Code and its contemporary significance

First, although the Code drew heavily on previous sources of law[32] it was intended that it should be interpreted in the light of

---

[28] During the *Consulat* period (1799–1804), draft legislation was prepared by the *Conseil d'Etat*, and then referred by the *Consuls* to the *Tribunat* for adoption or rejection. It then went before the *Corps Législatif* for adoption or rejection. It appears that only the *Consulat* actually had the power to initiate legislation.

[29] The members of the draft commission were Tronchet, President of the Court of Cassation, and representing the interests of the *droit coutumier*; Bigot de Préameneu, an advocate and member of the *Parlement de Paris*; Portalis, an administrative official, writer and public orator, who represented the interests of the *droit écrit*; and Maleville, a judge from the Court of Cassation.

[30] For detail on the procedure, see G. Marty & P. Raynaud, *Droit Civil: Introduction générale à l'étude du droit* (Sirey, Paris, 1972), Vol. 1, p. 128.

[31] The Code was enacted by the Act of 30 *ventose an* XII. Its title changed to the *Code Napoléon* in 1807, back to the *Code Civil* in 1816 following an ordinance of Louis XVIII, reverted to the *Code Napoléon* in 1852 under Napoleon III and then was finally renamed the *Code Civil* from 1870 during the Third Republic.

[32] For example the private law commentaries of Pothier, the collections of customs on property and succession, the *Corpus Juris Canonici* concerning marriage, royal ordinances on wills and gifts, and the ordinances prepared by Colbert concerning civil procedure and commercial transactions. See also G. Marty & P. Raynaud, *op. cit.* p. 132.

its own provisions and definitions.[33] Neither the content of the Code nor the idea of codification itself marked a total break with the past. However, as a source of law the Code became supereminent, replacing the courts and the king with a concise body of rules and principles which, theoretically at least, had been determined by the law-making function of the representative assembly of the people, thus reflecting a new relationship between legislators and those governed by the law.[34] The *Parlements* abolished during the Revolution, were replaced by a Supreme Court centralised in Paris and from 1810 onwards judges were required to give reasons for their decisions.[35]

Secondly, Napoleon's codification process was to have a wide impact on the rest of Europe, as a consequence of French political and military aggrandisement, with the result that a number of countries came to share a common legal heritage, not only of Roman law, but of the French Codes which were either imposed on them as a result of conquest, voluntarily adopted, or used as models for codes of their own.[36] This resulted in a geographical and conceptual distinction between codified and uncodified systems of law, differentiating even more clearly between Common law systems and Civil law systems.[37]

The codes have not remained unchallenged by time. On its centenary demands for reform were made, on the grounds that the provisions of the *Code civil* no longer reflected the positive law of France, and that the liberal and individualistic philosophy which had inspired it was in conflict with the more socialist

---

[33] The Act promulgating the Code and consolidating 36 previously separate statutes into the Code stated: "from the day when these laws come into force, the laws of Rome, the *ordonnances*, the general and local *coutumes*, the statutes, the regulations, cease to have the force of general or particular law in the matters which are the subject matter of the said laws composing the present Code". See M.S. Amos & F.P. Walton, *An Introduction to French Law* (Oxford University Press, 3rd ed., 1967), p. 6, n. 1.

[34] See K. Zweigert & H. Kötz, *An Introduction to Comparative Law* (Clarendon Press, Oxford, 1977), pp. 78–85.

[35] See art. 7 of the Act of April 20, 1810. Failure to comply with any of the procedural requirements concerning the number of judges, attendance at all hearings or publicity of the judgment, rendered the decision void.

[36] For example, it was imposed on Belgium, Luxembourg, Poland, parts of Italy and Egypt; adopted in Westphalia, Hanover, the grand duchies of Baden, Frankfurt and Nassau, and parts of Switzerland; and used as a model in Greece, Spain, the Netherlands, Quebec, parts of South America, Japan and Turkey.

[37] Nevertheless codes are found in common law systems, *e.g.* in India and California, and it can be argued that codification itself is not the distinguishing feature but the ideology that surrounds it. See J.H. Merryman, *The Civil Law Tradition* (Stanford University Press, 1985), p. 26.

thinking of the early twentieth century.[38] Moreover a new, more scientific model had emerged with the promulgation of the German Civil Code in 1900. Consequently an extra-parliamentary commission was appointed in 1904 to draft new provisions relating to the law of obligations. Its proposals were published in 1926 but nothing came of its work. Similarly demands for reform were made on the demise of the Vichy Government and the liberation of France in 1944. The following year a commission of 12 was created by a *décret* of June 7, 1945. Again no new code emerged, although some of the commission's work found its way into amendments of certain areas of the Code.[39] Thus, reform of the Civil Code has been piecemeal, retaining for the greater part the original numbering of the articles and incorporating by reference statutes passed subsequently. To date reforms have been made particularly in the areas of family law, matrimonial regimes and co-ownership.[40] More recently demands have been made for reform in the area of consumer law and credit sales. Some of the codes have been replaced, for example the 1806 Code of Civil Procedure was replaced in 1975, and the 1808 Code of Criminal Procedure replaced in 1959 and, more recently, reformed by Act No. 93–2 of January 4, 1993 (January 5, 1993: [1993] *JORF* 215 *et seq.*) and amended by Act No. 92–1336 of December 16, 1992 (December 23, 1992: [1992] *JORF*) as a result of the coming into force of the four Acts of Parliament reforming the Criminal Code which were adopted on July 22, 1992 (Nos. 92–683—92–686). The work of review and reform is a continuing one, nevertheless the impact of the Napoleonic Codes remains a significant and fundamental influence in French law.

2. THE FRENCH CONCEPTION OF LAW

LAW, MORALS AND SOCIAL STRUCTURE

In France, as in other western countries, law is seen as having an autonomous and vital role in society, separate from religion

---

[38] See F. Terré, *Introduction générale au droit* (Dalloz, Paris, 2nd ed., 1994), p. 64.

[39] Terré suggests that the reluctance to publish a totally new code was due to the rapid changes taking place at the time in so many aspects of life, *e.g.* social, economic, family, political, and international; *op. cit.* p. 62.

[40] For example by the Acts of December 14, 1964 (minority, guardianship and emancipation); July 13, 1965 (matrimonial regimes); July 11, 1966 (adoption); and June 4, 1970 (parental authority).

and politics. However, unlike the English, the French do not see the law primarily as a means of settling disputes or of restoring the peace, but adopt a rather more conceptual and abstract approach to the law, preferring to see it in terms of fundamental principles rather than a means of providing remedies for specific cases.[41] The reason for the difference in perspective is attributable to the difference in the historical development of the law, particularly the structural influence of Roman law, the conceptual role of the universities, and the diminished influence of the judges after the Revolution. Differences in the administration of justice were also significant. In England, the royal courts established after the conquest only had jurisdiction in exceptional cases — the county or hundred courts retaining their traditional jurisdiction. The administration of justice was therefore developed on a case-by-case basis with legal rules being closely connected to the facts of a particular case and not systematically. In France however, between the thirteenth and sixteenth centuries, reforms were introduced whereby an officer appointed by the king was in charge of each traditional court, and the procedural system was strongly based on a system of rational proof. Unlike the situation in England, procedure was not allowed to hamper the application of the rules of substance, and the task of judges and lawyers was to be first and foremost jurists, rather than proceduralists.[42]

Furthermore, the French conception of law is broader than that of England, encompassing political science and morality. Thus it is not just the preserve of lawyers and the courts, but permeates and concerns the whole of society. Law is not seen as being isolated from other intellectual disciplines but encompasses the study of political, social and economic sciences and public administration, and focuses on the rights and duties recognised in society according to an ideal of justice. Because each individual is recognised as having rights, the law has an important educative role to play in society. Emphasis is therefore placed on the importance of the rule of law, the safeguards of

---

[41] See B. Nicholas in his preface to D. Harris & D. Tallon, *Contract Law Today: Anglo-French Comparisons* (Clarendon Press, Oxford, 1989), p. 8; and R. David, *English Law and French Law* (Stevens and Sons, London, 1980), p. 4, who suggests that the basic axiom of the common law has always been "remedies precede rights".

[42] See R. David, *op. cit.* pp. 1–26.

individual rights and the accessibility of the law to non-lawyers. Revolution, a written constitution, codification and the anonymity of French judges have all helped towards this.

Nevertheless it may be argued that there is a distinction between the non-jurist's perception of the law and that of the jurist. For the former, law is synonymous with the idea of justice, the aim of which is to achieve a certain political, economic, and socially desirable order. The essence of law therefore lies in the general ideas it inspires, not in the technical rules by which it achieves these ends. The latter, more like their English counterparts, primarily see law as a body of rules of procedure and remedies which form the machinery of justice as administered by the courts, rather than statements of general principles and rules of ideal conduct.[43]

Although the French conception of law remains different from that of English law, today many of the distinctive characteristics of common law and civil law have been modified by legal evolution.[44]

THE CONCEPT OF *RÈGLE DE DROIT*

The French concept of *règle juridique* is not synonymous with the English idea of legal rule. In English law, legal rules are formulated by judges when adjudicating disputes and applied to specific, concrete situations. Where a distinguishable case arises a different legal rule may be applicable, thus making it more difficult for a systematic body of legal rules to emerge — although text-book writers endeavour to give form to this jumble of legal rules. In France, however, where the law is formulated by jurists and academics and finds expression through the legislator or the development of doctrine by the commentators, the approach is somewhat different. Rather than proceeding on a casuistic basis, the law seeks to establish general principles before considering specific cases. Thus the *règle de droit* exists at a more abstract and general level, which is superior to, and

---

[43] See R. David, *Les Systèmes de Droit Contemporains: le droit Français*: 1 (L.G.D.J., Paris, 1960), p. 66.

[44] For example the abolition of forms of action, and the merger of law and equity, in English law, together with increasing emphasis on statute law; and in France the development of codified law through the decisions of the courts, and the modification of the idea of absolute, subjective rights.

precedes, solutions awarded in specific cases. For the French, therefore, the English notion of legal rule is seen as emerging from the application of the law to a specific set of facts, while the *règle de droit* may be more closely compared to the English notion of general principles of law, which as such are rarely expressed by the legislator or judge, but find their place in legal text-books.

This distinction is not only of linguistic and theoretical importance, but also has practical consequences. First, French legislation is less detailed, leaving wide discretion to the judge who must refer to the general *règle de droit* to solve the case before him, and to fulfil his statutory duty under article 4 of the *Code civil*, whereby he is forbidden to refuse to apply the law on the grounds of the silence or ambiguity of the legislator. Because the judge's solution to a particular case will not be regarded as formulating a legal rule — indeed he is expressly forbidden from doing so by the *Code civil* — the *règle de droit* remains unaffected and may be applied differently in subsequent cases even if the facts are similar.

Following from this, a second consequence is that in France, as will be seen, the decisions of the courts are regarded in a somewhat different light from those in England, where failure to follow the precedent set by a previous decision can jeopardise the certainty of legal rules. In France the rejection or criticism of a previous decision, although it may cause slight uncertainty in predicting the outcome of individual cases, does not jeopardise the *règle de droit* because these are above specific solutions to cases. It is only when the *règle de droit* is itself questioned that the law needs reconsideration, and this is a matter for the legislator. Thus in French law, the role of precedent is less important for the development of legal rules and there is greater flexibility in the application of the *règles de droit*, which of course, has been necessary from time to time to keep the application of the Code up to date. Similarly, legal writers do not hesitate to challenge and criticise decisions of the courts and the particular application of a *règle de droit*.

The English law notion of a legal principle — *principe juridique* — may be described either as a *règle de droit* having emphasised importance, or a fundamental principle giving rise to a number of subsidiary *règles de droit*.[45]

---

[45] See R. David, *op. cit.* p. 71.

A third consequence of the difference in perception is that
what might be regarded as questions of law in English law are
simply regarded as questions of fact in French law, influencing in
turn matters which may be brought before the Court of
Cassation and those which may not.[46] Whereas in England there
may be a tendency to regard those questions brought before the
Court as raising questions of law, in France it is the legislator
who expounds the law and the judge who applies pre-established
principles to the facts before him.

While it is necessary to be aware of the differences in
perception between the two systems as regards the meaning and
role of legal rules, the difference should not be overemphasised.
Increasingly legislators in France are called upon to be more
specific in drafting laws, and in certain legal areas detailed
provisions are included and any liberal interpretation by the
courts is severely restricted — for example in criminal and fiscal
law. There have been a number of critics of the broad and
general terminology of the Civil Code, and although departures
from previous decisions may be made more easily in French law,
they are not made lightly.

RÈGLES DE DROIT IMPÉRATIVE ET SUPPLÉTIVE

French law distinguishes between mandatory or obligatory
rules, and supplementary or non-obligatory ones, depending on
the circumstances in which the rule is applied. Whereas there
are some rules which can be modified or specifically excluded
by the parties, there are others which cannot be departed from.
The former are the *règles de droit supplétives*, while the latter
are the *règles de droit impératives*. Where the legislator intends
the rules of a law to be *impérative* it will generally include
phraseology such as "notwithstanding anything to the contrary";
whereas a *supplétive* rule will be indicated by terms such as
"subject to any agreement or expression to the contrary". The
distinction only applies to private law. In public law all rules are
impératives. As a result there has sometimes been confusion
between the terms "rules of public law" and "imperative rules of
law". This has been aggravated by the increasing encroachment
of public law rules into the private law arena (discussed below).

---

[46] The issue is of course relevant in English law as regards what may or may not
be brought to the attention of a jury.

Nevertheless the distinction remains, and the main task facing the French jurist is to determine first whether the rules of law are *impératives* or *supplétives* and whether therefore the parties may in fact derogate voluntarily from them and secondly, whether in any given instance they have attempted or intended to do so. This necessitates interpreting the applicable law, considering the circumstances surrounding the transaction — including custom and conventions — and taking into account the expressions of intention in the specific instance. While the courts seek to uphold the right of individuals to determine their own legal relations, they will not recognise as valid any agreement that is contrary to public policy (article 6 *C.Civ.*).

3. Classification of laws

The Background to the Classification of Laws

One of the major tasks of the schools of law that emerged following the renaissance of legal learning in the twelfth century, was the systematisation of law. The purpose for doing this was not only to find the law more easily, but also to determine whether different approaches to different legal rules were required depending on their area of application. Roman law had distinguished between those legal institutions which were orientated to matters of public interest and those which were of private interest. This distinction between private law and public law was assimilated into Civil law.[47] French law, relying on the distinction made by Montesquieu — who differentiated between *droit politique* and *droit civil*[48] — consists of public law, which is that pertaining to the relationships between the Government and the governed, and private law, which pertains to those matters arising among individual citizens.

The distinction is not only important from a theoretical point of view, but has practical consequences relating both to the

---

[47] The distinction in Roman law was made by Ulpian in the 3rd century A.D. (Digest 1.2.1.1.) who stated *"publicum jus est, quod as status rei Romanae spectat; privatum, quod ad singulorum utilitatem"*.

[48] For Montesquieu public law was *"les lois dans le rapport qu'ont ceux qui gouvernent avec ceux qui sont gouvernés"*; while private law was *"les lois dans le rapport que tous les citoyens ont entre eux"*.

Diagram 1.1 **The Main Branches of French Public Law**

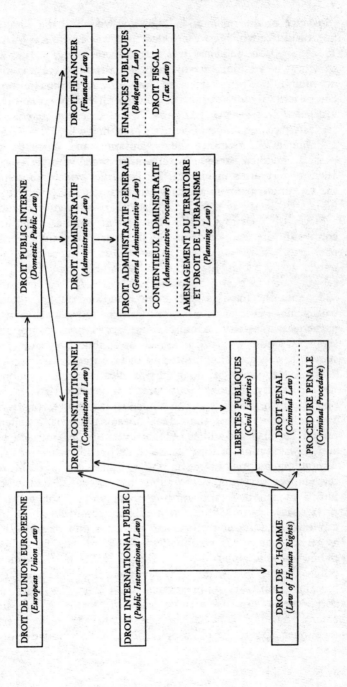

substance of the rights and duties involved, and the administration of justice which governs them. In terms of the Act of August 16–24, 1790, the judiciary was barred from ruling on the validity or otherwise of administrative acts. As a result there was initially no judicial body to review the acts of the administration, this being left to the executive power. Gradually however, the *Conseil d'Etat* became recognised as an independent court with separate jurisdiction (see Chapter Three, below).

Public law determines the organisation and scope of public powers and their exercise in relation to those who are governed. Such powers often include certain privileges which are unique to the Government or its agents — for example the power to make unilateral decisions concerning rules or regulations, and the exercise of executory action consequent to these. Public law confers on the State or its organs the power to grant government contracts, award concessions, control markets, etc. Moreover public law enables the State to do things which individuals cannot, such as expropriate land or services for public amenities and utilities. Even where the State or public authorities participate in legal transactions which individuals may also participate in — for example in the acquisition of property — the transaction will be governed by public law and may be subject to specific, often protective or favourable, legal regimes.

While the power of the State was weak the role of public law was relatively minimal compared to private law, and the philosophy of the Revolution to reduce the power of the State, and enhance that of individuals meant that for a long time private law had pre-eminence. However, the growth of the State and its institutions during the twentieth century has seen a corresponding increase in the importance of public law. Moreover the number of public corporations has multiplied and expanded into a range of sectors which were previously the preserve of private law bodies, for example the commercial, industrial, economic and social sectors, and the provision of services such as gas, electricity and communications. Where this has happened, public law still applies if one of the parties to the transaction is a public body, but many private law rules and practices are creeping into the administration of public law, and public corporations are assimilating the characteristics of private enterprises. The converse is true of private law, where, as mentioned above, the philosophy of unbridled individualism has been moderated by considerations of social welfare, public order, and greater interference in private law matters by the State.[49]

THE MAJOR AREAS OF PUBLIC AND PRIVATE LAW

The major areas of public law are: constitutional law — relating to the rules governing the form of the State, the constitution of the government and the organisation of public powers; administrative law — which determines the organisation of public bodies, the administrative structure of the State itself, including local government, *i.e.* in France the *régions*, *départements* and *communes*; the exercise of delegated power, and the operating and control of the public services and their relationship with individuals; financial law — relating to public finance; and criminal law — which establishes and governs the right of the State to punish individuals through those organs created under criminal procedure. As regards the latter it should be noted that criminal law includes some aspects which overlap with private law, for example it protects individuals' lives, reputations, property, etc., and in some senses could be regarded as the ultimate sanction of private law.[50] Also in French law it is possible to bring a civil law action simultaneously with a criminal one (see Chapter Five, below).

As indicated above, private law consists of those rules and institutions governing the relations between individuals. This includes private — as opposed to public — organisations such as companies and associations. The main branch of private law is civil law as found in the Civil Code, which has as its object the regulation of private relations imposing reciprocal obligations and rights. Thus it is concerned with questions relating to legal and civil status, the acquisition and determination of rights and obligations, and the sanctions available for upholding or enforcing these — as set out in the law relating to civil procedure or *droit judiciaire privé*.

During the past century certain branches of law have developed from the civil law acquiring their own autonomy, so that today civil law could more accurately be described as that branch of the law which governs private relations excluding those which are specifically commercial, industrial, social or

---

[49] See G. Marty & P. Raynaud who suggest that public law has invaded private law precipitating a crisis in both, *op. cit.* p. 67.

[50] See F. Terré, *op. cit.* p. 67.

agricultural, although many of these have influenced the body of civil law that remains.

Commercial law — *droit des affaires* or *droit commercial* — was treated as a distinct branch of private law early on. In 1673 Colbert drafted a Code of Commercial Law; in 1681 maritime commercial law was the subject of a special *Ordonnance*, and in 1807 the Code of Commerce was promulgated. Historically commercial law has been defined in different ways, being regarded subjectively as the law relating to those who conducted themselves as traders or merchants and had the *"qualité de commerçant"*, and objectively if the transaction was regarded as a commercial transaction, or a combination of both. Today commercial law may be classified under the broad category of business law — *droit des affaires* — which also includes tax, aspects of criminal law, accounting, employment, finance, economics, and administrative law; or under the separate headings of law that have developed from it, such as maritime law, transport law, insurance law, industrial property law, and banking law.

A further body of law which has developed from the ordinary civil law — particularly the law of contract — is employment, or labour law. Amalgamating the rules of law relating to individual and collective agreements between employers and employees, this branch of law developed considerably towards the end of the nineteenth and the beginning of the twentieth centuries with the victories of trade unions and the socialist movement.

HYBRID AND INDETERMINATE AREAS OF LAW

There have, from the outset, been areas of law which do not easily fall under either private law or public law. These are the law of civil procedure and that of private international law.

Civil procedure — *droit judiciaire privé* — is the body of rules governing the administration of civil law, and controls the process whereby parties to a dispute may have their rights recognised and remedies awarded. As such civil procedure includes aspects which fall into public law, for example the organisation and functioning of the courts, and aspects of private law, particularly the *locus standi* of the plaintiff to seek a remedy. Consequently civil procedure is viewed as being a collection of heterogeneous rules.

Similarly international private law is seen as combining aspects of both divisions of law. Questions relating to issues of

Diagram 1.2 **The Main Branches of French Private Law**

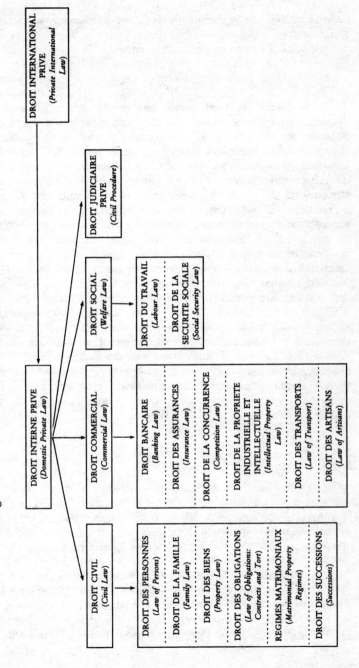

nationality and the rights of aliens is the domain of public law, while matters relevant to civil law, particularly issues arising under conflicts of law, are private in nature.

PROCEDURAL ASPECTS OF THE DIVISION

The distinction between public and private law is reflected in the administration of justice affecting individuals and the State. Because of the special legal regimes, powers and privileges afforded to the State and its organs under public law, litigation involving public authorities or public servants is heard by specialist administrative courts such as the *tribunaux administratifs*, the *cours administratives d'appel* and the *Conseil d'Etat* (see Chapter Three, below), with their own rules and procedures. In order to decide whether a matter is to go before the administrative courts or the private law courts, *i.e.* whether it is a matter of public or private law, judicial machinery in the form of the *tribunal des conflits* exists to determine questions of conflict, so that the court having correct jurisdiction may hear the matter. Moreover, in 1873 the long-held belief that the administration could not be judged by the principles applicable to individuals which had been established in the Code, was confirmed by the decision of the *tribunal des conflits* in the *Blanco* case. Further, in 1889 the *Conseil d'Etat* held that it had general power to review administrative acts without the need for special statutory powers. Thus the main body of public law developed over the past century has been that developed by the *Conseil d'Etat* in its review of administrative — rather than constitutional — law.

SIGNIFICANCE OF THE CLASSIFICATION

There have been a number of criticisms of the distinction made between public and private law. First, that the dividing line is imprecise and unable to adapt to the complexity and diversity of contemporary social and commercial transactions, with the consequence that a growing number of indeterminate areas arise, leading to increasing problems of determining jurisdiction.

Secondly, that the distinction between the individual and the State is false because the aims of both public law and private law should be to establish rules of law directed at the general interests of society. Thus private law, no less than public law, has to take into account the interests of individuals and the needs of society in general. This is reflected in the increasing incursion of imperative rules into private law (mentioned above), and the growing number of constraints being imposed on public law and the exercise of administrative powers.

There is also the view that as the public sector has expanded into industrial and economic activities which are characterised by private law rules, State organs ought to be subject to private law and not benefit from the special regimes of public law.

Nevertheless the distinction remains, perhaps primarily because the administration of government and matters falling within the public domain are regulated by rules and subject to jurisdictions which are different from those applicable to private individuals.

Also, it can be argued that differences other than the procedural consequences persist. The aim of public law is to fulfil the collective interests of the nation through the organisation of its government and the management of its institutions and public services, whereas that of private law is to ensure the maximum fulfilment of individuals' interests. Further, despite the encroachment of *impérative* rules into private law, the latter remains an area of law in which much is left to the individual wishes of the parties and, for the greater part, rules are suppletive, with individuals being free to depart from them in order to best achieve their own purposes. Moreover it remains the case that while the individual, private law plaintiff can seek the assistance of the courts if the law is unclear or unknown, the sanction of public law is more difficult to obtain, as the State is reluctant to condemn itself.[51]

---

[51] See F. Terré, *op. cit.* pp. 70 *et seq.*

Chapter Two
Sources of law

1. CODIFICATION[1]

The idea of collecting together a number of laws relevant to certain areas of law and arranging them in a structured whole, referred to as a code, pre-dates the Napoleonic period of codification.[2] Nor is the technique of codification unique to Civil law countries,[3] a number of codes having been drafted and compiled in Common law countries.[4] However, the distinction between the Civil law perception of codification and that to be found in Common law countries is the underlying ideology of the code. The aim of the Napoleonic codification was to repeal all existing and previous law, and to establish a new legal order which reflected the idea of the unified nation-state and could meet the needs of the new society and new government. The ideology of the codes reflected the philosophical belief in the law of reason. In reality, of course, as indicated in Chapter One, the codes contained much of the existing law drawn from a range of sources, and many of the more radical ideas of the *Droit Intermédiaire* were abandoned. Given the composition of the commission drafting the Code, and the influence of the *bourgeoisie* in achieving the ends of the Revolution, this was not surprising.[5]

---

[1] There is considerable academic discussion as to what exactly is meant by this term, see *e.g.* F. Lawson, *Many Laws Vol. IV: Selected essays* (European Studies in Law, Amsterdam, 1977), Vol. 1; and A.N. Yiannopoulus, *Civil Law in the Modern World* (1965). Even in France a distinction is made between classic codification and administrative codification. See F. Terré, *Introduction générale au droit* (Dalloz, Paris, 2nd ed., 1994), pp. 319–323.

[2] For example one of the earliest codes was that of Hammu-rabi, King of Babylon, dated around 2000 B.C.

[3] See J. Merryman, *The Civil Law Tradition* (Stanford University Press, 1969), pp. 27 *et seq.*

[4] For example India, Canada, and certain states of America.

[5] See *e.g.* the comments of K. Zweigert & H. Kötz, *An Introduction to Comparative Law* (Clarendon Press, Oxford, 1987), Vol. 1, pp. 87 *et seq.*

THE CODE CIVIL

The background to the Code, and the history of its passage has already been referred to in Chapter One. Suffice it to say that the Code itself has never contained all the law relating to that area of private law known as civil law, and that a number of written laws exist outside the Code, whose status is neither enlarged nor diminished because they have not been incorporated into the Code.[6] Moreover, from the outset, the compressed legislative style of the Code gave the courts scope to interpret its provisions so as to make the law applicable to unforeseen individual cases and to changes in the circumstances of society, which the legislators could not, and did not attempt to, envisage. Thus the Code sets out general principles and maxims of the law, leaving it to the judge and legislator to apply them or supplement these as necessary. The style is therefore, quite different from the more detailed provisions of the German Civil Code and others based on that model, and has sometimes been criticised for being too terse.[7]

The subject matter of the Code is divided into an introductory part and three books, subdivided in turn into articles. The first book is concerned with the law of persons (articles 7 to 515), the second (articles 516 to 710) with definitions and rights in property and the third (articles 711 to 2281) — which is twice as long as the other two books — deals with the acquisition of property, and includes such matters as succession, contract, delict, matrimonial property law, unjust-enrichment, etc. The arrangement and location of the subject matter of the Code frequently causes problems for non-French lawyers, who may expect to find related matters placed more logically together.[8]

THE OTHER NAPOLEONIC CODES

Four other Codes were passed following the *Code civil*. These were the *Code de procédure civile* (Code of Civil Procedure) in 1806, the *Code de commerce* (Commercial Code) in 1807, the *Code pénal* (Criminal Code), and the *Code d'instruction*

---

[6] See H. Roland & L. Boyer, *Introduction au droit* (Litec, Paris, 1991), p. 184.

[7] It should be noted that not only did the German Civil Code appear much later historically, but was influenced by a different philosophy, that of the German Pandectist School. See H. Kötz, (1987) 50 M.L.R. 1.

[8] Compare for example the views of K. Zweigert & H. Kötz, *op. cit.* pp. 94–95, and F. Terré, *op. cit.* p. 56.

criminelle (Code of Criminal Procedure) in 1810. Only the *Code civil* was ever known as the *Code Napoléon*, although all of them fall under the period and impetus of Napoleonic codification. Clearly, however, much law remained which was not codified, and remains so to this day.

MODERN CODES

The twentieth century has seen an abundance of new codes such as the *Code rural* (Rural Code), the *Code du travail* (Labour Code), *Code électoral* (Electoral Code), the *Code de la sécurité sociale* (Social Security Code).[9] Attempts have also been made to consolidate certain branches of the law, for example public health, customs, broadcasting, etc., and elsewhere summaries of the law have been made, but in either case it has been questioned whether such efforts can properly be called codes,[10] because their purpose is to consolidate and regroup a number of existing laws and regulations rather than to modify the law.[11] This era of codification, which has been extensive in terms of scope, time, and diversity of legal sources, has had two phases. The first was initiated in 1948, resulting in a number of codes in the 1950s, 1960s and 1970s. The second started in 1989 with the appointment of a new commission — by the *décret* of September 12, 1989.

The task of this second commission was slightly different in that it was to concentrate on the simplification and clarification of the law. Post-war legal development has therefore enabled a number of substantive changes to be introduced under the guise of administrative codification rather than through the usual procedure of legislative enactment.[12]

LEGISLATION

For a long time the Napoleonic Codes remained the most important source of law subject to very few amendments.

---

[9] For a detailed list see G. Marty & P. Raynaud, *Droit civil: Introduction générale à l'étude du droit* (Sirey, Paris, 1972), Vol. 1, p. 139–140.

[10] See R. David, *English Law and French Law* (Stevens, London, 1980), p. 18.

[11] This purpose is reflected in the *décret* of May 10, 1948 which initiated the process. See F. Terré, *op. cit.* p. 321.

[12] It has been suggested that this was the case with the *Codes des douanes* (Customs Code), and that relating to fiscal procedures. See M. Prelle: [1990] 2 Gaz. Pal. 622.

Gradually however, particularly during the latter part of the nineteenth and the beginning of the twentieth centuries, laws passed by Parliament became increasingly necessary to deal with the social, economic, political and industrial changes taking place. These consisted either of those passed by the legislature during times of peace, the *lois*; or those passed by the executive in times of crisis or war, in the form of *ordonnances* or *décrets*, for example the 1870 *décret* concerning national defence, or the *ordonnances* of the Vichy Government during the last World War. More recently, under the Fifth Republic, acts of the executive, the *règlements*, have acquired greater importance, being viewed no longer as secondary sources of law but acquiring the status of principal sources of law.[13] Today, therefore, codes are seen as being just one form of legislation, often incorporating or complemented by other sources of written and unwritten law.

2. SOURCES OF LEGALITY AND HIERARCHY OF SOURCES

Sources of law in France are divided into those that are authoritative — the primary sources of law — which give rise to legal rules; and those that are persuasive — the subsidiary sources of law — from which no binding rules can be derived. The former includes legislation and custom, the latter *jurisprudence* — the decisions of the courts — and *doctrine* — legal writings.

Above and beyond these sources of law exist certain supereminent principles — *les principes fondamentaux reconnus par les lois de la République* (fundamental principles recognised by the laws of the Republic). These fundamental principles underlie the law and are superior to all other sources.[14] Their existence is acknowledged in the preamble to the 1946 Constitution. The role of such fundamental principles is to fill the gaps in the law or to correct poorly conceived rules. As such they may be included in legislation or operate outside it. As judges in France are bound to decide a case, even if the law is

---

[13] H. Roland & L. Boyer, *op. cit.* p. 185.
[14] They are referred to as *principes généraux* or *principes supérieurs*, H.C. Gutteridge, *Comparative Law: An Introduction to the Comparative Method of Legal Study and Research* (Cambridge University Press, 2nd. ed., 1949), p. 94.

unclear or there appears to be no relevant law,[15] supereminent principles provide a means whereby such lacunae may be resolved without the judge having to rely solely on subordinate sources of law. The need to use such principles arises more often in areas such as administrative law, where there is no code, rather than civil law, where the general nature of the provisions allow a certain flexibility and discretion to the judge. Nevertheless, even in private law, the notion of *abus de droits* (abuse of rights) may be used to solve novel situations, and in public law consideration of fundamental principles such as *l'ordre public* (public policy), or *les bonnes moeurs* (good morals) may be referred to, to keep the exercise of administrative law in line with the general conception of social order and justice.[16] Thus, although French law knows no separate idea of equity, as in English law, these fundamental principles represent the commands of justice, as an integral part of the law.

(A)   AUTHORITATIVE SOURCES OF LAW

(1)   Written law

The *lois*

The emphasis placed on the separation of powers by the Revolution and the withdrawal of any law-making powers from the judiciary meant that written law, and more particularly that emanating from the legislature, became the primary source of law in France. Today this is still the case, with written law being used as the starting point of legal argument. In French law legislation is not seen as being opposed to immemorial custom or reason, but to exemplify the application of reason through law. While the term *législation* (legislation) exists, the word used to describe written laws is *loi*, which has both a broad meaning which encompasses the Constitution, international treaties, administrative *règlements* (regulations), etc.; and a narrower meaning equivalent to the English term "statutes",[17]

---

[15] Article 4 *C.Civ.* read with article 185 *C.P.* which sanctions breaches of the former with punishment.
[16] See R. David, *The Role of Judicial Decisions and Doctrine in Civil Law and in Mixed Jurisdictions* (Louisiana State University Press, J. Dainow ed., 1974).
[17] See M. Weston, *An English Reader's Guide to the French Legal System* (Berg, Oxford, 1991), pp. 60 *et seq.*

which is used to refer to legislation made by the legislature — as opposed to that made by the executive (see below). It is important to distinguish whether a piece of legislation is a *loi*, or not, because whereas a *loi* cannot be subject to any review once duly promulgated, other forms of legislation can.

As indicated, *loi* in its broadest sense can be used to describe all legal rules formulated in writing and given force and effect through compliance with recognised procedures and by an authority exercising its legislative or regulatory power.[18] *Loi* may be distinguished from *règles* (rules) because the former have three fundamental characteristics. First, they are general in nature, designed to provide for a range of similar situations rather than a single case. Secondly, they are abstract, because they are based on a formulation conceived with typical but abstract situations in mind. Thirdly, they are permanent, in the sense that the law applies to all successive relevant situations, until the law is abrogated. Not all written laws will have these characteristics, and so although a statute passed by the legislature to deal exclusively with a specific and individual situation may be a *loi* in the narrow, formal sense, it is not a *loi* in the wider sense.

The Constitution

In order to consider the hierarchy of sources of French law it is necessary to start with the Constitution, which establishes the law-making powers of the various organs of government. The first written Constitution of September 3, 1791 sought to clearly restrict the law-making powers of any institution other than those of the elected Parliament, although in French law both the legislature and the executive have certain law-making powers. The concept of separation of powers has continued through successive constitutions, although, as will be seen, at times the separation of powers between the legislature and the executive has become confused.

The Constitution serves three purposes. Firstly, it sets out the structure and function of public powers, for example the President, the Government, Parliament, etc., *i.e.* those aspects which might properly fall under the study of constitutional law.

---

[18] A further distinction may be made between *lois* in terms of substance, *i.e.* general measures issued by a duly constituted authority and *lois* in a formal sense, *i.e.* Acts of Parliament. See M. Weston, *op. cit.* p. 60.

Secondly, it contains by way of declarations and preambles statements relating to the economic and social organisation of the state. Thirdly, it includes declarations concerning the rights of individuals, a theme which in France has linked successive constitutions. Today, following a decision of the *Conseil Constitutionnel* on July 16, 1971, in order to decide whether an Act is unconstitutional, it is necessary to consider the 1958 Constitution in conjunction with the Declaration of the Rights of Man and the Citizen of 1789, the Preamble to the 1946 Constitution, and the fundamental principles of law recognised by the laws of the Republic. The scope and influence of the Constitution is not therefore limited solely to administrative matters but extends to all branches of law, and has been accompanied by an extension in the jurisdiction of the *Conseil Constitutionnel* (see Chapter Three, below).

In order to consider the different sources of law provided for under the Constitution it is useful to place the development of these in their historical context.

The 1875 Constitution created three categories of written law, which were applicable within the country. These were, first and foremost, in terms of hierarchy, *lois constitutionelles* (constitutional laws), which were directed at establishing the political organisation and structure, and the competence of the different powers within the constitutional framework. Subordinate to these were the *lois ordinaires* passed by the legislature, which could not be contrary to the Constitution — although under the Third Republic there was no effective sanctioning body (such as the *Comité Constitutionnel*, which was created under the 1946 Constitution, or the *Conseil Constitutionnel*, created under the 1958 Constitution). Although theoretically illegal if unconstitutional, the ordinary courts lacked jurisdiction to examine the constitutionality of *lois ordinaires* which had been passed according to due procedural form by a competent authority. Nor could the courts refuse to apply such a law. In the third category of written law were *règlements* made by authorities invested with executive power. These were inferior to the *lois ordinaires* of the legislature and could not include provisions contrary to law. Should this happen, either the *règlement* was annulled by an administrative court by way of a *recours pour excès de pouvoir*, or a *recours en annulation* (discussed in Chapter Five, below) or declared illegal by the ordinary courts by means of an *exception d'illégalité au contraire*.

The *décrets-lois*

The separation and balance of law-making powers between the legislature and the executive has from time to time been jeopardised — particularly in times of crisis — with the roles of the two becoming confused.[19] After the First World War successive governments sought to use the special power granted to the executive under the 1875 Constitution, which enabled the executive to take a wide range of broadly defined measures to deal with the post-war crises, for example to take any necessary steps to balance the budget, to fight against financial speculation, or to protect the French franc. A number of enabling laws were passed between 1919 and 1939 enlarging the powers of the executive. The measures taken were called *décrets-lois*. Often they modified the existing law and, although they were subject to tacit ratification by the legislature, in the interim they were regarded as having the force of law. The status of such *décrets-lois* was controversial. Essentially they were administrative acts, the legality of which could be recognised by a competent court, but the control of which was limited to the question of whether they had been passed *intra vires* and according to the proper procedures determined by law. However, despite this limited control, such *décrets-lois* had the force of law, and the modifications which they engendered were incorporated into the law. In effect they were seen as representing a delegation of its legislative power by Parliament to the executive.

Some effort was made to reverse this trend in the 1946 Constitution, in which article 13 stated that only the National Assembly could pass *lois* and could not delegate this right.[20] Nevertheless *décrets-lois* continued to proliferate, the provisions of the Constitution being avoided by the executive relying on its general power to pass *règlements* for effecting whatever measures were considered necessary for maintaining public order and the good functioning of services. At times such *règlements* became confused with the *règles* which the legislature were empowered to pass to effect *lois*, and excessive use by the executive of its power to take administrative measures resulted in the law-making powers of the executive being enlarged at the expense of those of the legislature.

---

[19] For historical examples see G. Marty & P. Raynaud, *op. cit.* p. 149; and F. Terré, *op. cit.* pp. 181 *et seq.*

[20] "*L'Assemblé nationale vote seule la loi. Elle ne peut déléguer ce droit.*"

The 1958 Constitution, which still applies today, sought to remedy the matter. Under article 34 the legislature may enact *lois* relating to those areas set out under the same article; while under article 37 the executive — the Prime Minister and his ministers who form the government and do not sit in the elected assemblies — may legislate by means of *règlements* in those spheres not reserved to the legislature under article 34.

Lois constitutionnelles, lois organiques, lois ordinaires

The 1958 Constitution distinguished the following forms of written laws. First are the *lois*, these can only be altered after a referendum vote initiated by the President of the Republic (article 12), or by a vote of the French Parliament. These can be divided into three categories: the *lois constitutionnelles* — constitutional laws including the Constitution itself — which are highest in superiority and cannot be altered or challenged, except according to a specific formal procedure; the *lois organiques* ("organic laws") which determine the establishment, function and form of public powers, and which are used to fill out the Constitution but not to amend it, and are subject to a particular form of voting procedure;[21] and the *lois ordinaires* which are passed by the National Assembly and the Senate in accordance with the procedures established by the laws relating to article 34 of the Constitution.

Although further distinctions are not made in the Constitution, *lois ordinaires* can be further divided into the *lois référendaires*, which are those acts passed subsequent to a referendum called by the President, concerning issues relating to the organisation of public powers, economic and social policies, public services or the ratification of certain treaties (article 11 as amended on July 31, 1995),[22] and may be used to revise the Constitution without resorting to the more cumbersome procedure laid down under article 89; the *lois de finances*, relating to the annual budget; the *lois de programme*, relating to the economic and social programmes of the State; and the *lois d'orientation*, which set

---

[21] See article 46 of the Constitution. Such laws do not have the status of constitutional laws, although they are referred to in the Constitution, but have a special status and domain among ordinary laws; see G. Marty & P. Raynaud, *op. cit.* p. 155. Note that M. Weston is critical of the term "organic laws" and as there is no accurate equivalent in English, it is probably preferable to leave the term untranslated, *op. cit.* p. 62.

[22] *e.g.* on September 20, 1992 the Treaty of Maastricht was ratified according to this procedure.

out a general policy in a specific area, for example the *loi d'orientation agricole* of August 5, 1960 relating to agricultural policy, or that of November 12, 1968 relating to higher education.[23] The characteristic of Acts of Parliament being either *lois impératives* or *lois supplétives*, has already been mentioned in the preceeding chapter.

A *loi* cannot be subject to judicial review of its legality or constitutionality once it has been duly promulgated. All *lois* start as bills, either as *projets de loi* — initiated by the Government — or *propositions de loi* — initiated by a Member of Parliament.

The *règlements*

The Constitution refers to *règlements*, of which there are a wide variety, including those passed to facilitate the implementation of any *lois* (*règlements d'application*) — which are subordinate to these and subject to annulment or a declaration of illegality. However, the *règlements* relating to those areas of competence established under article 37 are autonomous and not adjunct to any *lois* (*règlements autonomes*). The actual term used to describe a *règlement* depends on its origin. Those of the President of the Republic are called *décrets* (articles 13 and 19), as are those of the Prime Minister (article 21), whereas those of ministers or of various administrative authorities such as the *préfet* or *maire* are referred to as *arretés*.[24]

The *ordonnances*

Thirdly, article 92 of the Constitution provides that certain *ordonnances* (ordinances)[25] may have the nature and force of law. These may be made by the Cabinet following the advice of the *Conseil d'Etat*. Similarly under article 47, the Government, *i.e.* the executive, may make *ordonnances* in specific circumstances where Parliament has failed to act after a certain stipulated length of time.[26] Under article 38, the Government also has the power to ask Parliament's authority to pass an *ordonnance* for carrying out its programmes, even where such matters might normally fall into the domain of *lois*. Such a power

---

[23] For examples see F. Terré, *op. cit.* p. 181.
[24] *e.g. arrêtés préfectoraux and arrêtés municipaux.*
[25] This translation is not entirely satisfactory, therefore the French term is to be preferred.
[26] *e.g.* where Parliament fails to establish a national budget within a stipulated time.

will be for a limited period only,[27] and the enactments will be regarded as *règlements* until ratified by the French Parliament, when they will acquire the status and force of *lois*. Article 16 also confers on the President of the Republic emergency powers which may be exercised, subject to consultation with the Prime Minister and the Presidents of both assemblies and of the *Conseil Constitutionnel*, when the institutions of the Republic, her territory, independence, or the carrying out of her international commitments is seriously threatened and the normal functioning of the constitutional Government is disrupted. The form of any measures the President may take will depend on the domain in which he intends to operate. If he acts in a legislative way then his decrees will be *lois*, if in a regulatory way they will be *règlements*, etc.

Treaties and international agreements

As indicated above, treaties and international agreements are included in the broad definition of *lois*. Such treaties and agreements may not conflict with the provisions of the Constitution and are therefore inferior in terms of hierarchy to the Constitution, but superior to any *lois* which must conform with treaties and international obligations.[28] Should a treaty contain provisions conflicting with the Constitution then, under article 54, the Constitution must be altered prior to ratification of the treaty.[29]

---

[27] Such *ordonnances* revived the criticised *décrets-lois* found during the Third and Fourth Republics, but in a more regulated form. Moreover these may only be made under an enabling act, a *loi d'habilitation*.

[28] See arts. 26 & 28 of the 1946 Constitution, and art. 55 of the 1958 Constitution. This applies to those *lois* passed prior to a treaty or those passed subsequently. However there has been some problem over which court has jurisdiction to rule on this matter. In 1975 on a question concerning an alleged contravention between a proposed domestic law on abortion and art. 2 of the European Convention on Human Rights, both the *Conseil d'Etat* and the *Conseil Constitutionnel* held that they lacked competent jurisdiction, leaving the matter to the Court of Cassation.

[29] On June 23, 1992, the 1958 Constitution was amended to allow the ratification of the Maastricht Treaty. On the whole process of amendment of the Constitution and the ratification of the Maastricht Treaty, see in particular, F. Luchaire, *L'union europienne et la constitution*: [1992] R.D.P. 589, 933, 956, 1587 & [1993] R.D.P. 301; in this series of articles, the author comments successively on the decision of the Constitutional Court of April 9, 1992, the constitutional process of amendment, the constitutional law of amendment of June 25, 1992, the referendum of September 22, 1992 and finally the Rules of Procedures of the parliamentary assemblies.

Thus in French law treaties are automatically incorporated into domestic law provided they have been correctly ratified and published,[30] and cannot be abrogated, modified or suspended except in accordance with the rules of international law (article 28 of the 1946 Constitution). Since the 1958 Constitution such incorporation is subject to the principle of reciprocity whereby a treaty will only become part of French law if the other party — or parties in the case of a multilateral treaty — apply the provisions in a similar way (article 55 of the 1958 Constitution).[31]

Community law

The E.C. Treaty of March 25, 1957 to which France was one of the original six signatories,[32] the Treaty of Brussels of April 8, 1965, the Single European Act of 1986 and, more recently, the Maastricht Treaty of 1992 have had a significant impact on the development of French law and national legal order. Treaty stipulations concerning the free movement of workers, freedom of establishment or access to the professions and free movement of goods and services have given rise to a growing body of *lois* and *règlements* which have had to conform with obligations arising under the treaties, give effect to directives originating from the institutions of the Community, or amend existing law in the light of unfavourable rulings of the European Court of Justice, or the Commission.[33]

As regards the hierarchy of sources of law, Community law creates certain problems. In general terms, being of an

---

[30] This procedure is governed by the rules in Title VI of the Constitution. See C. Blumann, *L'article 54 de la constitution et le contrôle de constitutionnalité des traités en France*: [1978] R.G.D.I.P. 535 and F. Luchaire, *Le contrôle de constitutionnalité des engagements internationaux et ses conséquences relatives à la construction européenne*: [1979] R.T.D.E. 391.

[31] On the relationship between international law and French law, see notably R. Abraham, *Droit international, droit communautaire et droit français* (Hachette Supérieur, Coll. P.E.S., Paris, 1989) esp. 17–126; and *Les traités en droit interne* in *Conseil d'Etat, Rapport Public 1992* (*La Documentation Française, Etudes et Documents no. 44*, Paris, 1993) 279.

[32] The others being Germany, Italy, and the three Benelux countries.

[33] This body of legal response may be divided into *droit communautaire originaire* (primary E.C. law), deriving directly from the original treaties, agreements and conventions of the European Community, which may be equated with any international treaty; and *droit communautaire dérivé* (secondary E.C. law), emanating from the institutions of the Community. It is the latter which creates the greatest problems for incorporation into the legal rules of any national system.

international character it is ranked below the Constitution and above *lois*. However, *règlements* (regulations) issued by the Community are directly applicable in the Member States and no modification or obstacles to their uniform and immediate implementation are permitted.[34] Similarly, a decision of the institutions of the Community is binding on those who are party to it. Where the party to a decision is a State, the measures taken to comply with the decision — unlike with a directive — cannot be left to the discretion of the State. In order to accommodate this intrusion of Community law into the national sovereignty of the French State two phases may be considered. Under the 1946 Constitution, and prior to that of 1958, France agreed to consent to limitations on her sovereignty for the organisation and defence of the peace, although the Constitution made no provision for the control of the constitutionality of international treaties. The 1958 Constitution provided for this, but not retrospectively, thus excluding the provisions of the Treaty of Paris, the E.C. Treaty and any amendments or additions to these made subsequently and duly ratified. The *Conseil Constitutionnel* ruled in its decision of June 19, 1970: [1970] R.D.C.C. 15,[35] that the Treaty of Paris and the E.C. Treaty were regularly ratified and published and were therefore to be regarded as superior to ordinary laws within the meaning of article 55 of the Constitution. However European Community legislation emanating from the institutions cannot be subject to this control of constitutionality since it need not be ratified or approved by domestic law. It may then occur that such legislation could be in total contradiction to the Constitution.

The relationship between Community law and French ordinary legislation passed subsequently has been more complex. This is because French courts were inhibited by the traditional constitutional submission of the judiciary to the legislative power and were thereby prevented from verifying the conformity of ordinary laws with international obligations. However, the *Conseil Constitutionnel* removed this obstacle in 1975 and ordinary and administrative courts were free to recognise the

---

[34] See the decision of the European Court of Justice of February 7, 1973; 39/72, *Commission v. Italy*: [1973] E.C.R. 101 as well as decisions of December 14, 1972, 43/71, Politi: [1972] E.C.R. 1049 and October 10, 1973; 34/73, Variola: [1973] E.C.R. 990.

[35] See commentary by D. Ruzié: [1970] J.C.P. II 2354.

primacy of Community law over domestic legislation, in accordance with the case-law of the European Court of Justice, as developed in *Costa v. ENEL*[36] and *Amministrazione delle Finanze dello Stato v. Simmenthal SpA*,[37] even if French courts justified this, primarily or exclusively, on the basis of article 55 of the Constitution.

In its decision of January 15, 1975, the Constitutional Court, which was requested to rule on the constitutionality of a public bill on abortion and to examine whether article 55 had been infringed on the grounds of the alleged incompatibility of this bill with article 2 of the European Convention on Human Rights, ruled that it lacked jurisdiction as regards this issue on the grounds that, under article 61 of the Constitution, the Court only has the power to verify that ordinary laws comply with the Constitution and not with international treaties and agreements. It considered that there was a difference of nature between appraising ordinary laws in the light of the Constitution and appraising them in the light of a treaty.[38]

This decision left the Court of Cassation with no alternative but to hold that such a task fell within the jurisdiction of non-constitutional courts. It ruled in favour of the primacy of Community law over subsequent national legislation, first on the ground of article 55 of the Constitution (May 24, 1975, *Café Jacques Vabre*)[39] and subsequently, on the unique nature of the Community legal order (December 15, 1975, *Von Kempis*).[40]

By contrast, the *Conseil d'Etat* resisted the principle of primacy of Community law in the *Semolina* case of March 1, 1968.[41] In the view of this supreme administrative court, acknowledging the primacy of Community law over subsequent

---

[36] Case 6/64, *Costa v. ENEL*: [1964] E.C.R. 614, [1964] C.M.L.R. 425.

[37] Case 106/77, *Amminstrazione delle Finanze dello Stato v. Simmenthal*: [1978] E.C.R. 629, [1978] 3 C.M.L.R. 263.

[38] See commentary by L. Hamon: [1975] D. 529; G. Druesne, *Le Conseil constitutionnel et le droit communautaire, A Propos de la décision du 15 janvier 1975*: [1975] R. M. C. 285.

[39] [1975] 2 C.M.L.R. 336. For commentaries see G. Druesne, *La primauté du droit communautaire sur le droit interne, L'arrêt de la Cour de cassation du 24 mai 1975*: [1975] R.M.C. 379; J. Pirotte-Gerouville, *La primauté du droit international et la spécificité de l'ordre communautaire dans l'affaire Jacques Vabres*; [1976] R.T.D.E. 215.

[40] [1976] 2 C.M.L.R. 300, [1974] II J.C.P. 17556.

[41] [1970] C.M.L.R. 395, [1968] Rec. Lebon 149. See opinion of *Commissaire du Governement* N. Questiaux: [1968] A.J.D.A. 235.

domestic law would have been similar to verifying the constitutionality of national laws, which is clearly not within its jurisdiction (see Chapter Three, below). The *Conseil d'Etat* did not abandon its position until its decision in *Nicolo* of October 20, 1989,[42] in which it agreed to rule on the compatibility of an Act of 1977 with article 227(1) EEC and consequently to recognise the primacy of the latter. However, it only accepted to do so on the basis of article 55 of the Constitution. Similarly, in two subsequent decisions, the *Conseil d'Etat* acknowledged the primacy of Community regulations (September 24, 1990, *Boisdet*)[43] and that of directives (February 28, 1992, *SA Rothmans International France et SA Philip Morris France* and *Société Arizona Tobacco et SA Philip Morris France*[44]).[45]

---

[42] [1990] 1 C.M.L.R. 173, [1989] Rec. Lebon 190. See commentaries by P. Sabourin: [1990] D. 136 and L. Dubouis: [1989] R.F.D.A. 1003; see also J.-F. Lachaume, *Une victoire de l'ordre juridique communautaire: l'arrêt Nicolo consacrant la supériorié des traités sur les lois postérieures*: [1990] 337 R.M.C. 384; Ph. Manin, *The Nicolo case of the Conseil d'Etat: French constitutional law and the supreme administrative court's acceptance of the primacy of Community law over subsequent national statute law*: [1991] 28 C.M.L.Rev. 499.

[43] [1991] 1 C.M.L.R. 3, [1990] Rec. Lebon 250. See L. Dubouis, *Règlement communautaire et loi nationale postérieure (A propos de la décision du Conseil d'Etat du 24 septembre 1990)*: [1991] R.F.D.A. 172.

[44] [1993] C.M.L.R. 253. See commentary by J. Dutheil de la Rochère: [1993] 30 C.M.L.Rev. 187; see also D. Simon, *Le Conseil d'Etat, la directive , la loi, le droit, ad augusta per augusta*: [1992] 4 Europe 1, and *Le Conseil d'Etat et les directives communautaires: du gallicisme à l'orthodoxie*: [1992] R.T.D.E. 265; R. Kovar, *Le Conseil d'Etat et le droit communautaire: des progrès mais peut mieux faire*: [1992] Dalloz, Chron. 207; L. Dubouis, *Directive communautaire et loi française: primauté de la directive et respect de l'interprétation que la Cour de justice a donné à ses dispositions*: [1992] R.F.D.A. 425.

[45] On the relationship between Community law and French law, see notably R. Abraham, *op. cit.*, pp. 127–190 and B. Genevois, *Le droit international et le droit communautaire*, in *Conseil constitutionnel et conseil d'Etat* (L.G.D.J., Paris, 1988) 191; see also *Conseil d'Etat, Droit communautaire et droit français* (*La Documentation Française*, Paris, 1982); O. Audéoud, D. Berlin & Ph. Manin, *The application of Community law in France: review of French court decisions from 1974 to 1981*: [1982] 19 C.M.L.Rev. 289. *Conseil d'Etat, Rapport Public 1992, op. cit.* esp. 15–66, 235–266 and 305–312; and D. Simon & A. Rigaux, *Le Conseil d'Etat saisi par le droit communautaire: quelques réflexions sur le rapport public 1992*: [1993] 10 Europe 1. More specifically on the position of the *Conseil d'Etat*, see B. Genevois, *Le Conseil d'Etat et le droit communautaire*: [1979–1980] E.D.C.E. 73; V. Coussirat-Coustère, *Le juge administratif et le droit communautaire*: [1988] 46 Pouvoirs 85; P.-F. Ryziger, *Le Conseil d'Etat et le droit communautaire, de la continuité au changement*: [1990] R.F.D.A. 850; B. Stirn, *Le Conseil d'Etat et le droit communautaire*: [1993] A.J.D.A. 244; P. Sabourin, *Le Conseil d'Etat face au droit*

(2) Custom

Custom is the second authoritative source of law. Whereas the *loi* emanates from the State, either the legislative or executive power, custom originates from the people, but is recognised and safeguarded by the State. The French Civil Code does not include a definition of custom, and article 7 of the Act of March 21, 1804 (30 *ventose an* XII) which introduced the Civil Code, specifically provided that general or local customs were to cease to have effect in matters covered by the Code. The definition of custom is therefore left to doctrinal writers such as R. David who defines custom as "the continuing behaviour over a period of time of those governed by the law, with the understanding that their behaviour is required by the law".[46]

In order to be recognised as a formal source of law there are certain necessary elements that must be established — *les éléments nécessaires et constitutifs*.

First, custom must evolve through a slow, but spontaneous process of development — it cannot consist of a single occurrence, or be imposed on people other than by their own will, but must evolve through imitation and repetition. Secondly, it must have popular support and consent as to its usage, *i.e.* social approval and consensus. Thirdly, the obligatory nature of a custom must be recognised in the way it is regarded. This is the intellectual or psychological factor, whereby a custom is invested with judicial conviction both by those subject to it and others. Once these elements can be said to exist — and it is not always easy to determine when conventional usage becomes custom[47] — then a custom may be established.[48] It is not a requirement that custom be unwritten, and indeed a great part of customary

---

communautaire, méthodes et raisonnements: [1993] R.D.P. 397; J.-C. Bonichot, *Convergences et divergences entre le Conseil d'Etat et la Cour de justice des Communautés européennes*: [1989] R.F.D.A. 579; R. Kovar, *Le Conseil d'Etat et le droit communautaire: de l'état de guerre à la paix armée*: [1990] D. Chron. 57.

[46] R. David, *French Law; Its Structure, Sources and Methodology* (Louisiana State University Press, 1972), p. 170.

[47] See, *e.g.* the comments of Y. Loussouarn, "The Relative Importance of Legislation, Custom, Doctrine and Precedent in French Law", (1958) 18 La.L.R. 235 at 247 *et seq.*

[48] As G. Cornu states: "(a) custom is established when one can say that everyone does this" ("*La coutume est constituée quand on peut dire que tout le monde fait comme cela*"); see *Droit Civil* (Montchrestien, 4th ed., 1990), p. 39.

law was reduced to writing before the Revolution,[49] and some of it incorporated into the body of the *Code civil* (see Chapter One).

Despite the Code providing no definition of custom, reference is made to usages as a source of law in determining consensual transactions.[50] Also the Code made no provision for custom arising subsequent to codification and early interpretors of the Code maintained that as its provisions expressed the will of the people there was no place for custom.[51] However, today it is generally accepted that custom is a vital tool for interpreting the law and placing it in a contemporary social and normative context. Indeed in 1902 the *Cour de Cassation* held that a judge must take into account a custom if he is aware of its existence.[52]

French law recognises three types of custom. First, there is custom which supports the law — *consuetudo secundum legem* — which arises in the context of legislation to facilitate and direct its application, for example the customary use of terms such as date, signature, fault. In this respect French law places greater importance on custom as an interpretative linguistic guide than English Common law,[53] enabling changes of time, circumstance and social milieu to be taken into account. Secondly, there is custom which precedes the law — *consuetudo praeter legem*. Such custom is independent of, but not inconsistent with, legislation. The relevance of such custom varies depending on the legal area. Where the law has been codified it may be less relevant than where the law is constantly changing and adapting — for example commercial law and labour law. An area of law where such custom is never relevant is in the field of criminal law where the need for *a priori* legal sanctions is essential. Quite often such customs are referred to as "commercial usage" rather than custom.[54] Thirdly, there is

---

[49] For an interesting account see J. Dawson, "The Codification of the French Customs" (1940) 38 Mich.L.R. 765.

[50] For example articles 1135, 1159 & 1160 C.Civ.

[51] The status of custom as a source of law has therefore, been influenced by the various schools of legal reasoning. The post-revolutionary exegetical school denied it a place, while the later more liberal, scientific school advocated the role of custom in interpreting the law.

[52] This seems to be the case even if the litigants do not seek to rely on it.

[53] See R. David & H.P. de Vries, *An Introduction to Civil Law Systems: the French Legal System* (Oceana, New York, 1958), p. 107.

[54] As with the development of life insurance and hire-purchase contracts.

custom which is contrary to law — *consuetudo adversus legem*. Such a custom will not normally be openly acknowledged, but the rules of law will be circumvented either by flexible interpretation, if the law is a *loi impérative*, or by finding an intention to exclude it, if it is a *loi supplétive*.[55]

(B) SUBSIDIARY SOURCES OF LAW

The *Jurisprudence*[56]

The Act of August 16–24, 1790 abolished the power of the *Parlements*. Until the Revolution these French courts had had the power to establish legal rules and binding precedents. Title II, article 10 of this Act forbade them to issue general rules and commanded them to refer to the legislative body whenever they needed an Act interpreted or a new one enacted. Although this measure was subsequently modified by articles 4 and 5 of the Civil Code, the fundamental and far-reaching change in the position of the French courts remained.

Consequently the decisions of the courts do not have the same authority in French law as in English law,[57] and indeed, article 5 of the Civil Code expressly prohibits the establishment of rules of precedent by the judges. Nevertheless, not only do judges have a duty to decide all cases which come before them, but courts have to apply rules of law established by legislation — some of it several centuries old — to contemporary situations and give life to the law by adapting and updating the interpretation of the law. The difference between the application of the law by the judges in France and that of the judges in England, is that the text of a law, as interpreted by the courts, does not itself become law. Law-making remains the preserve of the legislature and indirectly, the people. The judge is to decide a case by reference to primary sources. Judicial precedent simply demonstrates past applications of a legal text. However, although

---

[55] An example is the situation regarding current accounts. Article 1154 *C.Civ.* forbids the charging of compound interest. In commercial law this is avoided by holding that such accounts are governed by custom alone.

[56] This term should not be confused with the English law use of the similar term jurisprudence relating to legal philosophy.

[57] Indeed J. Carbonnier, writing in the *Authorities in Civil Law in France*, states that "jurisprudence is not a source of civil law"; see J. Dainow (ed.), *op. cit.* p. 95.

a judge is not bound to follow a previous judicial decision, and may even depart from a decision of the Court of Cassation,[58] the need for continuity and certainty in the law tends to result in like following like. Thus a long line of similar decisions may amount to something resembling a rule of precedent under the doctrine of *jurisprudence constante* (settled jurisprudence). If such a doctrine is established then it may become a rule of customary law — which elevates it to an authoritative source — rather than merely a series of prior decisions. Also, in practice the collegiate response of the courts,[59] combined with considerations of economy of effort, legal predictability and stability, support a tendency for previous decisions to influence the determination of future cases. Moreover there is no restriction on referring to case decisions during the course of legal argument.

Although there is, as indicated, no rule of precedent whereby lower courts are bound by the decisions of higher courts, the origin of a decision may be important both in terms of its status, and as regards the right of appeal against it. Decisions of the courts of first instance (*tribunal d'instance* and *tribunal de grande instance*) are called *jugements*, while those of the Courts of Appeal and the Court of Cassation are called *arrêts*. As only published decisions can have any influence on the law, those of the courts of first instance, which are rarely published, are less likely to be reflected in the body of jurisprudence, whereas those of the Court of Cassation are published in an official bulletin, the *Bulletin des arrêts de la Cour de Cassation*.[60] That part of the decision which is relevant for other courts is the statement of legal reasons (*motifs de droit*) — rather than the reasons based on facts (*motifs de fait*) — or the actual court order (*le dispositif*).

---

[58] Y. Loussouarn suggests that in practice 90 per cent of judges adopt the position of the Court of Cassation, rather than risk the reversal of a court decision by appeal, *op. cit.* pp. 258–260.

[59] The decisions of judges are anonymous, and rarely do judges emerge as individuals. Most courts consist of more than one judge and the decision is that of the court, not the judge(s). See R. David & H. P. De Vries, *op. cit.* p. 117; and the comments of D. Pugsley, *Lawyers and Precedents* (University of Exeter, 1989), pp. 16–18.

[60] Published in two series — one for criminal law and one for civil — this became an official publication by the Act of July 23, 1947. Private publications also exist and have done for some time, *e.g.* Sirey (1791), *Dalloz* (1845), and the *Gazette du Palais* (1881).

Unlike its predecessor, the *Tribunal de Cassation* — created in 1790 — the Court of Cassation has the task of assuring the uniformity of case law, and of ensuring that decisions of the courts are soundly based on authoritative sources of law. In doing this the Court may well cite other case decisions — but not its own previous decisions. One of the reasons for the influence of the decisions of the Court of Cassation is that judges must state the grounds for the decisions indicating the juridical reasoning by which they were reached, thus providing the lower courts with a legal formula. However, a decision of the Court of Cassation will not become established until it has been adopted by the Courts of Appeal and the trial courts, through a series of consistent decisions.[61]

Occasionally the decision of a higher court is imposed on a lower one, for example when the former substitutes its opinion for that of the latter,[62] or when the lower court adjudicates in a manner which it knows represents the higher court's view. However, it can happen that a decision of a lower court influences that of the Court of Cassation, particularly if the matter is one not yet adjudicated upon by the Court of Cassation, or if it feels its previous decision to be no longer applicable.[63] Where there is not a relevant decision of the Court of Cassation then the geographical origin of a Court of Appeal's decision is relevant, lower courts tending to refer to the decisions of those courts in their region.

The *Doctrine*

One of the factors that has enhanced the significance of case-law has been the role of academic commentary as an influential authority in French law. The initial ideology surrounding codification denied the need for research and interpretation. As a model of rational thought, application of the written text was all that was necessary. At first there was a divergence between

---

[61] Even within the decisions of the Court of Cassation, a distinction is made between those based on the facts of the case (*arrêts d'espèce*) and those where the legal questions are subject to detailed examination and the solution posed in terms of general legal principles (*arrêts de principe*) with the latter being afforded greater prestige.

[62] For example in the case of an appeal or a *pourvoi en cassation*.

[63] In this respect it should be noted that greater weight is attached to the most recent decisions.

written commentary on the new code — which adopted the exegetical approach of expounding upon the text itself — and judicial decisions — which the exegetical writers ignored. Towards the end of the nineteenth century however, greater emphasis was placed on the need to not only construe the code in a logical and systematic way, but in doing so, to take into account actual usage and practice, and the needs of society.[64] As a result, sociological and comparative research was engaged in and jurists turned their attention to the decisions of the courts.

Traditionally legal scholarship has played a significant role in the development of French law (see Chapter One), and today *doctrine*, which may be defined as "the body of opinions on legal matters expressed in books and articles",[65] is regarded as influential, providing as it does, a systematic and critical exposition of positive law through written commentary. Moreover, *doctrine* does not consist solely of academic writings, but includes the comments of judges, practitioners and law teachers, and may be found in manuals, journals, legal periodicals, doctoral theses, and practical commentaries. Such jurists may work closely with practitioners, being consulted for opinions, or working on law reform commissions. Thus there is a broad range and variety of work which may be considered as falling into this area. *Doctrine* includes commentary on existing legislative acts, discussions on issues preceeding the promulgation of new legislation, suggested interpretation of new legal provisions and annotated reports and commentaries on decisions of the courts — including decisions of foreign courts applying a similar system of law — and the publication of text books for legal education. The influence and status of such jurists is greater in France than that afforded to their counterparts in England. In the nineteenth century jurists such as Aubry, Rau, Proudhon, Delvincourt and Demolombe had a significant impact on legal theory and practice, and some, such as Demolombe, Aubry and Rau remain influential today. This century great jurists have included Planiol, Colin, Capitant, Carbonnier, Marty and Raynaud, and it is not unusual to find their views cited in commentaries on the codes, or in the courts. Others have influenced the development of legislation, for example Carbonnier

---

[64] This school of thought was called the *Ecole de la Libre Recherche*. Eminent among its proponents were Gény and Saleilles.

[65] A.N. Yiannopoulos in J. Dainow (ed.), *op. cit.* p. 82.

on the reform of family law in the 1960s and 1970s — just as Pothier had done with the *Code Napoléon*.

Besides the historical development of the law, there are a number of practical reasons why the work of jurists is considered influential. First, as mentioned above, judges are anonymous and tend to act collegially, expressing a unanimous opinion which does not allow dissent or criticism to emerge within the judicial process. Secondly, the style of reporting case decisions tends to be brief and, to the common lawyer, cryptic. It is not always easy to find the legal reasons for the decision, and thus legal commentary, annotation and amplification helps to make individual cases more comprehensible, and also places them in the broader context of legal rules and institutions. Moreover, jurists do not hesitate to criticise decisions thereby re-enforcing the theoretical absence of a rule of precedent. Thirdly, jurists are traditionally seen as being impartial scholars whose task is to shape the law into a coherent body of legal principles,[66] thus both judges and legislators may take into account their views. *Doctrine* is not therefore, a source of law, but rather an inspiration and influence, which may be referred to either when there is no established *jurisprudence* on the matter, or when that which exists is deemed to be unsatisfactory.

---

[66] See for example the comments of J. Ghestin & G. Goubeaux, *Traité de droit civil*: (L.G.D.J., Paris, 1983), pp. 187 *et seq.*

Chapter Three
The courts' structure

1. THE FUNDAMENTAL PRINCIPLES OF THE COURTS' STRUCTURE

(A) THE PRINCIPLE OF SEPARATION OF THE COURTS

According to this principle, ordinary courts are not competent to hear disputes of an administrative character. The reasons for this separation between administration and courts are historical.

The principle of separation of powers as formulated by Montesquieu was interpreted dogmatically by the French revolutionaries. According to Montesquieu, there should be three distinct and separate powers: the executive power, the legislature and the judiciary. Their separation was a prerequisite for effective protection of individual freedoms.

The French draftsmen of the Revolution drew another principle from that formulated by Montesquieu: disputes involving the executive power and its members should not be heard by courts, otherwise the executive power would be subordinate to the judiciary.[1] In reality, behind this legal facade, there was a political reason: the revolutionaries did not trust the judiciary. They remembered and drew lessons from the experience of the Kings of France facing the conservative opposition of the *Parlements*.[2] The resistance of the *Parlements* to the legislative

---

[1] This argument is certainly not convincing from the legal point of view. The principle of separation of administrative and judicial authorities finds no justification either in history or in comparative law. In France, even systems of government which were not based on separation of powers (*e.g.* the Convention or the Empire) have maintained the above principle, while this principle is ignored in the United States whose political system is based on separation of powers.

[2] Under the Monarchy, the *Parlements* were sovereign courts of justice vested with certain political prerogatives. They were in charge of recording the royal *édits* and *ordonnances*. The *Parlements* could refuse to record these royal Acts and could address remonstrances to the King.

power of the King reached its height when the ministers of Louis XV wished to carry out some necessary reforms. The *Parlements*, determined to defend their privileges, prevented the achievement of these reforms. Turning this experience into dogma, the revolutionaries were determined to stop the resurgence of a strong judiciary. In their view, judges interfering with the State's affairs would go against the sound functioning of the State and the principle of separation of powers.

This principle of separation of administration and judiciary was established in two major legal texts. The first one was the Act of August 16–24, 1790. It governed the relationship between the judiciary and the two other powers and established the separation of the judiciary and the legislature. It also prohibited ordinary courts from preventing or suspending the application and implementation of Acts of Parliament. They were not allowed to take *arrêts de règlements* either, *i.e.* decisions by which a court could declare which rule to apply to future litigation.[3] Nor could a judge interpret Acts of Parliament. If laws were unclear, judges had to refer to the legislator for interpretation by way of *référé legislatif*.[4]

Moreover, article 13 of Title II of this Act provided that:

"The functions of the judiciary are and remain distinct and separate from those of the administration. Judges shall not, without incurring criminal liability, interfere in any manner whatsoever with the actions of the administration nor summon administrators to appear before them in order to account for their functions."[5]

---

[3] This prohibition was inserted later on in article 5 *C.Civ.*:
"Judges are forbidden from making general binding statements of law from the cases submitted to them" ("*Il est défendu au juges de prononcer par voie de disposition générale et réglementaire sur les causes qui lui sont soumises*").

[4] The *référé legislatif* shows how naive the authors of the 1790 Act were. In reality, this was rarely practised and was definitely abolished by art. 4 *C.Civ.* which provides that: "The judge who refuses to adjudicate on the ground of the silence, obscurity or insufficiency of the law, may be held liable for any miscarriage of justice" ("*Le juge qui refusera de juger, sous prétexte du silence, de l'obscurité ou de l'insuffisance de la loi, pourra être poursuivi comme coupable de déni de justice*").

[5] "*Les fonctions judiciaires sont distinctes et demeureront toujours séparées des fonctions administratives. Les juges ne pourront, à peines de forfaiture, troubler de quelque manière que ce soit les opérations des corps administratifs, ni citer devant eux les administrateurs pour raison de leurs fonctions.*"

This provision was aimed at protecting the executive power and was reiterated in a subsequent text, the *décret* of 16 *fructidor an* III (1795) which reads as follows:

"Courts are repeatedly forbidden by law from subjecting administrative acts, whatever their nature, to judicial review."[6]

These two texts are still in force today. The *tribunal des conflits* based its well-known *Pelletier* decision on them.[7] So did the *Conseil Constitutionnel* in its decision of January 23, 1987 even if it did not confer upon these texts constitutional value (see below). However, these texts simply prevented ordinary courts from interfering with administrative affairs and did not create any special court which could do so. This situation lasted until 1800 when, under the *Consulat* period,[8] the *conseils de préfecture* and the *Conseil d'Etat* were created. The former were presided over by the *préfets* and had limited judicial powers; the latter was not a real judicial body and could only suggest legal solutions to the Head of State. Therefore, from the legal point of view, the administration was its own judge since there was no independent court empowered to review its action.[9] It was only in 1872 that the *Conseil d'Etat* was definitively recognised as a court when *justice déléguée*, *i.e.* the power to review administrative action, was conferred upon it by the Act of May 24, 1872.

(B) THE CONSTITUTIONAL FOUNDATION OF THE DUAL SYSTEM OF COURTS

As a result of this historical evolution, nowadays France has a dual system of courts which consists of two *ordres*[10] *de juridictions*[11]: the *ordre judiciaire*, *i.e.* ordinary courts and the *ordre administratif*, *i.e.* administrative courts.

This principle of a dual system of courts has a constitutional foundation. In other words, the merger of the two *ordres juridiques* would be impossible under the 1958 Constitution. On

---

[6] *"Défenses itératives sont faites aux tribunaux de connaître des actes d'administration, de quelqu'espèce qu'ils soient, aux peines de droit."*

[7] (T.C.), July 30, 1873: (G.A.), p. 22.

[8] Political regime established between November 9–10, 1789 and May 18, 1804 by Napoléon Bonaparte after the coup of 18–19 *brumaire an* VIII.

[9] This was called *"justice retenue"* (by the Government).

[10] The word *ordre* has to be understood in the sense of hierarchy or system.

[11] In French, *juridiction* is another word for *cour* or *tribunal*. Any *cour* or *tribunal* is a *juridiction* whereas a *juridiction* is either a *cour* or a *tribunal*.

the one hand, the existence of an independent system of ordinary courts is expressly provided for in Title VIII of the French Constitution. On the other hand, although the principle of a system of administrative courts is not laid down in the Constitution, it was recognised by the *Conseil Constitutionnel* in its decision of July 22, 1980 ([1980] R.D.C.C. 2) which referred to the "fundamental principles recognised by the laws of the Republic"[12] and, in particular, to the Act of May 24, 1872 on the organisation of the *Conseil d'Etat*. Subsequently the Constitutional Court was called on to examine the constitutionality of an Act of Parliament providing that the *Conseil de la concurrence* — an administrative body in charge of repressing anti-competitive practices — could be subject to an appeal before the *cour d'appel* of Paris, an ordinary court. In its decision of January 23, 1987 ([1987] R.F.D.A. 287) the Constitutional Court ruled that the principle of separation of ordinary and administrative courts had no constitutional value *per se* but that there was however a principle recognised by the laws of the Republic according to which:

"with the exception of those matters which by nature are reserved for the judicial authority, the annulment or amendment of decisions taken, in the exercise of public power, by the executive authorities, their agents, local governments, or those bodies under their authority or control, fall, in the last resort, within the jurisdiction of the administrative courts."[13]

Therefore, the *Conseil Constitutionnel* has considered that the existence of a system of administrative courts with distinct powers of judicial review of acts of public authorities is a fundamental principle recognised by the laws of the Republic. Indeed, the role of the *Conseil d'Etat* as an administrative court was confirmed by a series of laws adopted during the Second, Third and Fourth Republics.[14]

---

[12] "*Les principes fondamentaux reconnus par les lois de la République.*"

[13] "*A l'exception des matières réservées par nature à l'autorité judiciaire, relève en dernier ressort de la compétence de la juridiction administrative l'annulation ou la réformation des décisions prises dans l'exercice de prérogatives de puissance publique, par les autorités exerçant le pouvoir exécutif, leurs agents, les collectivités territoriales de la République, ou les organismes placés sous leur autorité ou leur contrôle.*"

[14] See the Acts of March 3, 1849 and May 24, 1872 and the *ordonnance* of July 31, 1945.

(C) JURISDICTION OF ORDINARY AND ADMINISTRATIVE COURTS

(1) Civil and criminal jurisdiction of ordinary courts

The courts of the *ordre judiciaire* have two functions: on the one hand, they adjudicate disputes between individuals in the sphere of civil law; on the other hand they pass sentences against perpetrators of offences. These two functions are exercised jointly by the same courts. This contributes to the unity of civil and criminal courts. For instance, the *tribunal d'instance* hears minor disputes of civil law and, as the *tribunal de police*, minor criminal offences. In the same way, the *tribunal de grande instance* and the *cour d'appel* deal with the most important civil disputes and, respectively, as the *tribunal correctionnel* and as the *chambre correctionnelle* of the *cour d'appel*, with major offences. The *cour d'assises* which is competent to try crimes is the only exception to this principle of unity.

Another link between civil and criminal courts can be found in the principle according to which general criminal courts can deal with actions for damages following harm caused by a criminal offence. In such a case, the victim has two alternatives: either to bring an action for damages before a civil court (either the *tribunal d'instance* or the *tribunal de grande instance* depending on the monetary value of the claim), or to bring the same action before the criminal court.

(2) Jurisdiction of administrative courts

With the exception of a few costs, the courts of the *ordre administratif* have exclusive jurisdiction in cases relating to public law and involving individuals in the *juridictions de droit commun* on the one hand, and the State, a civil servant, a State corporation or any public authority on the other.

2. *JURIDICTIONS DE DROIT COMMUN* AND *D'EXCEPTION*

The *juridictions de droit commun*[15] are those courts which have jurisdiction to try all cases other than those for which other courts have been given special jurisdiction by statute. The latter courts, *i.e.* the *juridictions d'exception*, can hear only cases for which they have been given express jurisdiction.

---

[15] As M. Weston suggests, this term can be better rendered in English by "general courts" or "courts of general jurisdiction" as opposed to "specialised courts" or "courts of limited jurisdiction" for *juridictions d'exception*; see *op. cit.* p. 71.

Diagram 3.1 Court Structure

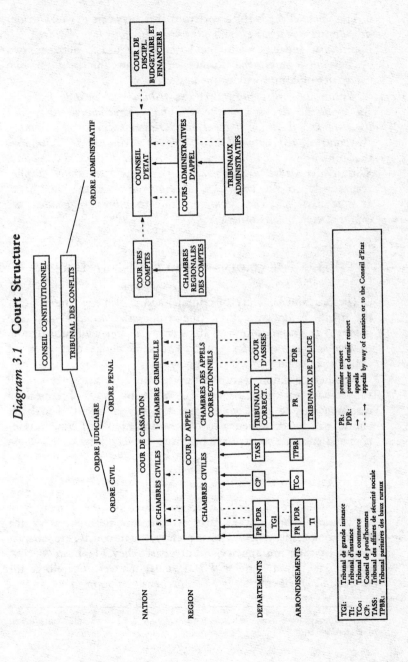

This distinction is different from that between the *juridictions de l'ordre judiciaire* and the *juridictions de l'ordre administratif*. Indeed, while the latter distinguishes between two systems of courts, the former draws the line between two categories of courts within one system of courts.

Within the *ordre judiciaire*, the *tribunal de grande instance*, the *tribunal de police*, the *tribunal correctionnel*, the *cour d'assises* and the *cour d'appel* are *juridictions de droit commun*. By contrast, the *tribunal d'instance*, the *tribunal de commerce*, the *conseil de prud'hommes*, etc., are *juridictions d'exception*. Within the *ordre administratif*, the same distinction applies respectively to the *tribunaux administratifs* on the one hand, and to the *cour des comptes*, the *chambres régionales des comptes*, etc., on the other.[16]

3. THE ORDINARY COURTS' STRUCTURE

The principle of unity of criminal and civil justice implies that the main ordinary courts (the *tribunal d'instance* and the *tribunal de grande instance*) have criminal and civil jurisdiction. In the smallest of these courts, the same judge may even sit either as a criminal or a civil judge.

Another common feature of these courts is that they are all subordinate to the *Cour de Cassation* by way of appeal in cassation and to the *cour d'appel* by way of *appel*. The latter courts will be examined after the organisation and functions of civil and criminal courts have been successively described.

(A) CIVIL COURTS

The structure of civil courts is based on the principle of *adéquation*, which means that disputes are dealt with by the most competent judge. Consequently, civil courts are characterised by their multiplicity and diversity; they adjudicate in civil, commercial, rural, industrial and social matters. Therefore, the expression "civil courts" is a comprehensive notion in so far as it

---

[16] In administrative law, *juridictions d'exception* are also called *juridictions d'attribution*.

embraces courts which have jurisdiction to hear civil disputes (in the narrow sense) including the status of persons (for example family, filiation, etc.) or property (for example acquisition, successions, etc.) as well as disputes occurring in a professional and social context (for example social security, employment, etc.).

Civil courts can be classified into two categories: general and specialised courts.

(1) General court: the *tribunal de grande instance*

The *ordonnance* of December 22, 1958 created two courts of first instance within the *ressort* (territorial jurisdiction) of each Court of Appeal. These are the *tribunal d'instance*, a single judge court, and the *tribunal de grande instance*. The *tribunal de grande instance* alone has to be regarded as a court of general jurisdiction.

Composition

The *tribunal de grande instance* is organised according to the principle of *collégialité* (article L 311–6 *C.O.J.*). Under this principle, ordinary cases are adjudicated by a bench of three judges. When this court has more than five judges (for example as in Paris, 165; Marseille, 28; and Nanterre, 55), it is divided into *chambres* (Divisions), each being a *formation de jugement* (sitting as a court).

However, under the Act 70–613 of July 10, 1970, the President of the court has the power to allocate cases to a single judge (articles 801–805 *N.C.P.C.*). Nevertheless, if the litigants request, or the President of the court considers it to be more appropriate, a case formerly allocated to a single judge may be referred back to a bench of three judges (article L 311–10 *C.O.J.*). These single judges are:

— the *juge des enfants* who specialises in young offenders (articles L 531–1—L 531–3 *C.O.J.*).
— the *juge de l'exécution* who is responsible for enforcing judgments passed by French courts and for authorizing the enforcement in France of foreign judgments and decisions reached by arbitration in France or abroad (see the Act of July 9, 1991 and articles L 331–11 *et seq. C.O.J.*). His

functions are carried out by the President of the court
(article L 311–12 *C.O.J.*).

— a *juge délégué aux affaires familiales* who, since February
1, 1994, replaces the former *juge délégué aux affaires
matrimoniales* (see the Act of January 8, 1993, article L
312–1 *C.O.J.* and article 247 *C.Civ.*), and who is competent
in divorce and related matters, as was his predecessor, and
in all family matters (marriage obligations, parental
authority, filiation, request for change of surname of an
illegitimate child and litigation relating to parental choice of
a child's first name).[17]

— a *juge de l'expropriation* who is responsible for awarding
expropriation compensation (article L 431–1 *C.O.J.*).

— a single judge who was made competent, under the Act of
July 5, 1985 on traffic accidents, to deal with litigation
arising from road accidents (article L 311–10(1) *C.O.J.*).

Within the *tribunal de grande instance*, the prosecution or
parquet consists of the *procureur de la République* assisted by
one or two *substituts*.[18] The administration is carried out by a
secretariat-greffe headed by a *greffier en chef* (see Chapter Four,
below).

Organisation

In 1958, the *tribunal de grande instance* was created to
replace the *tribunal de première instance* (Court of First
Instance) which had been created in 1789[19] and the territorial
jurisdiction of which was confined to an *arrondissement*.[20] In
principle, there is one *tribunal de grande instance* per
département, located in its *chef-lieu* (main town). In reality, this
is the case in only 32 *départements*, most of them having two or
more courts.[21] Overall, there are 181 *tribunaux* in metropolitan
France and the overseas territories.

---

[17] See C. Maillard, *La réforme sur le juge aux affaires familiales. La loi du 8
janvier 1993*: [1994] 51 Les Petites Affiches 15.

[18] In courts dealing with a high number of cases, *e.g.* that of Lyon, the *procureur*
is assisted by a *procureur-adjoint* and by *premiers substituts*.

[19] See J. Martin de la Motte, *La réforme des juridictions civiles du 22 décembre
1958* (Mélanges Maury), Vol. 1, p. 252.

[20] The *arrondissement* is an administrative and geographical unit between the
département and the *canton*, which has no legal personality.

[21] For instance, the *département du Nord* has seven courts.

The *tribunaux de grande instance* have judicial as well as administrative functions. For this purpose, they are organised into *formations juridictionnelles* (Judicial Divisions) and *formations administratives* (Administrative Divisions). There are two judicial divisions and the court usually sits *en audience publique*, *i.e.* three judges sit together in an open court (article L 311–6 & 7 C.O.J.).[22] More rarely, the court sits *à huis clos* (*in camera*) when only the parties and their lawyers have access. In such a case the court sits as a *chambre du conseil* (in the judge's chambers). The court may also sit like this with one single judge where the law provides so (for example matrimonial affairs, expropriation, traffic accidents, etc.).

The court also has administrative functions regarding the working of the court (for example, the appointment of the *juge de l'application des peines* who is in charge of the enforcement of sentences and the allocation of cases between the different divisions). These functions are carried out by a number of *assemblées*[23] whose composition and scope are governed by the *décret* of December 23, 1983. This law has permitted the whole personnel of the court to take part in its operation and administration. It has at the same time reduced the powers of the President of the court.

Jurisdiction

In principle, it is the *tribunal de grande instance* of the defendant's home which is territorially competent (articles 42 & 43 *N.C.P.C.*).[24] This is an old principle which can be traced back to Roman law ("*Actor sequitur forum rei*"). However, there are some exceptions where the law confers powers upon another court: for example, in matters of immovable property, the court in the territory of which the property is situated, is competent. In other cases, the plaintiff may have a choice. In tort, the plaintiff may choose the court of the place where the defendant lives or where the damage has occurred. In contract disputes the

---

[22] If a judge cannot sit, art. L 311–9 provides that the court may be completed by an *avocat* who belongs to the Bar of that court.

[23] These are the *assemblée des magistrats du siège et du parquet*, the *assemblée des magistrats du siège*, the *assemblée du parquet*, the *assemblée des fonctionnaires du secrétariat-greffe*, and the *assemblée plénière des magistrats et fonctionnaires*.

[24] As a natural person, the defendant's home is the domicile or residence and for legal persons, this is their place of establishment or of registration.

plaintiff may choose the court of the place where the defendant resides or where the contract has been carried out (*i.e.* where the goods are delivered or the service supplied).

According to article L 311–1 of the *Code de l'organisation judiciaire*:

> "Subject to appeal, the *tribunal de grande instance* is competent to hear all disputes, unless jurisdiction has been expressly conferred upon another court on account of the nature of the dispute or the sum involved."[25]

The *tribunal de grande instance* is undoubtedly a court of general jurisdiction, *i.e.* it has jurisdiction to try any private law litigation within the limits of its territorial jurisdiction. However, this general competence is limited in a few instances both as regards the nature of the case (commercial or employment cases are dealt with by specialised courts) or the amount of money involved (litigation arising to less than 30,000 FF falls within the competence of the *tribunal d'instance*).

The *tribunal* enjoys exclusive jurisdiction in certain matters such as marriage, divorce and separation, filiation, nationality, patents, immovable property, road accidents, etc. In all these cases, the *tribunal* adjudicates *en dernier ressort* (without appeal) when the amount of money involved is less than 13,000 FF. Above this amount, its judgments are appealable.

Apart from his administrative and disciplinary powers, the President of the court is vested with specific powers and accordingly may make an *ordonnance sur requête* or an *ordonnance de référé*. In the former procedure, the plaintiff requests the President of the court to make an order authorising a measure (for example a *saisie conservatoire* — which is directed at preserving assets) without the opposing party being informed. If the opponent was informed, the procedure would loose its efficacy. Such a procedure may be requested from the President of the court when a debt collection is jeopardised and an authorisation to distrain the bank account of the debtor is necessary. However, once the order has been carried out, the opposing party may appeal against it (articles 493–498 &

---

[25] "*Le tribunal de grande instance connaît, à charge d'appel, de toutes les affaires pour lesquelles compétence n'est pas attribuée expressément à une autre juridiction, en raison de la nature de l'affaire ou du montant de la demande.*"

812–813 *N.C.P.C.*). The latter procedure is different from the former since the opposing party is informed of it.[26] In cases of urgency, this procedure allows the plaintiff to obtain an immediate decision from the President of the court which cannot be suspended by an appeal. The President acting as *juge des référés* may authorise the plaintiff to take a *mesure conservatoire*, intended to prevent imminent damage from occurring, or to proceed to a *remise en état* in order to stop disorders (for example towing away trucks which have been left by strikers in front of the garage of an employer thereby obstructing its entrance). Before the final judgment, the President may also grant a creditor a *provision* (provisional payment of a sum of money, such as damages or payment of salary in the case of redundancy) when the obligation of the other party is not in dispute (for example accident allowances, allowances under succession rights, etc.). The *juge des référés* may also be requested to intervene where there is difficulty in enforcing a court decision or any other writ of execution (article 811 *N.C.P.C.*).

Due to the position the *tribunal de grande instance* occupies in the court system both procedures confer important powers on its President. Nevertheless these are used in all ordinary civil courts.

(2) Specialised courts

Amongst the numerous courts of limited jurisdiction, five of these deserve to be analysed owing to their practical importance. These are the *tribunal d'instance*, the *tribunal de commerce*, the *conseil de prud'hommes*, the *tribunaux des affaires de sécurité sociale* and the *tribunaux paritaires des baux ruraux*.

(a) The *tribunal d'instance*
In 1958 the *tribunal d'instance* replaced the old *juges de paix* created under the French Revolution.

Composition
The *tribunaux d'instance* do not have their own personnel. Judges of the *tribunaux de grande instance* are appointed for

---

[26] This can be traced back to ancient law and is now provided for in arts. 482–491 and 808–811 *N.C.P.C.*

three years to serve in the *tribunaux d'instance* (articles L 321–5 & R 321–33 to 321–43 *C.O.J.*).

Unlike the *juges de paix*, the *tribunal d'instance* consists of more than one judge, the number varying according to the size of its territorial jurisdiction and the number of cases it deals with (for example nine in Lyon, 13 in Bordeaux). However, judgments are made by a single judge (article L 321–4 *C.O.J.*). The *parquet* has no permanent representative but the *procureur de la République of the tribunal de grande instance* may assume these functions on any matter. However, the *tribunal d'instance* does have its own *secrétariat-greffe*.

Organisation

Like that of the *tribunal de grande instance*, the territorial jurisdiction of the *tribunal d'instance* is defined by *décret*. This usually corresponds to the *arrondissement*.[27] There are 473 *tribunaux d'instance* including the overseas courts.

In courts having two or more judges, the judge who is highest in rank is in charge of the administration of the court and of allocating cases to the other judges. In the situation where judges are of the same rank, it is for the President of the *tribunal de grande instance* to appoint one of them to this function.

Jurisdiction

The competent court is that which is the nearest to the defendant's home (articles R 321–24 to 321–30 *C.O.J.*).

The *tribunal d'instance* has administrative and judicial functions. For instance, as regards the former, the court may issue nationality certificates, *actes de notoriété*,[28] affix and remove seals, receive the oath of gamekeepers, etc. One of its judges is *juge des tutelles* who supervises the administration of property of minors under wardship and ensures the protection of mentally handicapped adults.

With respect to its judicial powers, article 321–1 *C.O.J.* reads as follows:

> "...in civil matters, the *tribunal d'instance* hears all personal and moveable property disputes without appeal when the

---

[27] The *arrondissement* is an administrative subdivision of the *département*.

[28] These are acts directed at registering declarations of persons certifying facts which are publicly known.

value is no more than 13,000 FF. and, subject to appeal, when the value is up to 30,000 FF."[29]

Table 3.1 **Proceedings of *tribunaux de grande instance* from 1985 to 1992**

	1985	1986	1987	1988	1989	1990	1991	1992
cases lodged	417,552	427,404	432,496	450,112	470,357	488,680	492,391	523,026
cases decided	425,493	435,077	477,143	454,710	460,022	463,075	462,326	475,775
référé procedures						95,886	96,184	110,132

Source: *Annuaire statistique de la justice* 1989–1990 at pp. 53–44 and 1988–1992 at p. 21

Table 3.2 **Proceedings of *tribunaux d'instance* from 1985 to 1992**

	1985	1986	1987	1988	1989	1990	1991	1992
cases lodged[1]	395,019	417,053	445,921	508,391	541,396	532,702	547,890	609,190
cases decided[2]	382,001	406,138	445,493	444,412	474,113	501,578	518,732	588,126
référé procedures				70,323	82,380	87,910	91,596	93,178

[1] These figures do not include cases decided through special procedures.
[2] Since 1988, *tribunaux d'instance* also deal with cases relating to the protection of minors.

Source: *Annuaire statistique de la justice* 1989–1990 at p. 55 and 1988–1992 at p. 23

---

[29] "... *le tribunal d'instance connaît, en matière civile, de toutes actions personnelles ou mobilières, en dernier ressort jusqu'à la valeur de 13 000 F et, à charge d'appel, jusqu'à la valeur de 30 000 F.*"

Various powers have been conferred upon the court: for instance, *actions possessoires* (claims for possession of real estate), *actions en bornage* (actions for marking out land), actions regarding professional and residential renting, claims for allowances for necessaries, distraint, *redressement judiciaire civil* (administration of a private insolvent debtor's affairs — Act 89–1010 of December 31, 1989) and debt collection by means of an *injonction de payer* (injunction to pay).

Within the limits of their powers, judges of the *tribunaux d'instance* may make any *ordonnance sur requête* and *en référé* except in a case where enforcement causes difficulty. They may also use the procedure of *injonction de faire* (mandatory injunction) for the specific performance of obligations (articles 1425–1 to 1425–5 *N.C.P.C.*).

(b) The *tribunal de commerce*

The *tribunal de commerce* or *juridiction consulaire* is an institution of the *Ancien droit*. Cases relating to trade by land and trade by sea used to be tried by the *tribunaux consulaires* and the *amirautés* respectively. Commercial courts survived the French Revolution and only the *amirautés* were abolished. A number of reforms were envisaged but none of them has been successful. Indeed commercial courts have a lot of advantages arising from the specific character of commercial law and, particularly the lack of court costs owing to judgments being rendered by lay judges and justice rendered by peers.

The legal texts which govern the *tribunal de commerce* are to be found mainly in the Act of July 16, 1967 and three *décrets* of 1988 (articles L 412–1 *et seq.* & R 412–1 *et seq.* *C.O.J.* and Book IV of the *Code de commerce* (*C.Com.*)) and in the *nouveau Code de procédure civile* (*N.C.P.C.*) (articles 853–878).

Composition

The *tribunal de commerce* is composed of elected judges. However, in Alsace-Moselle, commercial disputes are dealt with by a commercial division of the *tribunal de grande instance* which consists of one professional judge and two elected traders (articles L 913–1 *et seq.* *C.O.J.*).[30] In the overseas *départements* of Guadeloupe, Réunion, Martinique and Guyana, there are mixed courts of commerce composed of the President of the *tribunal de grande instance* and three elected judges (articles L 921–4 *et seq.* *C.O.J.*).

Table 3.3 **Proceedings of *tribunaux de commerce* from 1985 to 1992[1]**

	1985	1986	1987	1990	1991	1992
cases lodged	278,390	274,238	281,076	275,651	298,632	307,910
cases decided[2]	269,452	277,071	287,328	233,314	259,062	266,305
référé procedures				49,831	54,378	56,853

[1] Figures for 1988 and 1989 are not available
[2] Up to 1990 these include cases decided by way of *référé*

Source: *Annuaire statistique de la justice* 1989–1990 at p. 57 and 1988–1992 at p. 27

Table 3.4 **Proceedings of *conseils de prud'hommes* from 1985 to 1992**

	1985	1986	1987	1988	1989	1990	1991	1992
cases lodged	150,922	144,033	142,991	145,522	151,161	152,955	156,928	172,883
cases decided	153.711	150,961	150,580	147,733	148,970	145,935	148,547	161,128
référé procedures	40,997	36,987	37,402	38,164	40,631	40,822	43,078	49,268

Source: *Annuaire statistique de la justice* 1989–1990 at p. 57 and 1985–1992 at p. 29

The *juges consulaires* are initially elected for two years and then for four years but are not eligible for a year if they have been judging continuously for 14 years (articles L 412–7 & L 413–4 *C.O.J.*). Anyone who is at least 30 years old, has been registered as a trader for at least five years and is not currently

---

[30] This is a transplant of the German model of *échevinage*.

subject to a procedure of *redressement judiciaire* (administration of a business under judicial supervision)[31] or *liquidation judiciaire* (liquidation), is eligible for the functions of *juge consulaire*. The elections are in two stages: the *juges consulaires* are elected by a body of *délégués consulaires* who themselves are elected every three years by tradesmen.

The *juges consulaires* are subject to disciplinary rules. For this purpose a *Commission nationale de discipline* was created in 1987. It is presided over by the President of a division of the Court of Cassation and can rule on liability and disqualification (articles 414–1 *et seq. C.O.J.*).

The office of *procurum* of the *tribunal de commerce* is held by the *procureur de la République* of the *tribunal de grande instance* (article 412–5 *C.O.J.*). Each commercial court has a *greffier* with the status of *officier public et ministériel* (see Chapter Four, below) (article L 821–1 *C.O.J.*).

Organisation

Commercial courts are created by a *décret en Conseil d'Etat*[32] which determines their seat and territorial jurisdiction (article L 411–2 *C.O.J.*).[33] The powers of the commercial court are usually territorially limited to the *arrondissement*.[34] Where there is no commercial court, commercial disputes are dealt with by the *tribunal de grande instance* which then adjudicates according to the rules of commercial procedure (articles 640 *C.Com.* & L 311–3 *C.O.J.*).

Unless provided expressly by law, judgments of commercial courts are rendered by at least three judges. Courts with more

---

[31] The procedure of *redressement judiciaire* is a single procedure established by Act 85–98 of January 25, 1985 and intended to replace the old procedures of *règlement judiciaire* (administration of the insolvent debtor's business), *liquidation des biens* (liquidation of an insolvent debtor's property) and *suspension provisoire des poursuites* (provisional suspension of action) created in 1967. It applies to all traders, artisans and legal persons of private law who are in *cessation de paiement* (in default) and may lead to either the continuation of the business, *cession* (alienation) or its liquidation.

[32] This is a *décret* which is adopted after having been submitted for the opinion of the *Conseil d'Etat*.

[33] The creation of a commercial court depends on the commercial activities of a region. The *décret* of July 14, 1986 created the court of Bobigny whilst a *décret* of 1985 merged those of Roubaix and Tourcoing. The courts of Douai and Foix were created in 1988 and 1989 respectively.

[34] A table showing the seats and territorial jurisdiction of all commercial courts was appended to *décret* 88–38 of January 13, 1988.

than eight judges are subdivided into *chambres* as is the case in Marseille where the commercial court has 16 divisions.

Jurisdiction

The competent commercial court is, in principle, that of the defendant's home. However, in contract disputes, the plaintiff may bring an action to the court of the place where the obligations have been performed.

Commercial courts are specialised courts. Their powers are defined by articles 631–640 *C.Com.* They are competent to try all disputes between tradesmen and all disputes between individuals concerning commercial transactions.[35] They may deal with disputes between partners on matters relating to the creation, the operation or the liquidation of a business (article 631–2 *C.Com.*), with *cessations de paiement* (defaults of payment) and with *redressement* and *liquidations judiciaires* of businesses when the debtor is a trader or an artisan (article 7 of the Act of January 25, 1985).

The *tribunal de commerce* is competent when a business has less than 50 employees and its turnover is inferior to a limit fixed by *décret*.[36] The most important cases are reserved for a limited number of commercial courts.[37]

The President of the court may adjudicate *en référé* or make *ordonnances sur requête* and use the procedure of injunction to compel payment.

(c) The *conseil de prud'hommes*

The *conseil de prud'hommes*, the equivalent of English industrial tribunals, are mixed (*paritaires*) courts, the function of

---

[35] The *actes de commerce* may have a commercial character by nature (*e.g.* buying goods in order to resell them) or in its form like a *lettre de change* (bill of exchange). With respect to mixed acts such as the sale of goods by a trader to a private individual, the latter may sue the former either in a commercial or a civil court; on the other hand, the trader may only sue the private individual in a civil court.

[36] This limit was set at 20 million FF by *décrets* 85–1387 of December 27, 1985 and 86–859 of July 17, 1986.

[37] These are listed in an appendix to the 1985 *décret*: *e.g.* the commercial court of Lyon is competent to hear such cases although there are three commercial courts in the *département* of the Rhône. However, this limited reform has not been very successful since it causes legal discrimination against the smallest courts and divergences of interpretation about the size limit of businesses. This list was therefore extended (by a *décret* of 1987) to most of the courts although the previous distinction remains.

which is to conciliate and, failing to do so, to adjudicate on individual employment disputes.

The origins of this industrial tribunal can be traced back to an old *cour des arts et métiers* (tribunal of arts and crafts) in Lyon. Abolished under the Revolution, it was re-established in Lyon by Napoleon in 1806. Its name comes from the medieval French *prud'hommes*, meaning men of loyalty, wisdom and integrity. Until the 1979 reforms, these tribunals were only established in part of France and their powers were limited. Act 79–44 of January 18, 1979 (as amended by Act 80–4 of January 5, 1980) has increased their number and enlarged their powers according to a uniform model.[38]

Composition

This industrial tribunal consists of elected representatives of employers and employees in five *sections* (divisions) each having eight members, *i.e* 40 members in total. This number is higher in large cities.[39]

The conditions for being a voter are identical for employers and employees: to have a professional activity or to be involuntarily unemployed and to be over 16. Under article L 513–1 of the *Code du travail* (*C.Trav.*) foreigners also have the right to vote.

In order to stand as a candidate, one must be of French nationality, over 21 and be registered on the employment electoral roll (article L 513–2 *C.Trav.*).

The composition of the tribunal is based on the principle of *parité i.e* of equal representation of both socio-professional categories. As a result, there is an equal number of representatives of employers and employees, and the presidency is held alternately by an employer and by an employee.

Organisation

There is at least one *conseil de prud'hommes* in a *département*[40] and 282 tribunals in total, including those in the overseas territories.

---

[38] On this reform see *inter alia*: B. Alibert, *La loi du 18 janvier 1979 sur les conseils de prud'hommes*: [1979] D. Chron. 169; F. Rochon, *Les nouveaux conseils de prud'hommes*: [1979] Rev. Prat. de Dr. Soc. 69.

[39] There are 140 court members in Bordeaux, 164 in Lyon, 184 in Marseilles and 740 in Paris.

[40] Article L 511–3(2) *C.Trav.* provides that more than one tribunal may be created within the territorial limits of a *tribunal de grande instance*: *e.g.* in the *département* of Loire, there are six *conseils de prud'hommes* for three *tribunaux de grande instance*.

The five *sections* (divisions) of the tribunal correspond to different sectors of the economy (management, industry, commerce, agriculture, miscellaneous activities). The jurisdiction of each division in a particular case is determined by the main activity of the employer, or of the business in which the litigating employee works (article L 512-2 *C.Trav.*). The divisions may be subdivided into *chambres* (sections) amongst which one specialises in redundancies arising for economic reasons. Each of the divisions or sections sits either as a *bureau de conciliation* (conciliation panel) or as a *bureau de jugement* (adjudication panel). The conciliation panel, which consists of two judges, not only has the function of settling disputes (article R 516-13 *C.Trav.*) but also of taking urgent measures such as delivering work certificates and pay slips, ordering the employer to pay provisional salaries when the existence of such an obligation is not contested, preparing the case, scheduling the investigation, and fixing the date for the hearing of the adjudication panel (article R 516-18 *C.Trav.*). The adjudication panel, which consists of four judges renders judgments on cases in which conciliation has proved impossible.[41]

Each *tribunal* may sit in chambers and hear applications *en référé* (articles L 516-1 & R 516-30 to 516-35 *C.Trav.*).

Since the 1979 reform, the *conseils de prud'hommes* have their own *secrétariat-greffe* whose members have the same status as those of the general courts.

A *conseil supérieur de la prud'homie*, attached to the Minister of Justice and the Minister of Labour, was created in 1982. Consisting of 23 members (five representatives of the State, 18 representatives of employers and employees), this has a purely consultative role on bills and draft regulations relating to industrial tribunals, and may undertake research and studies on the organisation and operation of these (article R 511-4 *C.Trav.*).

Jurisdiction

In principle, the competent *conseil de prud'hommes* is that within whose territorial jurisdiction the activity is carried out (article 517-1(1) *C.Trav.*).

It deals with all individual disputes between employers and employees and its main task is to settle a dispute through conciliation or adjudication, irrespective of the monetary value

---

[41] Due to the principle of *parité*, it may happen that the panel must reconvene under the presidency of a judge from the *tribunal d'instance* who will settle the vote (art. L 515-3 *C.Trav.*).

of the case. Up to 19,360 FF, a judgment is not appealable (article D 517–1 *C.Trav.* as amended by *décret* 93–1364 of December 30, 1993). It adjudicates on employment and apprenticeship contracts provided that the dispute is of an individual character (collective disputes are not dealt with by this tribunal), has a direct link with employment (for example this excludes any dispute about a loan granted by the employer to an employee) and involves the two parties to the employment contract (social security matters and industrial injuries do not fall within the jurisdiction of this tribunal), and the litigants are individuals (disputes between the state, a local authority or an *établissement public* and their staff are excluded).

Table 3.5 **Proceedings of *tribunaux des affaires de sécurité sociale* from 1985 to 1992**

	1985	1986	1987	1988	1989	1990	1991	1992
cases lodged	93,100	96,012	115,639	108,847	109,434	99,927	94,046	103,050
cases decided	90,390	93,064	103,855	109,573	112.749	97,432	93,860	83,741

Source: *Annuaire statistique de la justice* 1989–1990 at p. 57 and 1988–1992 at p. 25

Table 3.6 **Proceedings of *tribunaux paritaires de baux ruraux* from 1985 to 1992**

	1985	1986	1987	1988	1989	1990	1991	1992
cases lodged	4,934	4,903	4,761	4,981	4,907	4,859	4,566	5,605
cases decided	4,852	4,872	4,588	4,841	4,894	4,576	4,590	6,042
référé procedures				582	405	325	297	541

ource: *Annuaire statistique de la justice* 1989–1990 at p. 55 and 1988–1992 at p. 25

(d) The *tribunal des affaires de sécurité sociale*

The *tribunal des affaires de sécurité sociale* consists of three judges, two lay judges — one representing employees and one representing employers and the self-employed — and one judge from the *tribunal de grande instance* acting as President, who is appointed for three years by *ordonnance* of the President of the *Cour d'Appel*. This court,[42] which is similar to the English social security appeals tribunal, hears social security disputes of first instance, such as social security registration, contributions, benefits entitlement, etc. whatever the nature of the scheme (for example a general, special or agricultural scheme), and irrespective of the monetary value of the dispute, although up to 13,000 FF judgments are not appealable (article R 142–25 *C.O.J.*).

Its territorial jurisdiction is set out by an *arrêté ministériel* and corresponds in whole or partially to the territorial limits of the authority of a social security authority (article R 142–13 *C.O.J.*). There are at present 110 social security tribunals.

(e) The *tribunal paritaire de baux ruraux*

Created in 1944 and governed by the *décret* of December 22, 1958 (article 441–1 *C.O.J.*), the *tribunal paritaire de baux ruraux*, which is similar in composition, function and jurisdiction to the English agricultural land tribunal, is competent to hear disputes between landlords and tenants.

It consists of five members: a judge from the *tribunal d'instance*, acting as President, and four lay judges — two representatives of tenants and two of landlords — who are elected for six years by their respective peers. Therefore it is a *juridiction échevinale et paritaire*, like the social security tribunal described above.

It sits in two different compositions: either as a single judge court in which the President has the general power to hear urgent applications *en référé* or *sur requête*; or as a full bench which is divided into two *sections* (divisions), the *section du métayage* (the division dealing with the share-cropping system) and the *section du fermage* (the division dealing with the system of leasehold rents).

---

[42] This court was reorganised by the 1985 Act. Before 1985, it was called *commission de première instance de sécurité sociale*.

Its territorial jurisdiction is similar to that of the *tribunal d'instance*.[43]

(B) CRIMINAL COURTS

The *juridictions pénales* or *juridictions répressives* are not fundamentally distinct from the civil courts. Indeed, they are composed of the same judges acting in the same way as criminal or civil judges. However, the criminal justice system has a unique structural difference as a result of the three-stage proceedings which contrasts clearly with the unity of civil proceedings. These three stages are the pre-trial stage, which subdivides into the *poursuite* (public prosecution) and the *instruction* (investigation), and the trial stage or *jugement*. Each stage is separate and distinct according to the principle of *séparation des fonctions judiciaires* (judicial functions are separate) and only the latter two take place in a court. These will be examined in this section.[44]

(1) The *juridictions d'instruction*

In French criminal law not all cases proceed directly to trial. Before they are tried, some of them, the most serious or the most complex ones, are examined by a *juridiction d'instruction* (pre-trial investigatory court).

The main *juridictions d'instruction*[45] are the *juge d'instruction* or *magistrat instructeur* (investigating judge) and the *chambre d'accusation* (Indictment Division).[46]

---

[43] However, in practice there are less agricultural land tribunals (413) than *tribunaux d'instance* (471).

[44] The stage of the *poursuite* is examined in Chapter Five, below.

[45] Some pre-trial bodies are attached to criminal courts of limited jurisdiction. Crimes tried by the *Haute Cour de Justice* and the *Cour de Justice de la République* are investigated by a *commission d'instruction* which consists of judges from the Bench of the *Cour de Cassation*. In cases involving young offenders, serious crimes are exclusively investigated by an ordinary investigating judge while major and minor offences are concurrently investigated by the *juge des enfants* and the investigating judge. In military courts, the investigation is conducted by an investigating judge, who either comes from an ordinary court or is a military judge, and by a *chambre de contrôle de l'instruction*, which mainly consists of judges from ordinary courts.

[46] Their respective powers are considered in Chapter Five, below.

Table 3.7 Civil Courts of First Instance

	NUMBER OF COURTS	COMPOSITION	LOCATION	TERRITORIAL JURISDICTION	JURISDICTION	FORMATIONS DE JUGEMENT			APPEALS IN COURTS OF APPEAL		
						Public hearings	In camera	Single judge	Under 13,000FF	From 13,000FF	From 30,000FF
T.G.I.	181	Three judges at least	Chief town of a département	One at least per département	General jurisd. in civil matters	yes	yes	yes	no	yes	yes
T.I.	473	Variable number of judges	Chief town of a département or arrondissements	One at least per arrondissement	Civil matters up to 30,000 Ffr.	yes	no	yes	no	yes	n.a.
T.Co.	229	Three lay elected judges at least	Variable	Variable	Commercial matters	yes	yes	yes	no	yes	n.a.
T.A.S.S.	110	One judge + Two lay judges	Variable	One within the area of a social security authority	Social security matters	yes	no	no	no	yes	n.a.
T.P.B.R.	413	One judge + Four lay judges	Variable	One within the territorial jurisdiction of a T.I.	Agricultural land disputes	yes	yes	yes	no	yes	n.a.
C.P.	282	Elected lay judges	Variable	One at least in a T.I.'s territorial jurisdiction	Employment disputes	—conciliation panel —adjudicating panel			No appeal under 18,200Ffr.	Appeal over 18,200Ffr.	n.a.

T.G.I.: Tribunal de grande instance
T.I.: Tribunal d'instance
T.Co.: Tribunal de commerce
T.A.S.S.: Tribunal des affaires de sécurité sociale
T.P.B.R.: Tribunal paritaires des baux ruraux
C.P.: Conseil de prud'hommes

(a) The *juge d'instruction*

Under article 50 of the *Code de procédure pénale* (*C.P.P.*), the *juge d'instruction* is a judge from the *tribunal de grande instance* and is therefore a *magistrat du siège* (judge of the Bench) (see Chapter Four, below). In principle, he is appointed by a *décret* of the President of the Republic[47] and, consequently, can be removed from this function by a similar *décret* without, however, loosing his status as judge. There is one investigating judge in each *tribunal de grande instance* but many of the largest courts have more than one of them.[48]

Originally, in the *Code d'instruction criminelle*, the investigating judge was simply a police officer in charge of the investigation, only becoming a judicial authority since the Act of July 17, 1856. The expression *"juge d'instruction"* clearly reflects his role in criminal proceeedings: like a police officer, he conducts investigations with the view to collecting evidence and, like a judge, he issues orders which can be appealed against before the Indictment Division. The investigating judge is regarded as a court in its own right which performs its functions fully independently from the prosecution, the Indictment Division and the parties.

(b) The *chambre d'accusation*

For long called *chambre des mises en accusation*, the *chambre d'accusation* is a special division of the *cour d'appel* composed of three judges. Its main role is that of a *juridiction d'instruction du second degré* (pre-trial investigatory Appeal Court). It re-examines the investigation of serious crimes (article 181 *C.P.P.*) and, if it confirms the decision of the investigating judge, it sends the case for trial at the Assizes (articles 214 & 215 *C.P.P.*). It also hears appeals against orders issued by the investigating judge (articles 185–187 & 207 *C.P.P.*), acts as a disciplinary body for the police (article 224 *et seq. C.P.P.* supervises extraditions (article 4 of the Act of March 10, 1927), and decides on rehabilitation (article 783 *C.P.P.*) and amnesty.

(2) The *juridictions de jugement*

While *juridictions d'instruction* investigate cases, *juridictions de jugement* try them and deliver either a judgment of

---

[47] Articles 50(2), (3) & (4) *C.P.P.* provide for other temporary and exceptional cases where another *juge d'instruction* may be appointed.

[48] *e.g.* the court of Paris has 70 investigating judges.

conviction or acquittal. As is usual in French law, there is a distinction between courts of general jurisdiction and courts of limited jurisdiction.

(a) General courts

There are three criminal courts which deal separately with each category of offences (see Chapter Five). These are the *tribunal de police* (Police Court), the *tribunal correctionnel* and the *cour d'assises* (Court of Assize).

The tribunal de police

In accordance with the principle of unity of civil and criminal justice, the *tribunal de police* is the *tribunal d'instance* sitting as a criminal court. It is therefore the lowest criminal court. There is one court per *arrondissement*.[49] This is a single judge court in which the *juge d'instance* sits alternatively as a civil and a criminal judge, but as most *tribunaux d'instance* have more than one judge, one of them specialises in criminal cases.

The functions of prosecutor are performed by a police officer and, in the case of *contraventions de la 5ème classe*,[50] by the *procureur de la République* of the *tribunal de grande instance* (articles 45–48 C.P.P.).

The jurisdiction of the *tribunal de police* is limited to *contraventions* (minor offences) which are punishable by a fine not exceeding 20,000 FF (article 521 C.P.P. as amended by article 43 of the Act of December 16, 1992 on the coming into force of the new Criminal Code).[51] The competent court is that of the place where the offence has been committed or recorded or where the offender resides (article 522 C.P.P.).

The tribunal correctionnel

When exercising its criminal jurisdiction the *tribunal de grande instance* is referred to as the *tribunal correctionnel* or

---

[49] However, three courts specialising in criminal matters have been created in Paris, Lyon and Marseille (art. L 623–2 C.O.J.).

[50] Minor offences are classified into five categories. Those offences of the fifth category are punishable by the highest penalties for minor offences, *i.e.* fines between 10,000 and 20,000 FF or restrictions or deprivation of rights (arts. 131– 12 to 131–14 of the Criminal Code).

[51] The jurisdiction of the French Police Court combines roughly that of the English magistrates and county courts.

chambre correctionnelle. In most courts, a single division adjudicates on civil and criminal cases whilst larger courts have one or more criminal divisions dealing specifically with criminal cases.[52]

This criminal court is usually composed of three judges (article 398 *C.P.P.*) but in order to speed up the proceedings, the Act of December 29, 1972 provides that certain offences (for example cheque frauds, reckless driving causing death or incapacitating injuries, game related offences) may be tried by a single judge unless the accused is in pre-trial detention (article 398–1 *C.P.P.* as amended by article 32 of the Act of December 16, 1992). More recently, under the Act of February 8, 1995 — which came into force on March 6, 1995 — the list of offences which can be tried by a single judge was extended to, *inter alia*, assault with intent which has incapacitated someone from working for more than eight days (including aggravating circumstances), aggravated thefts, malicious telephone calls, indecent exposure, abandonment of family, interference with parental authority, etc.[53]

This criminal court is competent to try *délits* (major offences) which have been committed within its territorial jurisdiction —

---

[52] In Paris, there are 20 criminal divisions, and five in Marseille and Lyon.

[53] According to a circular of the Minister of Justice of February 14, 1995, the jurisdiction of the single judge was extended only to relatively simple and recurrent cases amounting to no more than 20 per cent of judgments passed by *tribunaux correctionnels*. In reality, these offences, which are not all minor ones, account for a third of the cases dealt with by the Court of Paris and for even more in smaller courts (*e.g.* 70 per cent in the Court of Avranches and up to 83.7 per cent in the Court of Aurillac). Furthermore, the sentencing power of single judges is not negligible: they may pass sentences of up to five years' imprisonment for first-time offenders and, in principle, sentences of up to ten years' imprisonment for recidivists (however, in the latter case, the offender is more likely to be summoned to appear immediately before a court or to be remanded in custody by the investigating judge, in which case he will be tried by a bench of three judges). Basically, the purpose of this reform is to lighten the workload of judges and release some of them for other important tasks. However, this reform was not approved of unanimously by judges: some of them, like Jean Bastelica, the President of the Court of Valence, considered that it was far from being time-saving; others, like Michel Lernout, a member of the *Union syndicale des magistrats*, believe that the fundamental principle of *collégialité*, which is regarded as a procedural safeguard for the defendant and a guarantee of the independence of judges, is sacrificed for budgetary reasons and that this reform will encourage a two-speed justice (see *Le Monde*, March 7, 1995, p. 10).

that is the *département* — or outside it, if the perpetrator resides or has been arrested in this *département* (article 382(1) *C.P.P.*). A *délit* is an offence punishable by a sentence of imprisonment of six months or more, or by a fine of, or above, 25,000 FF (article 381 *C.P.P.*). They may also deal with minor offences associated with a major one, and certain special minor offences (for instance under articles 624 and 1867 of the *Code général des impôts* (*C.G.I.*) in matters of indirect taxes). Highly complex cases of an economic and financial nature (for example tax, customs, banking, stock exchange offences, misleading advertising, etc.) are tried by a special division (articles 704 and 705 *C.P.P.*). Similarly, since the Act of July 21, 1982 which abolished the *tribunaux permanents des forces armées* (military courts in peacetime), military offences (for example desertion, insubordination, desertion of one's post, etc.) fall within the jurisdiction of the criminal court situated in the same town as the *cour d'appel* (article 697 *C.P.P.*).

The cour d'assises

The *cour d'assises* (Court of Assize)[54] is usually described by French legal writers as the most distinctive court amongst the French courts. It is indeed distinctive with respect to its territorial jurisdiction, its composition, its operation and its competence.

There is one court in each *département* (article 232 *C.P.P.*). It bears the name of the *département* (for example *cour d'assises de Paris, du Bas-Rhin*, etc.) and generally has its seat in the chief town. Consequently, it may share premises with a *cour d'appel* or a *tribunal de grande instance*, and certain personnel may overlap (for example the prosecution or the *greffe*). There are 99 Courts of Assize altogether.

Unlike other criminal courts, the Court of Assize consists not only of professional judges but also of a jury of nine lay *jurés*. This is why this court is commonly called the *juridiction populaire* (the people's court). The court itself has three judges: a President who is either the Division President or a *conseiller* of a *cour d'appel* (article 244 *C.P.P.*) — or very rarely, its first President (article 247 *C.P.P.*) — and two judges chosen from the

---

[54] See D. Vernier and M. Peyrot, *La cour d'assises* (Coll. Que-sais-je? PUF, Paris, 1989).

conseillers of a *cour d'appel* or the judges of the *tribunal de grande instance* (article 249 *C.P.P.*). According to the principle of strict separation between the prosecution, the investigation and the adjudication, these judges cannot be appointed from amongst those who have participated in the first two functions (article 253 *C.P.P.*).

The Court of Assize usually sits only once every quarter unless more hearings are needed due to the number of cases to be tried, as is the case in Paris (article 236 *C.P.P.*). Since the Act of November 25, 1941, the jury and the court consider and decide questions of law and fact together to determine whether the accused is guilty or not and the sentence to be passed (articles 356 and 362 *C.P.P.*). In order to prevent the jury from being influenced by the judges, the Code of Criminal Procedure provides that any decision concerning guilt which is unfavourable to the accused must be approved by a qualified majority of eight (therefore including five jurors) against four (article 359 *C.P.P.*). A majority of seven votes is therefore not sufficient and if five votes are favourable to the accused he will be acquitted or be given the benefit of any extenuating circumstances according to the principle of the *minorité de faveur* (favourable minority). For the sentence, an overall majority of seven votes is required.

However, the highest applicable *peine privative de liberté* (custodial sentence) (see Chapter Five, below) must be approved of by a majority of eight votes. If this majority is not reached, a sentence of more than 30 years' imprisonment may not be passed if the maximun applicable sentence is life imprisonment, nor may a sentence of more than 20 years' imprisonment be passed where the highest applicable sentence is 30 years' imprisonment. The same principle applies to *détention criminelle* (detention) (see article 362(2)).

If after two ballots, no majority is reached, a third ballot is conducted, the heaviest sentence proposed in the preceeding vote being excluded, and so on until agreement on a sentence is reached (article 362(3)).

The Court of Assize is competent to try *crimes* (serious crimes) — excluding those perpetrated by minors, high treason by the President of the Republic and crimes committed by ministers — and offences connected with a serious crime. Moreover, according to the principle of *plénitude de juridiction* (full jurisdiction), the Court of Assize must try minor and major offences for which it has been wrongly seized by the Indictment

Division, the latter having wrongly classified the offence (article 231 *C.P.P.*). Indeed, the *arrêt de mise en accusation* (committal for trial on indictment) delivered by the Indictment Division is said to be *attributif de competence* in that it makes the Assize Court fully competent to try these offences (article 594 *C.P.P.*).[55] The principle of full jurisdiction also allows the Court of Assize to award damages to the *partie civile* (civil party) even in the case of acquittal or *exemption de peine* (exemption from punishment) (article 372 *C.P.P.*).

Whatever the offence being tried is, judgments of the Court of Assize cannot be appealed against to the *chambre des appels correctionnels* (Criminal Division of the Court of Appeal). Only an appeal in the form of a *pourvoi en cassation* to the Court of Cassation is available. Indeed, the people's verdict is not to be censured.

Table 3.8   **Sentences Passed by Criminal Courts of General Jurisdiction from 1987 to 1992**

	1987	1988	1989	1990	1991	1992
Cours d'assises	2,410	2,648	2,626	2,567	2,553	2,443
Tribunaux correctionnels	413,884	277,379	389,952	410,134	390,961	398,199
Tribunaux de police	1,288,960	810,365	1,089,567	1,049,094	1,048,764	904,971

Source: *Annuaire statistique de la justice* 1988–1992 at pp. 91, 93 and 97

(b)   Specialised courts

Some criminal courts have a limited jurisdiction based either on the personality of the offender (minors, members of the forces, the President of the Republic and members of Government) or the nature of the offence (for example offences related to marine mercantile law).

---

[55] However, this principle does not apply to offences committed by minors since minors cannot be tried by courts of general jurisdiction.

In the 1980s, two specialised courts were abolished: in 1981, the *cour de sûreté de l'Etat* (State Security Court), competent to try major offences and serious crimes against the State; and, in 1982, the *tribunaux permanents des forces armées* competent to try offences punished by the *Code de justice militaire* (Military Code of Justice) and non-military offences perpetrated by servicemen (for example theft or crimes committed on military premises).

The cours d'assises spéciales

As a remarkable departure from the principle of mixed composition, a number of specialised Courts of Assize without a jury have been created. This has been the case since 1982 for military crimes and crimes committed against State security (see below). Since the Act of September 9, 1986, a specialised court has been established which is competent to try adults responsible for crimes committed either individually or collectively against public order by means of intimidation or terror (article 706–25 *C.P.P.*). More recently, as a result of the reform of the Criminal Code, the Act of December 16, 1992 created another special Assize Court responsible for trying drug trafficking offences (article 706–27 *C.P.P.*).

The juridictions pour mineurs

The existence of Youth Courts can be explained by the specific character of juvenile delinquency and the need for preventive and educative measures. Only minors under 13 are subject to such measures whereas minors under 18 may face ordinary sentences although of a lower quantum than adults. Minors are only tried by Youth Courts when they have committed *contraventions de la 5ème classe* (see footnote 50, above), *délits* and *crimes*. They are tried by Police Courts, like any adult offender, for minor offences of the first four categories.

These Youth Courts are the *juge des enfants* (judge specialising in dealing with young offenders), the *tribunal des enfants* and the *cour d'assises des mineurs* (Youth Assize Court).

The juge des enfants

The *juge des enfants* is appointed for an unlimited period from amongst judges of the *tribunal de grande instance* on the basis of his interest in children and his personal aptitude (article L 532–1 *C.O.J.*). He is competent to deal with *contraventions de la 5ème classe* and any *délits* committed by minors under 18 (article L 531–2 *C.O.J.*). As an exception to the principle of separation of judicial functions, a *juge des enfants* who has investigated a case may also choose to adjudicate it alone in *chambre du conseil* instead of forwarding it to the *tribunal des enfants* (article 8(3) of *ordonnance* 45–174 of February 2, 1945 on Juvenile Delinquency). Where a judge regards himself as competent, he may subject the minor only to educative measures or supervision (for example by sending him back to his family or a third person, and/or by taking a measure of *liberté surveillée* [supervision order]) but may not send him to a state or private educational institution (article 8 *in fine* of 1945 *ordonnance*). In practice, if the judge considers that a simple educative measure is sufficient, he will then adjudicate alone. If he reckons that a sentence must be imposed or the minor must be sent to a specialised institution, he must then adjudicate with the two other judges.

The tribunal des enfants

This Youth Court is made up of one *juge des enfants* — as its presiding judge — and two lay judges, appointed for four years by an *arrêté* of the Minister of Justice from amongst French citizens over 30 years old who have shown competence and interest in matters relating to children (articles L 522–2 & 522–3 *C.O.J.*).

There is at least one Youth Court in each *département* having the same seat and territorial jurisdiction as the *tribunal de grande instance* (130 courts altogether listed in Table III of the *Code de l'organisation judiciaire*).

This court has the same jurisdiction as the *juge des enfants* but, in addition, deals with crimes perpetrated by minors under 16. Unlike the *juge des enfants*, it may decide to send a juvenile offender to a specialised institution or even sentence him, although the penalty is lighter than for an adult offender (articles 15, 16 & 2 of the 1945 *ordonnance*).

The cours d'assises des mineurs

Youth Assize Courts are organised on the same model as that of the ordinary Courts of Assize: their territorial jurisdiction, seats and sittings follow the same pattern. Even their respective compositions are basically identical: a Bench of three judges and a jury of nine. However the Bench consists of a *conseiller à la cour d'appel* and two *juges des enfants*.

They are competent to try serious crimes perpetrated by minors over 16 (article L 511–2 *C.O.J.*). If the Indictment Division decides so under article 9(3) of the 1945 *ordonnance*, they also have jurisdiction to try adult offenders who have been parties to a serious crime committed by a minor.

According to the principle of restricted publicity, the *débats* (hearings) are open to only a few people (article 20(8) *ord.*); but the reading of the questions to the jury and the judgment are in open court. Judgments of the Youth Assize Court are appealable only to the Court of Cassation by way of a *pourvoi en cassation*.

The juridictions militaires

Offences committed by members of the armed forces have for a long time been tried by a number of military courts. When the *Code de justice militaire* (Code of Military Justice) was promulgated on July 8, 1965, only two courts remained: the *tribunaux permanents des forces armées* sitting in peacetime and the *tribunaux militaires aux armées* sitting in wartime or in peacetime when forces were operating outside French territory. Often subject to criticism, the *tribunaux permanents des forces armées* in peacetime were abolished under the Act 82–621 of July 21, 1982. Military courts in wartime were maintained.

Military justice in peacetime

Offences falling within the jurisdiction of the old *tribunaux permanents des forces armées* (those defined by Title III *C.J.M.*; for example desertion, insubordination, treason, and non-military major offences and serious crimes committed by members of the forces) are now dealt with by criminal courts of general jurisdiction (article 1 of the 1982 Act). Within the territorial jurisdiction of each Court of Appeal, a specialised division of the *tribunal de grande instance* is competent to conduct the investigation, and in the case of major offences, to try offences committed by members of the armed forces (article 697 *C.P.P.*). A special Court of Assize, composed of seven judges but without a jury, deals with serious crimes (article 697(3) *C.P.P.*).

Nevertheless, when French armies are operating outside French territory, the offences referred to above are tried by military courts such as the *tribunaux aux armées en temps de paix* and the *tribunaux prévôtaux*, the latter being competent to hear minor offences.

Military justice in wartime

In wartime, there are two categories of courts: military courts established on French territory (the *tribunaux territoriaux des forces armées* and the *haut tribunal des forces armées* which tries high ranking officers), and those outside the territory (the *tribunaux militaires aux armées*).

The tribunaux maritimes commerciaux

Re-established in 1939 in the main ports (Dunkirk, Le Havre, Boulogne, Marseille etc.), these criminal courts, composed mainly of members of maritime trade, are competent to try maritime offences (ship desertion, usurpation of command, refusal to salvage, etc.).

Table 3.9 **Sentences Passed by Criminal Courts of Limited Jurisdiction from 1985 to 1992**

	1985	1986	1987	1988	1989	1990	1991	1992
Tribunaux pour enfants	30,698	28,592	22,597	8,759	14,538	19,550	20,657	22,594
Juges pour enfants	30,254	28,559	21,170	8,653	15,891	18,535	19,238	16,985
Cours d'assises pour mineurs	244	198	226	164	205	155	186	177
Tribunaux aux armées	1,329	1,971	1,984	1,274	2,164	2,102	1,986	1,761
Tribunaux maritimes commerciaux	53	40	154	176	273	251		

Source: *Annuaire statistique de la justice* 1989–1990 at pp. 121, 123 and 125 and 1988–1992 at pp. 91, 95 and 99

The Haute Cour de Justice

This is a court of a political nature competent to try the President of the Republic, if he is suspected of the crime of high treason (article 68 of the 1958 Constitution). It consists of 24 M.P.s elected by the two Houses of Parliament (article 67 of the Constitution and article 1 of *ordonnance* 59–1 of January 2, 1959). The Prosecution Department is represented by an *avocat général près la Cour de Cassation* assisted by the *premier avocat général* and two *avocats généraux* (article 13 of the 1959 *ordonnance*). Judgments of the *Haute Cour* are not appealable (article 35).

The Cour de Justice de la République

The 1958 Constitution was amended so as to add a new Title X on criminal liability of Members of Government. This provides that Members of Government may be tried by a new court called "*Cour de justice de la République*" (new article 68–1(2) of the Constitution)[56]. This court is composed of 15 judges, 12 of them being appointed from amongst Members of Parliament and three from amongst judges of the Court of Cassation, and is presided over by one of the latter judges (new article 68–2(1)). The innovation lies in the fact that under new article 68–2(2) of the Constitution, anyone who claims to be the victim of a serious crime or a major offence committed by a Member of Government in the performance of his official functions may bring an action before a *commission des requêtes* (complaints committee), the role of which is, under article 68–2(3), either to dismiss the case or transfer it to the *procureur général* of the

---

[56] Former art. 68(2) of the Constitution gave powers to the *Haute cour de justice* to try Members of Government. However, since 1918, not a single Member of Government has ever been tried by the *Haute cour*. As long as they could be brought before ordinary courts, as was the case on few rare occasions during the Third Republic (1875–1940), this had never had major consequence as far as justice was concerned. Since 1958, Members of Government enjoyed a *de facto* criminal immunity. Even the Court of Cassation interpreted former article 68(2) of the Constitution as meaning that present or former Members of Government could be tried by the *Haute cour de justice* only for crimes and major offences committed in the performance of their governmental functions, thus letting politicians try politicians. Although the investigation was carried out by judges of the Court of Cassation, judgments were delivered by a court composed of Members of Parliament. These were therefore of a strong political nature. It is then not surprising that, until the recent affair of contaminated transfusion blood, no parliamentary majority has ever committed any Member of Government for trial before this political court. It was only after the case concerning haemophiliacs contaminated by Aids through blood transfusions that it was felt necessary to amend the procedure for investigating the criminal liability of Members of Government.

Table 3.10 Main Criminal Courts of First Instance

	NUMBER OF COURTS	COMPOSITION	LOCATION	TERRITORIAL JURISDICTION	JURISDICTION	FORMATIONS DE JUGEMENT			APPEALS TO THE COURTS OF APPEAL / APPEALS BY WAY OF CASSATION
						Public hearings	sessions in camera	single judge	
COURS D'ASSISES	102	Three judges + Nine jurors	Chief town of départements	One per département	Serious crimes	yes	Trials in continuance	no	Court of Cassation
TRIBUNAUX CORRECTIONNELS	186	Three judges	Chief town of departments	One at least per département	Major offences	yes	no	yes	Chambre des appels correctionnels
TRIBUNAUX DE POLICE	460	One judge	Chief town of départements or arrondissements	One at least per arrondissement	Minor offences	yes	no	yes	Chambre des appels correctionnels
JUGE DES ENFANTS	279	One judge	One specialist judge in tribunaux de grande instance	One at least per département	Minor offences of the fifth category and major offences committed by minors	no	yes	n.a.	Chambre spéciale of a Court of Appeal
TRIBUNAUX POUR ENFANTS	136	One juge des enfants + Two lay judges	Chief town of départements	One at least per département	As above plus serious crimes committed by minors under 16	limited	no	no	Chambre spéciale of a Court of Appeal
COUR D'ASSISES POUR MINEURS	102	Three judges + Nine jurors	Chief town of départements	One per département	Serious offences committed by minors over 16	no	yes	no	Court of Cassation

Court of Cassation with the view to further taking it to the *Cour de justice de la République*. The *procureur de la République* may also forward the case directly to the *Cour de justice de la République* with the assent of the *commission des requêtes* (article 68–2(4)).

(C) THE COURTS COMMON TO CIVIL AND CRIMINAL MATTERS

The general and specialist ordinary courts described so far try cases in the first instance. These are the *juridictions du premier degré* (courts of first instance). Of course, any party who has lost a case before one of these courts (except the Court of Assize, the *Haute cour de justice* and the *Cour de justice de la République*) has the right to appeal to a higher court, the *cour d'appel* (Court of Appeal) and have the case re-examined. This is by virtue of the rule of *double degré de juridiction* (appeal court system).

Besides this appeal, which lies in the re-examination of the facts and the law of a case, there is another possible appeal, the *pourvoi en cassation* or *recours en cassation* (appeal in *cassation*) the purpose of which is quite different, as it is to set aside a judgment solely on legal grounds, and to assure the uniformity of case law.[57] The *Cour de Cassation* is *juge du droit* since it does not examine the facts but only the legality of those decisions of the lower courts which are referred to it.

The *cour d'appel* and the *Cour de Cassation* will be examined in turn.

(1) The *cour d'appel*

Originally, the French revolutionaries did not want to create any higher courts over the newly established district courts. Under the Act of August 16–24, 1790 a circuit appellate system called *appel circulaire* was established but proved to be a failure. The *cours d'appel* appeared only in 1800 and their decisions were called "*arrêts*" as opposed to the "*jugements*" of the courts of first instance.

The *ordonnance* of December 22, 1958 reorganised the Courts of Appeal which were too varied and numerous, and

---

[57] Appeal and appeal in *cassation* are examined in Chapter Five, below.

created single and common Courts of Appeal which hear appeals from all courts of first instance situated within their territorial jurisdiction.

Composition

A Court of Appeal consists of judges called *"conseillers"*[58] working under the authority of a *premier président* (or *chef de cour*). These appeal judges are high-ranking and well-experienced judges. Their number is greater or lesser depending on the importance of the court and the number of cases to be tried, but there must be at least three judges (there are 132 of them in Paris). The State Counsel's Office is headed by a *procureur général*, one or more *avocats généraux* and the *substituts du procureur général* (*substituts généraux*).

Each court is normally composed of several *chambres* (divisions) headed by a *président de chambre* (for example 28 in Paris, 16 in Aix-en-Provence, seven in Lyon, but only two in Bastia and in Chambéry). Each division has general jurisdiction except for those divisions created by the legislator for a specific purpose such as the *chambre sociale* (Social Security and Employment Division), the *chambre des appels correctionnels* (Criminal Division), the *chambre spéciale* (Juvenile Division), the *chambre d'accusation* (Indictment Division) and the *assemblée des chambres*.[59]

Organisation

There are 34 Courts of Appeal in metropolitan and overseas France, these being regional courts the territorial jurisdiction of which corresponds on average to three *départements*.[60]

Jurisdiction

In civil matters, the Court of Appeal hears appeals from all civil courts (article R 211–1 *C.O.J.*), whatever the nature of the decision (*jugement, ordonnance de référé* or *ordonnance sur requête*), and re-examines the facts and the legal points of a case.

---

[58] The term *"conseiller"* comes from the time when justice was rendered by the King after seeking advice from his counsellors or *"conseillers de longue robe"*.

[59] This *assemblée* consists of the first two or three divisions of the Court of Appeal and is competent in matters relating to the judicial professions (*e.g.* it receives judges' oaths, it may annul Bar elections, it hears appeals against the decisions of the *Conseil de l'ordre des avocats*, deals with disciplinary cases involving *avoués* and *huissiers*, etc.).

[60] However, the court of Paris covers six *départements* and that of Metz, only one (Moselle).

However the Court of Appeal does not hear appeals from cases tried *en premier et dernier ressort* and those having a monetary value under the level fixed by *décret*.

In criminal matters, appeals from the criminal courts go to the *chambre des appels correctionnels* or the *chambre spéciale* in the case of juvenile offenders. Appeals against decisions of investigating judges are heard by the Indictment Division. By way of exception, no appeal lies from Courts of Assize.

In principle, *arrêts* of a Court of Appeal are passed *en audience ordinaire* and, exceptionally, *en audience solennelle* (sitting with five judges instead of three) — in the case of an action against a judge who has committed a *faute personnelle*, or when a case has been remitted to the Appeal Court after it has been quashed by the Court of Cassation.

Table 3.11 **Proceedings of Courts of Appeal in Civil and Commercial Matters from 1985 to 1992**

	1985	1986	1987	1988	1989	1990	1991	1992
Cases lodged	147,264	146,745	148,441	153,509	161,406	167,803	173,777	182,794
Cases decided	138,059	142,533	149,464	158,271	163,973	169,010	168,011	171,082

Source: *Annuaire statistique de la justice* 1989–1990 at p. 53 and 1988–1992 at p. 31

Table 3.12 **Sentences Passed by *Chambres des Appels Correctionnels* and *Chambres Spéciales* from 1985 to 1992**

	1985	1986	1987	1988	1989	1990	1991	1992
Chambres des appels correctionnels	31,009	33,278	33,389	23,291	25,289	26,660	27,109	27,299
Chambres spéciales	472	518	357	159	165	212	228	257

Source: *Annuaire statistique de la justice* 1989–1990 at p. 121 and 1988–1992 at p. 101

(2) The *Cour de Cassation*

The Court of Cassation is the highest court of the *ordre judiciaire*[61] and is often referred to as the *"Cour Suprême"* (Supreme Court)[62] although this is not an official title.

It is a single court which sits in Paris in the *Palais de Justice, quai de l'Horloge*. Its origins can be traced back to the old *Conseil des Parties* which was one of the divisions of the *Conseil du Roi* and which was competent to examine applications lodged against judgments of the old *Parlements*. These were abolished during the Revolution and replaced by the *Tribunal de Cassation* in 1790 which was founded on the fundamental principle of the uniform interpretation of the rule of law. Indeed, the role of the Court of Cassation is to ensure that, in its interpretation and application, the rule of law is observed by inferior courts.[63] This is why the Court of Cassation does not deal with the facts of a case but only with points of law and examines whether the law has been properly applied to the facts.[64] If it considers that the law has been properly applied, it rejects the appeal; if it *casse* (quashes)[65] the decision challenged, it remits it to the same, or another, Court of Appeal.

Composition

Headed by a *premier président*, the Court of Cassation is composed of six divisional Presidents, 85 *conseillers* (judges), 39 *conseillers référendaires* (auxiliary judges), 18 *auditeurs* (administrative assistants), a *procureur général*, the *premier avocat général* and 19 *avocats généraux*; in total 169 judges (*décret* 94–128 of February 11, 1994).

The *premier president*, who is the highest judge in the ordinary courts' hierarchy, has no specific judicial power but has important functions:
— he presides over the First Division, the *chambre mixte*, the *assemblée plénière* and the *formation spéciale pour "avis"* (see below);

---

[61] See G. Picca and L. Cobert, *La Cour de Cassation* (Coll. Que-sais-je? PUF, Paris, 1986).
[62] *Ibid.* pp. 24–29.
[63] For this reason, the *Cour de cassation* is also called *"Cour régulatrice"*.
[64] *"(L)a Cour de cassation ne juge pas l'affaire, elle juge le jugement"*; ("the Court of Cassation does not try the case, it tries the judgment").
[65] Hence the word *"cassation"*.

— he supervises the working of the court, allocates its members to the different divisions, determines the powers of each division, decides whether a case should be referred to the *chambre mixte* or the *assemblée plénière*, etc.
— he presides over the *Conseil supérieur de la magistrature* when it sits as a disciplinary body.

The Division President conducts the proceedings of his division and assigns the files to his *conseillers*. He belongs to the *bureau* of the court and is an *ex-officio* member of the *assemblée plénière*.

The *conseillers* (also unofficially called *"hauts conseillers"*) are judges of the Bench, at the height of their career, who take part in the proceedings and the adjudication of a case.

The task of the *conseillers référendaires* (created by the Act of July 3, 1967) is to examine the files and to prepare a report on relatively simple cases. They may take part, in an advisory capacity only, in the proceedings of cases or have a right to vote in cases they have reported on.

As for the *auditeurs* (created in 1984), these are young judges who have mainly administrative duties directed at the preparation of the decisions of the Court (article R 131–14 *C.O.J.*).

The role of the *ministère public* of the Court of Cassation, headed by the *procureur général* who is assisted by the *avocats généraux*, is to ensure a proper application and a uniform interpretation of the law.[66]

Organisation

The Court of Cassation is organised into administrative services and judicial divisions.

Administrative services

The members of the Court of Cassation may sit in *assemblée générale* under the authority of the *premier président* (article R 131–8 *C.O.J.*). Its powers are not defined in any provision. Article R 131–9 *C.O.J.* only provides that the minutes of the *assemblée générale* must be drawn up.

---

[66] They do not conduct a prosecution like their colleagues from inferior courts; this is why the *procureur général* of the Court of Cassation has no direct authority over the *procureurs généraux* of the Courts of Appeal.

Table 3.13 **Proceedings of the *Court of Cassation* (all Divisions) from 1987 to 1994**

	1987	1988	1989	1990	1991	1992	1993	1994
Cases lodged	26,178	25,345	27,186	27,279	26,471	25,827	25,981	25,502
Cases decided	25,407	24,144	26,780	25,951	26,144	24,900	24,714	24,295
Cases still pending on December 31	30,923	32,124	32,530	33,858	34,015	34,942	36,209	37,416

Source: *Rapport de la Cour de Cassation* 1994 at p. 508

Table 3.14 **Proceedings of the *Court of Cassation* (Civil, Social and Commercial Divisions) from 1987 to 1994**

	1987	1988	1989	1990	1991	1992	1993	1994
Cases lodged	18,467	17,667	19,977	19,395	19,386	18,947	20,076	19,283
Cases decided	18,126	16,402	19,255	18,613	18,427	18,049	18,569	18,456
Cases still pending on December 31	26,569	27,754	28,476	29,258	30,047	30,945	32,452	33,279

Source: *Rapport de la Cour de Cassation* 1994 at p. 509

Table 3.15 **Proceedings of the *Court of Cassation* (Criminal Divisions) from 1987 to 1994**

	1987	1988	1989	1990	1991	1992	1993	1994
Cases lodged	7,711	7,670	7,209	7,884	7,085	6,851	5,905	6,219
Cases decided	7,281	7,662	7,525	7,338	7,717	6,880	6,145	5,839
Cases still pending on December 31	4,354	4,370	4,054	4,600	3,968	3,997	3,757	4,137

Source: *Rapport de la Cour de Cassation* 1994 at p. 510

The *bureau* of the Court of Cassation assists the *premier président* in supervising the working of the Court and in drafting its Rules of Procedure.

The Court also has a *service de documentation et d'études* (Documentation and Studies Department) in charge of classifying the applications lodged at the Court[67] and of publishing the *Bulletins civils et criminels de la Cour de Cassation* in which the most interesting cases are reported

Judicial divisions

The Court of Cassation currently has five *chambres civiles* (Civil Divisions)[68] and one *chambre criminelle* (Criminal Division) which is subdivided into three sections. Cases must be heard by at least five judges in order for decisions to be valid (article L 131-6 *C.O.J.*). However, the *premier président* or the Division President may decide to refer the case to a *formation restreinte* (Division sitting with only three judges) but this formation may refer it back to the division.

When a case raises complex and important issues of law and affects more than one division, it is heard by a *chambre mixte* (Mixed Bench) consisting of at least 13 judges including two *conseillers* from at least three divisions, the *premier président* and the Presidents and the most senior judges of the divisions concerned (article 121–5 *C.O.J.*). A case is referred to the *chambre mixte* either by the *premier président*, or by the division dealing with the case, or *ipso jure*, at the request of the *procureur général* (article L 131–3 *C.O.J.*).

When a case which has been quashed is referred again to the Court of Cassation by the Court of Appeal to which it was remitted, it is examined by the *assemblée plénière* (Full Court) which consists of 25 judges from all six divisions and is presided over by the *premier président*. Moreover, since 1979, the *assemblée plénière* may hear cases referred to the Court for the

---

[67] For this reason, this department is commonly called the *"fichier"* ("catalogue").

[68] The First Division (persons, contracts), the Second Division (divorce, civil procedure, tort), the Third Division (real rights, property, town planning), the *chambre commerciale et financière* (Commercial and Financial Division; business law), and the *chambre sociale* (Social Division; employment and social security law).

first time which raise issues concerning principles of law, in particular in the case of conflicts either between the Court of Cassation and the inferior courts, or between inferior courts (article L 131–2(2) *C.O.J.*). The decisions of the Full Court are binding on the *juridiction de renvoi* (court to which the case has been remitted) as regards points of law. Therefore the *juridiction de renvoi* must interpret the law in accordance with the Full Court's decision (article L 131–4(2) *C.O.J.*).

An inferior court may obtain an opinion from the Court of Cassation before delivering its judgment. The opinion is then delivered within three months by the *Formation spéciale "pour avis"* consisting of the President of the Court, the six Division Presidents and two judges from the divisions concerned.

4. THE ADMINISTRATIVE COURTS' STRUCTURE

The structure of the administrative courts is quite different from that of the ordinary courts. Whilst the *ordre judiciaire* consists of a few courts of general jurisdiction, the administrative judicial hierarchy is characterised by a number of specialised courts with diverse and specific jurisdiction. The only common feature of both court structures is the existence of a supreme court at the top of each *ordre*: the *Cour de Cassation* in the *ordre judiciaire* and the *Conseil d'Etat* in the *ordre administratif*. However, the Act of December 31, 1987 on the reform of the administrative courts' structure, has made the two *ordres* resemble each other more closely by creating the *cours administratives d'appel*.

The *Conseil d'Etat*, the *tribunaux administratifs*, the *cours administratives d'appel* and finally a few specialised courts will be examined in turn.

(A) THE *CONSEIL D'ETAT*

The *Conseil d'Etat* is an old institution which originated from the King's Council but was abolished under the Revolution. Re-established in 1800 (by the Constitution of 22 *frimaire an* VIII), it was resurrected as a court by the 1872 Act. The *Conseil d'Etat* sits at the *Palais Royal* in Paris. Although it is no longer a court of general jurisdiction, since the creation of the *tribunaux administratifs* by the *décret* of September 30, 1953, it remains the keystone of the administrative courts' structure.

Composition

The *Conseil d'Etat* consists of less than 300 members among whom 100 exercise their functions outside the *Conseil*. Members are mainly recruited from the *Ecole Nationale d'Administration* (E.N.A.) (National Civil Service College — see Chapter Four, below).

It is officially presided over by the Prime Minister but, in reality, by its vice-President, appointed by the Cabinet.

Apart from the vice-President and six Presidents of *sections* (Divisions), the *Conseil d'Etat* consists of *auditeurs, maîtres des requêtes* and *conseillers d'Etat*. The *auditeurs* and the *maîtres des requêtes* are responsible for preparing cases for trial. *Auditeurs* act as *juges rapporteurs* with the principal task of managing the case through the various stages of the procedure and of drafting the judgment, whilst *maîtres des requêtes* are *commissaires du gouvernement*,[69] whose role is to represent the interests of law and submit to the *Conseil* opinions in which they suggest, in the light of the existing case-law of the court, a solution to the pending case.[70] The *conseillers d'Etat* are the senior members of the *Conseil* (see Chapter Four, below) and it is they who actually decide the cases. A *secrétaire général* appointed from among the *maîtres des requêtes* supervises the working of the court and undertakes the role of a registrar.

Although they are not protected by the principle of irremovability, the permanent members of the *Conseil d'Etat* are actually very independent.[71]

Organisation

The *Conseil d'Etat* is organised into six *sections*: five *sections administratives* (Administrative Divisions) and one *section contentieuse* (Judicial Division). Four administrative divisions cover

---

[69] This term is a misnomer since this member of the *Conseil d'Etat* does not speak for the Government. His mission is identical to that of the Advocate-General in the European Court of Justice.

[70] See R. Guillien, *Les commissaires du gouvernement près les juridictions administratives*: [1955] R.D.P. 2.

[71] See O. Dupeyroux, *L'indépendance du Conseil d'Etat statuant au contentieux*: [1983] R.D.P. 565.

different areas of policy: finances, home affairs, civil engineering and public works, and social affairs. These areas of policy correspond to the scope of activities of different government departments. A new division, the *section des rapports et des études* (Report and Research Division) was created in 1985 with the task of drawing up and presenting to the Government proposals for reforms and drafting annual reports of activities.

The Administrative Divisions carry out the advisory functions of the *Conseil d'Etat*. The opinion requested from the *Conseil* is in principle delivered by the competent division. When the issue falls within the competence of more than one *section*, the opinion is given by the *sections réunies* (Combined Divisions) or by a *commission commune*, *i.e.* a committee composed of a few members from the different divisions concerned. The most important issues are heard by the *assemblée générale* which sits either as a *formation ordinaire* with 35 members or as a *formation plénière*, consisting of all the senior members of the court.

The *section du contentieux* is itself divided into 10 *sous-sections* (Sections) which specialise in different types of cases.[72] The simplest cases are tried by one *section* but the majority of cases are usually heard by two different *sections* sitting together in *sous-sections réunies* (Combined Sections), one of which is responsible for the investigation in order to prepare the case for trial. Cases presenting greater difficulty are heard by the *section du contentieux, formation de jugement* consisting of the President of the Judicial Division, the three vice-Presidents, 10 section Presidents, two *conseillers* from the Administrative Divisions and the *rapporteur* of the case. This composition of the Court must not be confused with the Judicial Division itself since it is a particular composition of this Division. Indeed, this is the Judicial Division sitting *en formation de jugement* (sitting in an adjudicating capacity). If a case has major political or administrative implications, it is heard by the *assemblée du contentieux* (Judicial Assembly) which consists of the vice-President of the *Conseil d'Etat* acting as President, the Division Presidents, the vice-Presidents of the *section du contentieux*, the President and the *rapporteur* of the *section* which has prepared the case. This

---

[72] The *décret* of September 9, 1968 abolished the specialisation of the *sous-sections*. However, the distinction between general *sous-sections* numbered 1, 2, 3, 4, 5, 6 & 10 and the fiscal *sous-sections* numbered 7, 8, & 9 still remains.

assemblée has to be distinguished from the *assemblée générale du Conseil d'Etat (ordinaire* or *plénière)* mentioned above.

The increasingly important role of the President of the Judicial Division should be emphasised. Indeed, not only does he allocate the different cases to the *sections* but he is also vested with specific powers which he exercises on his own (for example *référé, sursis* (see Chapter Five, below) and has the task of solving problems of jurisdiction between the administrative courts).[73]

Jurisdiction

The *Conseil d'Etat* is both an advisory and a judicial body. As an advisory body, it delivers opinions to the Government on legislative and administrative matters and, as such, takes part in the law-making process.[74] As a judicial body, it deals with disputes between citizens and the administration.

The *Conseil d'Etat* has to be consulted on legislative matters in two cases: first, according to article 39 of the 1958 Constitution, the Government must consult the *Conseil d'Etat* on public bills before they are discussed in Cabinet; secondly, according to article 38 of the Constitution, the *Conseil d'Etat* must be consulted about *ordonnances* the Government is authorised to make by Parliament in the domain of law. As far as the regulation-making power of the administration is concerned, the opinion of the *Conseil d'Etat* is required when a regulation modifies a statute adopted before 1958 on a subject matter which now falls within the scope of application of regulations as defined by article 37 of the present Constitution. The same procedure is to be followed when a statute provides that an implementing measure, for example a *décret*, shall be adopted after consulting the *Conseil d'Etat*. If the Government fails to consult the *Conseil d'Etat* when this is required, its measure is declared void on the ground of lack of competence. Except in a few rare cases where the assent of the *Conseil d'Etat* is required, its opinion is not binding on the Government. However, the Government, which has some room for manoeuvre between the initial bill and that as amended by the Court, may not table a

---

[73] See M. Carraud, *Le rôle du President de la section du contentieux*: [1980] R.D.P. 1403.

[74] See M. Long, *Le Conseil d'Etat et la fonction consultative: de la consultation à la décision*: [1992] R.F.D.A. 787.

third draft on which the Court has not been consulted. The Government may also ask for the opinion of the *Conseil d'Etat* either on a regulation or on a decision applying to an individual. It may also request advice on a specific point of law or ask the Court to undertake some research.

The *Conseil d'Etat* is in a unique position since it may act as *juge de premier degré* (at first instance), a *juge d'appel* (in appeal) and *juge de cassation* (in cassation).

Until 1953, it had general jurisdiction and sat as a *court de premier et dernier ressort*, *i.e.* its judgments were final. Nowadays, the *Conseil d'Etat* sits as *juge d'attribution* and has special jurisdiction conferred by statute in highly important matters such as[75]:

— *recours pour excès de pouvoir* (judicial review of administrative action) brought against *décrets* (either of general or specific application);
— disputes involving civil servants appointed by *décret* of the President of the Republic (for example members of the *Conseil d'Etat* and of the *Cour des comptes*, judges of ordinary courts, army officers, *préfets* (*i.e.* chief administrative office in a *département* or a *région*), *recteurs d'académie* (regional director of education, university professors, etc.);
— judicial review of *actes réglementaires* adopted by members of the Cabinet;
— judicial review of administrative acts (*réglementaires*, which are of general application, or *non-réglementaires*, which are of individual application) adopted by members of the Cabinet, where consultation with the *Conseil d'Etat* is compulsory;
— judicial review of decisions of *organes administratifs collégiaux à compétence nationale* (administrative bodies with nation-wide competence) such as professional boards or national examination boards, the *Commission Nationale Informatique et Libertés* (a data information watchdog), and boards of directors of State-owned corporations like the *S.N.C.F.* (railways) or *E.D.F.* (electricity);

---

[75] The jurisdiction of the *Conseil* in first and last resort remained untouched under the Act of 1987 on the reform of the administrative courts' structure.

— *recours en interprétation et en appréciation de légalité* (application for interpretation and for review of legality);[76]
— challenge of the election of French M.E.P.s (see article 25 of the Act of July 7, 1977; (C.E. Ass.), October 22, 1979: [1980] A.J.D.A. 39 and *Nicolo* (C.E.), October 20, 1989: [1989] A.J.D.A. 788);
— challenge of the election of members of regional councils (article L 361 of the Electoral Code);
— action against unilateral administrative acts falling within the territorial jurisdiction of more than one *tribunal administratif*;
— administrative disputes arising outside the national territory (for example, disputes arising on the high sea, as in *Ministère de la Défense Nationale v Starr* (C.E.), December 4, 1970: [1970] Rec. Lebon 733; or in a foreign State, as in *Société Neptun Transport* (C.E.), November 17, 1965: [1965] Rec. Lebon 614.

Since 1953, the *Conseil d'Etat* has been competent to hear appeals against judgments of the *tribunaux administratifs*. However, following the passing of the 1987 Act, which transferred some of its powers to the *cours administratives d'appel*, the *Conseil d'Etat* is no longer *juge de droit commun* in appeal and remains competent only as regards[77]:

— appeals against judgments of the *tribunaux administratifs* following a *recours en appréciation de légalité* (application for review of legality by way of preliminary rulings);
— disputes relating to elections of city, town and *canton*[78] councils; and
— appeals from some specialised administrative courts (see below, section on specialised courts).

As *juge de cassation*, the *Conseil d'Etat* can quash judgments of lower courts on the grounds of lack of competence, of a *vice de forme* (procedural impropriety) or misinterpretation of law. After quashing a judgment, the *Conseil d'Etat* remits the case to

---

[76] This procedure is similar to that of art. 177 under E.C. law.
[77] From October 1, 1995, the *Conseil d'Etat* is no longer competent to hear appeals from *tribunaux administratifs* in the field of judicial review of *actes individuels* (or *non-réglementaires*) as well as of *actes réglementaires* (see below, section on the jurisdiction of Administrative Courts of Appeal).
[78] A *canton* is an administrative unit between an *arrondissement* and a city or a town. It has no legal personality.

another court of the same category as the court which has had its judgment overruled. An appeal in *cassation* can be made against judgments of administrative courts adjudicating as courts of last resort. There are about 30 such courts. Indeed, it is well established in administrative case-law following the *Aillières* decision[79] that any judgment of such courts is subject to an appeal in *cassation* even if no law provides so.

Under article 10 of the 1987 Act, appeals also can lie from the *cours administratives d'appel.*[80]

Table 3.16 **Proceedings of the *Conseil d'Etat* from 1989 to 1993**

	1989	1990	1991	1992	1993
Cases lodged	8,205	8,069	9,843	10,705	10,335
Cases decided[1]	8,437	9,269	9,907	9,976	10,395

[1] This includes interim judgments, decisions referring a case to the *Tribunal des conflits* or an ordinary court and decisions following a request for a stay of execution.

Source: *Rapport Public du Conseil d'Etat* 1991 at p. 55 and 1993 at p. 117

(B) THE *TRIBUNAUX ADMINISTRATIFS* AND THE *COURS ADMINISTRATIVES D'APPEL*

The *tribunaux administratifs* were created by the *décret* of September 30, 1953 to replace the old *conseils de préfecture*

---

[79] (C.E.), February 7, 1947: [1947] Rec. Lebon 50. See also (C.C.), May 18, 1988 according to which appeals in *cassation* are a "fundamental guarantee" under article 34 of the Constitution.

[80] This provision has considerably extended the jurisdiction of the *Conseil d'Etat* which can now be regarded as *juge de cassation de droit commun*. See J. Massot & O. Fouguet, *Le Conseil d'Etat, juge de cassation* (Berget-Levrault, Paris, 1993).

established in 1800. The *cours administratives d'appel* were established by the Act of December 31, 1987.[81] In both cases, the creation of these new courts was intended to remedy the ever-increasing work-load of the *Conseil d'Etat*. Before the 1987 reform, there were about 25,000 cases pending before the *Conseil d'Etat*. Out of the 10,000 applications lodged every year, only 6,000 to 7,000 judgments are delivered. The average length of proceedings is not less than three years. In the *tribunaux administratifs*, 100,000 cases are lodged every year and only 50,000 adjudicated and the average length of proceedings is two years.

The 1987 Act laid down the principle of unity of both courts with respect to recruitment, career and status of their members.[82] This is why the composition of the two courts will be examined jointly before focusing on the organisation and the jurisdiction of each of them.

(1) Composition

Members of both courts are part of one single entity: the *corps des tribunaux administratifs et des cours administratives d'appel*, which is distinct and separate from the *corps du Conseil d'Etat*.[83] Mainly recruited from the *ENA*, members of these administrative courts are appointed and promoted by *décret* of the President of the Republic. They are first recruited as members of a *tribunal administratif* and may become members of a *cour administrative d'appel* only after being promoted as *conseillers de première classe* and having served the administration for six years or a court for four years.[84]

---

[81] On administrative justice before 1953, see Liet-Veaux, *La justice administrative au ralenti*: [1948] D. Chron. 133; and J. Rivero, *Sur la réforme du contentieux administratif*: [1951] D. Chron. 163.

On the 1953 reform, see J. Rivero, *La réforme du contentieux administratif*: [1953] R.D.P. 926 and *Le Conseil d'Etat, cour régulatrice*: [1954] D. Chron. 157; Gazier, *Perspectives ouvertes par la réform*: [1954] R.D.P. 669.

On the 1987 reform, see: [1988] A.J.D.A. Feb. Spec. Issue: [1988] R.F.D.A. Spec. Issue; and M. Pinault, *Perpectives ouvertes par la loi de 1987*: [1988] 40 E.D.C.E. 215.

[82] See R. Abraham, *Les magistrats des tribunaux et cours administratives d'appel*: [1988] R.F.D.A. 207.

[83] By contrast, the members of the *ordre judiciaire* belong to a single *corps* and are subject to the same status.

[84] The *corps* consists of the following ranks:

— President of the *tribunal administratif* of Paris
— Vice-President of the *tribunal administratif* of Paris

The independence of the members of these administrative courts is guaranteed by the Act of January 6, 1986, which created a *conseil supérieur des tribunaux administratifs*[85] chaired by the vice-President of the *Conseil d'Etat* and consisting of, *inter alia*, representatives of members of the *tribunaux administratifs*. This body plays an important role in personnel management, *i.e.* promotion, or appointment to a new post, etc. Moreover, since January 1, 1990, members of these courts are no longer subordinate to the Home Office but to the Ministry of Justice and are supervised by the *secrétaire général* of the *Conseil d'Etat* who sits in the *Conseil supérieur* (article 3 of the 1987 Act).

(2) The *tribunaux administratifs*

Organisation

This court is a regional court, the territorial jurisdiction of which covers 2 to 6 *départements*. There are 33 of them of which 26 are located in metropolitan France and seven in overseas territories. They consist of two to five *chambres* (Divisions), each comprising three judges. By way of exception, the Court of Paris consists of seven sections divided into two *chambres* each.[86]

Under article 4 of the *Code des administratifs et cours administratives d'appel* (*C.T.A.*), judgments are usually passed by one Division but cases presenting greater difficulty are heard by the *formation plénière*, *i.e.* the full assembly of the Court (except in the Court of Paris where the *formation plénière* consists of the President, the *rapporteur* and the seven Presidents of the *sections*). Also, following the adoption of Act 95–125 of February 8, 1995 on the organisation of courts and civil, criminal and administrative procedures, new article 4–1 *C.T.A.*, lists a series of cases which are automatically adjudicated by the President of the court alone (or a judge appointed by him from *conseillers*

— President *hors-classe* of a *tribunal administratif*
— President of a *tribunal administratif*
— *Conseiller hors-classe*
— *Conseiller de première classe*
— *Conseiller de seconde classe*.

[85] See M. Long, *Le Conseil supérieur des tribunaux administratifs et cours administratives d'appel*: [1988] 40 E.D.C.E. 227.
[86] See Landron, *Le tribunal administratif de Paris*: [1967] 19 E.D.C.E. 267.

Grade I), in public hearings and after the *commissaire du gouvernement* has delivered his opinion.

Jurisdiction

Like the *Conseil d'Etat*, the *tribunal administratif* is an advisory as well as a judicial body. These functions used to belong to the *conseil de préfecture*. However, the advisory role of the *tribunal administratif* is more restricted than that of the *Conseil d'Etat*. Administrative courts may give opinions at the request of the *préfets* of a *département*. This happens very rarely however.[87]

With respect to their judicial functions, article L 3 *C.T.A.* states that:

"The administrative courts are courts of general jurisdiction which, subject to appeal, hear administrative litigation at first instance."[88]

It appears clear from the above that these courts have general jurisdiction and try all administrative cases unless the case comes before the *Conseil d'Etat*, or a specialised court when stipulated by statute. They are also administrative courts of first instance, the judgments of which can be subject to an appeal of the *cours administratives d'appel* or the *Conseil d'Etat*. *Tribunaux administratifs* may also adjudicate as *cours de dernier* ressort (for example on fiscal matters or with respect to conscientious objectors). These judgments are then subject to an appeal in *cassation* before the *Conseil d'Etat*.[89]

Each tribunal has limited territorial jurisdiction[90] and is competent to try cases which originate within the area where it is situated (article R 46 *et seq. C.T.A.*).

(3) The *cours administratives d'appel*

Organisation

Only five Administrative Courts of Appeal have been created: those of Paris, Lyon, Bordeaux, Nantes and Nancy (*décret* 88–155

---

[87] See R. Ludwig, *Considérations sur le rôle non juridictionnel des tribunaux administratifs*: [1966] A.J.D.A. 594; C. Courtine, *Les attributions consultatives et administratives des tribunaux administratifs*: [1967] E.D.C.E. 299.

[88] "*Les tribunaux administratifs sont en premier ressort et sous réserve d'appel, juges de droit commun du contentieux administratif.*"

[89] See (C.E.), November 4, 1988, *Mme Schott*: [1988] Rec. Lebon 394.

[90] See G. Braibant, *La compétence des tribunaux administratifs régionaux dans la jurisprudence du Conseil d'Etat*: [1955] A.J.D.A. 98; R. Drago, *La compétence territoriale des tribunaux administratifs*: [1961] A.J.D.A. 183.

Table 3.17 **Proceedings of *tribunaux administratifs* from 1988 to 1993**

	1988	1989	1990	1991	1992	1993
Cases lodged	68,285	70,629	69,853	78,061	84,082	87,632
Cases decided[1]	54,478	57,900	60,195	70,819	72,176	79,449

[1] This includes interim judgments, decisions referring a case to the *Tribunal des conflits* or an ordinary court and decisions following a request for a stay of execution.

Source: *Rapport Public du Conseil d'Etat* 1991 at p. 56 and 1993 at p. 117

of February 15, 1988). They are organised in divisions: four divisions in the first two courts and three in the last three (see article 5 of the *décret* of March 17, 1992). Each division is composed of one President, five *conseillers* and two *commissaires du gouvernement*. The President of an Administrative Court of Appeal is a *conseiller d'Etat*.

Jurisdiction

The 1987 Act provided that Administrative Courts of Appeal have judicial powers only. In principle, they hear appeals in all matters and could therefore be considered as courts of general jurisdiction.[91] However their jurisdiction is still limited with respect not only to the categories of courts from which they can hear appeals, but also to the kinds of proceedings (*compétence ratione materiae*). They hear appeals from one specialised court only — the *commission du contentieux de l'indemnisation des*

---

[91] See Ch. Debbasch & J-Cl. Ricci, *Contentieux administratif* (Dalloz, Paris, 6th ed., 1994), 176 *et seq.*; J. Rivero & J. Waline, *Droit administratif* (Dalloz, Paris, 15th ed., 1994), 174 *et seq.*; B. Pacteau, *Contentieux administratif* (PUF, Droit Fondamental, Paris, 3rd ed., 1994) 71.

Français dépossédés (created in 1970)[92] — and from the *tribunaux administratifs*. The transfer of powers from the *Conseil d'Etat* to the *cours administratives d'appel* has in fact been only partial. For these reasons it could be suggested that, in reality, they are specialised courts.[93]

As seen above, the *Conseil d'Etat* remains competent to hear appeals in three areas. However, the *cours administratives d'appel* now have exclusive jurisdiction to hear appeals from the *tribunaux administratifs* in applications for judicial review against *actes réglementaires* (acts of general application) and *non réglementaires* (acts of individual application)[94] as well as in all actions of *pleine juridiction*[95] (such as those concerning administrative liability, administrative contracts etc.).[96]

Each Administrative Court of Appeal is territorially competent to hear appeals from the *tribunaux administratifs* which are located within its territory.[97]

---

[92] This is a court specialising in repatriation claims by French nationals living in French overseas territories.

[93] See G. Vedel & P. Delvolvé, *Droit administratif* (PUF Thémis Droit, Paris, 12th ed., 1992), Vol. 2, 118.

[94] This transfer of jurisdiction became effective on October 1, 1995 as a result of the adoption of *décret* 92–245 of March 17, 1992 which supplemented art. 1(2) of the 1987 Act. Originally, the latter provision gave jurisdiction to Administrative Courts of Appeal only to hear appeals in the field of judicial review of *actes non-réglementaires*. Eventually, article 75 of the Act of February 8, 1995 on the organisation of courts and civil, criminal and administrative procedures, extended their jurisdiction to applications for judicial review of *actes réglementaires*.

See B. Pacteau, *L'achèvement de la réforme du contentieux de 1987. L'extension des compétences des cours administratives d'appels*: [1992] R.F.D.A. 857; D. Mandelkeen, *Les conditions du transfert de l'excès de pouvoir aux cours administratives d'appel*: [1992] R.F.D.A. 860; and Chr. Huglo & C. Lepage, *Le titre IV de la loi 95–125 du 8 février 1995 consacré à la juridiction administrative contient-il des dispositions révolutionnaires?*: [1995] 33 Les Petites Affiches 9, esp. 11.

[95] This is also called *plein contentieux*; see Chapter Five, below.

[96] For a survey of the work of Administrative Courts of Appeal in their first years of existence, see *Deuxième année d'activité des cours administratives d'appel*: [1991] R.F.D.A. 431 *et seq.* and *Troisième année d'activité des cours administratives d'appel*: [1992] R.F.D.A. 643 *et seq.* With respect to their working procedure, see D. Chabanol, *La pratique du contentieux administratif devant les tribunaux administratifs et les cours administratives d'appel* (Litec, Paris, 2d ed., 1991) and H. Isaia, *Les cours administratives d'appel, Approche critique* (Economica, Paris, 1993).

[97] As provided in *décret* 88–155 (art. 7 C.T.A.), the territorial jurisdiction of each Administrative Court of Appeal is as follows:

— Bordeaux: Bordeaux, Limoges, Montpellier, Pau, Poitier and Toulouse;

Table 3.18 **Proceedings of Administrative Courts of Appeal from 1989 to 1993**

		1989	1990	1991	1992	1993
Cases lodged	Paris	2,948	1,130	1,214	1,448	1,453
	Lyon	2,024	982	1,137	1,616	2,014
	Bordeaux	2,016	776	977	1,284	1,537
	Nantes	1,563	687	944	1,163	1,271
	Nancy	1,605	709	799	1,040	1,278
	Total	10,156	4,284	5,071	6,551	7,553
Cases decided	Paris	685	1,556	1,473	1,447	1,709
	Lyon	623	1,007	1,242	1,388	1,746
	Bordeaux	490	807	1,079	1,117	1,421
	Nantes	510	677	908	1,104	1,193
	Nancy	397	864	1,049	1,013	1,008
	Total	2,705	4,911	5,751	6,069	7,077

Source: *Annuaire statistique de la justice* 1991–1992 at p. 209 and *Rapport Public du Conseil d'Etat* 1991 at p. 56, 1992 at p. 76 and 1993 at p. 117

(C) Specialised Courts

Due to the complexity of some matters which need to be dealt with by specialist judges, a great number of specialised administrative courts were created.

Two categories of specialised courts can be distinguished:

— those from which the *Conseil d'Etat* hears appeals: the *conseil des prises* (Prize Court); the *conseil du contentieux administratif* in the overseas territories of Wallis and Futuna, and Mayotte; and the *commissions d'arrondissement des dommages de guerre* (District Courts for War damages); and

— those from which the *Conseil d'Etat* hears appeals by way of *cassation*, namely the *Cour des comptes*, the *Cour de discipline budgétaire* and disciplinary courts.

— Lyon: Bastia, Clermond-Ferrand, Grenoble, Lyon, Marseille and Nice;
— Nancy: Amiens, Besançon, Chalons-sur-Marne, Dijon, Lille, Nancy and Strasbourg;
— Nantes: Caen, Nantes, Orléans, Rennes and Rouen;
— Paris: Paris, Versailles and overseas.

Multiplicity and diversity are the main features of these administrative courts of limited jurisdiction.[98] For this reason the analysis of them will be limited to the second category of courts mentioned above and, amongst these, to the most important ones.

(1) Financial courts

(a) The Cour des comptes

Created in 1807, the *Cour des comptes* (Court of Auditors)[99] has constitutional status (article 18 of the 1946 Constitution and article 47 of the 1958 Constitution).

It is governed by the Act of May 22, 1967 and the *décret* of February 11, 1985. Its composition and organisation are fairly similar to those of the *Conseil d'Etat* but, unlike the latter, the former has a *ministére public service* headed by a *procureur général*. It is made up of seven *chambres*, each of them divided into *sections*. The court may sit *en audience solennelle*, *i.e.* all its members wear a ceremonial robe, on special occasions such as the first sitting of the year; *en chambre du Conseil* (First President, Division Presidents and *conseillers-maîtres*) when it carries out administrative functions only; or *toutes chambres réunies* (all divisions combined) which brings together under the authority of the First President, the Division Presidents and two *conseillers-maîtres* for each division.

The Court of Auditors has both administrative and judicial functions. As an administrative body, the Court supervises *ordonnateurs*, *i.e.* ministers and other higher officials who are responsible for expenditure and make orders to pay these. Its observations and opinions are expressed in a public annual report. It also assists the Parliament in supervising the

---

[98] Created by statute or acknowledged by the *Conseil d'Etat*, they are either permanent or temporary. There is however no complete inventory of them; see Theis, *Essai de recensement des juridictions relevant du Conseil d'Etat par la voie de recours en cassation*: [1952] E.D.C.E. 79; R. Odent has identified 43 courts; see *Cours de contentieux administratif* 1970–1971, 694.

Also due to the obscurity of legislative provisions, it is sometimes difficult to determine whether a body is a purely administrative body or a judicial one. On the notion of administrative court, see R. Chapus, *Qu'est-ce qu'une juridiction? La réponse de la jurisprudence administrative* (Mélanges Ch. Eisenmann) 265.

[99] See J. Reynaud, *La Cour des comptes* (PUF, Coll. Que-sais-je?, Paris, 1980); J. Magnet, *La Cour des comptes* (Berget-Levrault, Paris, 3rd ed., 1986) and *La Cour des comptes est- elle une juridiction?*: [1978] R.D.P. 1537.

implementation of the budget (article 47 of the 1958 Constitution), and supervises the accounts of social security authorities and state-owned companies.

As a judicial body, the Court may order rectification of errors made by *comptables publics*, *i.e.* those civil servants responsible for the recovery and payment of debts owed to or by public authorities and for administering the public purse. On its own motion, the Court audits accounts of the *comptables publics*. It delivers judgments which may be in the form of *arrêts de décharge* — when no error has been made — or *arrêts de débet* — when expenditure have been incurred in an irregular way or revenues have not been received. However, the jurisdiction of the Court is limited to examining the correctness of accounts, not the liability of the *comptables*. Furthermore, it has no jurisdiction over the action of *ordonnateurs*.

Appeals lie from the Court of Auditors to the *Conseil d'Etat* by way of *cassation* for lack of competence, procedural irregularity or infringement of the law. Following the Act of March 2, 1982,[1] it hears appeals from the *chambres régionales des comptes* (regional Courts of Auditors)[2] which were established by two Acts of 1982. The function of the regional courts is to examine public expenditure incurred by regional and local authorities and to supervise public funds at regional and local level.[3]

(b) The *cour de discipline budgétaire et financière*

Created in 1948 and reorganised by the Act of July 13, 1971,[4] this court consists of six members appointed for three years and is presided over by the First President of the *Cour des comptes*. It is competent to impose sanctions for irregularities committed

---

[1] Act 82–213 relating to the rights and liberties of the *régions*, *départements* and *communes*.

[2] Or "regional audit boards", as suggested by M. Weston, *op. cit.* p. 89.

[3] See J. Raynaud, *Les chambres régionales des comptes* (Coll. Que-sais-je?, PUF, Paris, 1984); P.M. Gaudemet, *Les chambres régionales des comptes*: [1983] A.J.D.A. 102; F.J. Fabre, *Réflexions sur l'institution des chambres régionales des comptes* (Mélanges P.M. Gaudemet), p. 521; Ph. Limouzin-Lamothe, *La réforme des chambres régionales des comptes: amélioration ou amputation?*, [1988] A.J.D.A. 427; J.-L. Chartier & A. Doyelle, *L'activité des chambres régionales des comptes: le contrôle des comptes produits par les comptables des collectivités et établissements publics locaux*: [1992] A.J.D.A. 194; *L'activité des chambres régionales des comptes: les collectivités locales en grave difficulté financière*: [1992] A.J.D.A. 717.

[4] See J.C. Maitrot, *Jouvence pour une inconnue? La réforme de la Cour de discipline budgétaire et financière*: [1971] A.J.D.A. 507.

by officials — civil as well as military — involved in the implementation of the Government budget, the budget of local authorities and that of *établissements publics*.[5] However, ministers and elected officials are not subject to its supervision.[6]

(2) Disciplinary courts

A number of courts exist to sanction disciplinary irregularities committed by members of public institutions. Only the main courts will be mentioned here.

(a) The *conseil supérieur de la magistrature*

The Superior Council of Judges of the Bench and Members of the State Counsel's Office is a constitutional body intended to guarantee the independence of the judiciary. When it sits as a disciplinary body, it is regarded, in the case-law of the *Conseil d'Etat*, as a specialised administrative court,[7] although it sits at the Court of Cassation.[8]

When President Mitterrand chaired this Council for the first time on June 21, 1981, he made it clear that the effective independence of the judiciary would eventually necessitate a constitutional reform. In the early 1980s, this was strongly supported by 67 per cent of the judiciary and, in 1989, reform was demanded by the Congress of trade unions of lawyers, judges and *greffiers*. This reform was adopted on July 19, 1993 by the French Parliament, convened in Congress.[9]

Under the new article 65 of the Constitution, the President of the Republic still remains the head of the *Conseil* but is no longer solely responsible for appointing its members. According to the second paragraph of this article, the *Conseil* consists of two *formations* (Divisions) which are responsible for *magistrats du siège* (judges of the bench) and *magistrats du parquet* (State Counsel's Office) respectively.

---

[5] An *établissement public* is a "legal person" of public law in charge of a public service.
[6] See G. Vedel, *La responsabilité des administrateurs devant la Cour de discipline budgétaire et financière*: [1964] Rev. Sc. Legisl. Fin. 774.
[7] See (C.E. Ass.), July 12, 1969, *L'Etang*: [1969] Rec. Lebon 388.
[8] See art. 40 of *décret* 94–100 of March 9, 1994.
[9] On this reform, see notably commentaries by NGuyen Van Tong: [1993] J.C.P. I 3703; Ch. Bigault & J.P. Lay: [1993] D. Chron. 275; Cadiet: [1993] J.C.P. I 3723; Picard: [1994] J.C.P. I 3736.

Table 3.19 The Main Administrative and Financial Courts

	NUMBER OF COURTS	COMPOSITION	LOCATION	TERRITORIAL JURISDICTION	JURISDICTION	APPEALS AND APPEALS IN CASSATION
CONSEIL D'ETAT	1	Vice-President, 6 Division Presidents, conseillers d'Etats, maîtres des requêtes and auditeurs	Paris	Nationwide	—judicial review of decrees or measures from the Cabinet —disputes involving civil servants appointed by presidential decree —review of nationwide measures —interpretation and review of legality judgments of tribunaux administratifs and some specialised courts —bears appeals in cassation from all administrative courts passing final judgments	
COURS ADMINISTRATIVES D'APPEL	5	A Court President, Division Presidents, conseillers de première classe	Bordeaux, Lyon, Nancy, Nantes, Paris	Hear appeals from 5 to 7 tribunaux administratifs	Hear appeals from tribunaux administratifs except from those heard by the Conseil d'Etat	Appeal in cassation to the Conseil d'Etat
TRIBUNAUX ADMINISTRATIFS	33	A Court President conseillers de première et deuxième classe	Chief town of a département	From 2 to 7 départements	General jurisdiction in administrative disputes	Administrative Court of Appeal, and to the Conseil d'Etat —Appeal in cassation to the Conseil d'Etat
CONSEILS DU CONTENTIEUX ADMINISTRATIF	2	A Court President + 5 civil servants	Wallis & Futuna Mayotte	Geographical limits of the oversea territory concerned	—General jurisdiction in administrative disputes —Limited jurisdiction in disputes between the State and its agents	Appeals to the Conseil d'Etat
COUR DES COMPTES	1	A Court President, 7 Division Presidents, conseillers-maîtres, and conseillers-référendaires	Paris	Nationwide	—General jurisdiction with respect to audit of accounts of the State and public authorities —Hearsay appeals from the chambre régionales des comptes	Appeal in cassation to the Conseil d'Etat
CHAMBRES REGIONALES DES COMPTES	25	A Court President + conseillers	Chief town of a région	1 per région	General jurisdiction with respect to public expenditures of local authorities	Appeal to the Cour des comptes
COUR DE DISCIPLINE BUDGETAIRE ET FINANCIERE	1	First President of the Cases des comptes + 6 members appointed for 3 years	Paris	Nationwide	Irregularities committed by public officials responsible for the implementation of the budgets of the State, local authorities and établissements publics	Appeal in cassation to the Conseil d'Etat

The first *formation* is composed of: the President of the Republic and the Minister of Justice, five *magistrats du siège* and one *magistrat du parquet*, one *conseiller d'Etat* and three public persons, who are not members of the Parliament nor of the judiciary and are appointed respectively by the President of the Republic and by the Presidents of the chambers of Parliament (article 65(3) of the Constitution). This division is competent to make nominations for the highest functions in the Court of Cassation, the posts of First Presidents in Courts of Appeal and the posts of Presidents in *tribunaux de grande instance*. Its *avis conforme* (assent) is required for the appointment of ordinary judges of the Bench. It also sits as a disciplinary body for *magistrats du siège*, in which case it is headed by the First President of the Court of Cassation (article 65(6)).

The composition of the second *formation* is similar to that of the first one but consists of five *magistrats du parquet* and only one *magistrat du siège* (article 65(4)). This division delivers opinions on appointments of *magistrats du parquet* — except on those decided in Cabinet — (article 65(7)), and on disciplinary sanctions applied to these members of the judiciary, in which case it is presided over by the *procureur général* of the Court of Cassation (article 65(8)). In its disciplinary role, this second division seems to have less powers than the first one, which delivers final binding judgments instead of mere opinions. However, in practice, it would be very unlikely that a member of the Government would take the risk of ignoring an opinion of this second division and, as a consequence, challenge the moral authority of the *Conseil supérieur de la magistrature*.[10]

(b) The *conseils universitaires*

Besides their administrative or consultative functions, these bodies have disciplinary jurisdiction. Those involved in education are judged by their peers. These *conseils* are the *conseils départementaux* in primary education, the *conseils académiques*

---

[10] This important reform came into force following the passing of the *loi organique* 94–100 of February 5, 1994. This *loi organique* determines the conditions for appointment of members of the *Conseil* and for the exercise of its powers. See also *décret* 94–199 of March 9, 1994 on the rules for the election of members of the *Conseil*, the role of the administrative secretariat and the working of the *Conseil*. See commentaries by Cadiet: [1994] J.C.P. I 3755 and Ch. Bigault & J.-P. Lay: [1994] D. Chron. 129.

in secondary education and the *conseils d'université* in higher education.

(c) The *juridictions professionnelles*

Since the *de Bayo* judgment of the *Conseil d'Etat* in 1953 ((C.E. Ass.) [1953] Rec. Lebon 544), *conseils nationaux* of professional associations (*e.g.*, of doctors, pharmacists and chemists, and architects) have been regarded as administrative courts when they exercise their disciplinary powers.[11]

(d) The *commission bancaire*

As a disciplinary body, this supervisory banking authority — known as *commission de contrôle des banques* before the coming into force of the Act of January 24, 1984 — is a specialised administrative court, the decisions of which can be challenged by way of *cassation* in the *Conseil d'Etat*.

(3) Other specialised courts

There are a number of *juridictions sociales*, the decisions of which can be appealed against by way of *cassation*. The *Commission centrale d'aide sociale*, which adjudicates on rights to social benefits, is one example of such courts. This commission hears appeals from local *commissions d'aide sociale*.

Another important specialised court is the *Commission des recours des réfugiés*. This court hears appeals against decisions of the *Office français des réfugiés et apatrides* (known as OFPRA) which refuse refugee status to foreign citizens. Owing to the growing number of applications for refugee status, it has become the most important administrative court in quantitative terms, *e.g.* in 1991, it adjudicated 60,000 cases.

5. THE *TRIBUNAL DES CONFLITS*

The existence of a dual system of courts reflecting the principle of separation of administrative and ordinary courts is

---

[11] By way of exception, disciplinary decisions taken by the *Conseil national de l'Ordre des avocats* can be challenged by an appeal in an ordinary Court of Appeal.

not without its drawbacks. In principle, this separation seems to be clear cut. As soon as a State authority is involved in a dispute, ordinary courts are not competent. However, ordinary courts remain competent in a number of cases (for example road accidents involving a vehicle belonging to an administrative authority, etc.). There are many cases where it is unclear whether a given action should be brought before an ordinary or an administrative court. There are also cases where both courts have a different interpretation of the principle of separation of their respective functions.

In order to settle disputes concerning jurisdiction, a *Tribunal des conflits* (Jurisdiction Disputes Court), lying outside and above the two *ordres de juridictions*, was created in 1849 and re-established by the Act of May 24, 1872, after it was abolished following the *coup d'etat* of December 2, 1851.

(A) Composition

The *Tribunal des conflits* is composed of three *conseillers en service ordinaire* from the *Conseil d'Etat* and three *conseillers* from the Court of Cassation. These six elected members, together with the Minister of Justice — who is the *de jure* President of the Court — elect in turn two other judges from the two Supreme Courts, and again, all nine elect two substitutes from those two courts.

As the Minister of Justice only sits in the *Tribunal des Conflits* on the rare occasions when his casting vote is needed,[12] the Court is presided over by a vice-President elected from his brethren. Its members hold office for three years.

Commissaires du gouvernement are appointed each year equally from *maîtres des requêtes* of the *Conseil d'Etat* and *avocats généraux* of the Court of Cassation.

(B) Organisation

The *Tribunal des conflits* is located at the *Palais Royal* in Paris. Its procedure is modelled on that of the *Conseil d'Etat* but is also based on the principle of equal representation of both the highest courts.

---

[12] This has happened only nine times since the *Blanco* decision in 1872.

Cases are heard by five judges at least. Each case is prepared by a *juge rapporteur* and the opinion on each case is presented by a *commissaire du gouvernement*.[13]

It may happen that the Court does not reach a decision, in which case another hearing presided over by the Minister of Justice takes place in order to *"vider le partage"* (to settle the vote).[14]

(C) Jurisdiction

Originally, this Court was intended to settle dispute concerning jurisdiction. Its own jurisdiction was later enlarged in 1932 to include *contrariétés de decisions* (resolution of conflicting decisions).

(1) Conflicts of jurisdiction

Conflits de compétence may arise in two ways and lead to two procedures known as *conflit positif (d'attributions)* and *conflit négatif*.

The *conflit positif*

A *conflit positif*[15] occurs when the administration (not the administrative judge) challenges the competence of an ordinary civil court (except the Court of Cassation)[16] before which a case was brought. The parties themselves cannot take the case to the *Tribunal des conflits*. Only the local *préfet* may *élever le conflit* (raise the question of jurisdiction) by entering a *déclinatoire de compétence* (plea of no jurisdiction) intended to prevent the civil court from hearing the case. If this court ignores the plea, the *préfet* will then bring the matter to the *Tribunal des conflits* by means of an *arrêté de conflit*. The Jurisdiction

---

[13] Cases with an even filing number are dealt with by a member of the Court of Cassation; the opinion will then be delivered by a *commissaire du gouvernement* chosen from amongst members of the *Conseil d'Etat*.

[14] See A. Oraison, *Le partage d'opinions au Tribunal des conflits* [1971], A.J. 585; and Fr. Chouvel, Th. Lambert & D. Pelissier, *Les cas de partage au tribunal des conflits et la répartition des compétence*: [1983] R.D.P. 1313.

[15] See J.F. Flauss, *La pratique administrative du conflit positif d'attribution de 1962 à 1977*: [1979] R.D.P. 1591.

[16] Apart from a few exceptions, the question of jurisdiction cannot be raised in a criminal court (*ord.* of June 1, 1928).

Disputes Court will then have three months to settle the dispute, during which the ordinary court must *surseoir à statuer*, *i.e.* stay the proceedings. The Court may either annul the *arrêté de conflit* or accept it. In the latter case, the ordinary court is relieved of the case and the plaintiff must bring the case to an administrative court (the transfer of the file to this court is not automatic).

Judgments of the *Tribunal des conflits* — called *arrêts* — are not appealable.

The *conflit négatif*

There is *conflit négatif* when an ordinary and an administrative court duly seized of a case, have disclaimed jurisdiction on the grounds that the other court was competent.

In such a case, the parties have no other alternative than to apply to the Jurisdiction Disputes Court. However, in practice, this has rarely occurred since the *procédure de renvoi* was created by the *décret* of July 25, 1960. According to this procedure, when a court has disclaimed jurisdiction in a final judgment, the other court must refer the issue of jurisdiction to the *Tribunal des conflits* if it regards itself as incompetent. The latter court cannot disclaim jurisdiction. This procedure is therefore intended to settle a *conflit négatif* before it has fully arisen.

Another procedure was set up by the same *décret* in order to settle serious difficulties of jurisdiction. Only the *Conseil d'Etat* or the Court of Cassation may, of its own motion, refer any question raising such difficulty to the *Tribunal des conflits* for a binding decision on the matter. The purpose of this procedure is to avoid future conflicts of jurisdiction arising.

(2) Conflicting decisions

The *conflit de décisions* (or *contrariété de jugements*) is different from a conflict of jurisdiction. Here, an administrative court on the one hand, and an ordinary court on the other, both claiming jurisdiction, have reached conflicting decisions on the same case. The individual plaintiff is then in a prejudicial situation verging on a miscarriage of justice. Following the famous *Rosay* case of 1932, the Act of April 20, 1932, extended the jurisdiction of the *Tribunal des conflits* to such conflicts. The plaintiff has two months from the last court decision to bring the matter to the *Tribunal des conflits*. The *Tribunal* does not *rule on a jurisdictional issue but au fond, i.e.* on the merits.

6. THE *CONSEIL CONSTITUTIONNEL*

Unlike the United States and other European States, judicial review of constitutionality has always been seen in the French constitutional tradition as being contrary to the principle of *souveraineté absolue de la loi* (similar to the principle of English parliamentary supremacy), the *loi* being the *expression de la volonté générale* (the law as supreme expression of the people's will).[17] It was only in 1958 that a constitutional court, the *Conseil Constitutionnel*, was created under the Constitution of the Fifth Republic. This was indeed a real innovation in French constitutional law.

The *Conseil Constitutionnel* is governed by Title VII of the 1958 Constitution and the *lois organiques* of November 7, 1958 and December 26, 1974.

(A) Composition

The *Conseil Constitutionnel* has nine members appointed for a nine-year term — three, including the President of the Court, being appointed by the President of the Republic, three by the President of the National Assembly and three by the President of the Senate.

Former Presidents of the Republic are also *de jure* members — although so far only Presidents Auriol and Coty have sat in this Court.

Once appointed, members of the Constitutional Court enjoy full independence since their term is not renewable and they cannot be dismissed.

(B) Jurisdiction

The *Conseil Constitutionnel* has a wide range of powers which it exercises as an adjudicative or an advisory body. However, as an adjudicative body, it does not examine all issues

---

[17] As expressed by the French philosopher J.-J. Rousseau in *Le Contrat Social* (1762).

relating to the interpretation of the Constitution. Unlike the American Supreme Court or the German Federal Constitutional Court it has only limited jurisdiction. Therefore, a number of constitutional issues — such as, for instance, the risks of conflicts between the President of the Republic and his Prime Minister during the "cohabitation" period (1986–88) — do not fall within its jurisdiction.

The adjudicative functions of the *Conseil Constitutionnel*

The first task of the *Conseil Constitutionnel* is to ensure that both Parliament and the Government keep within their respective spheres of legislative competences as laid down in articles 34 and 37 of the Constitution (see Chapter Two, above). First, article 41 of the Constitution gives the Government the right to challenge Parliament's ability to legislate on a given matter and, in the case of a disagreement between Parliament and the Government, to refer the matter to the Constitutional Court which must give its ruling within a week. This is the preventative procedure of *irrecevabilité*. Secondly, article 37(2) provides that a statute on a regulatory matter passed by Parliament after 1958 may be amended by a *décret* only after the *Conseil* has ruled that the subject matter falls within the legislative sphere of the Government.[18] This is called the *délégalisation* by which an Act of Parliament becomes an *acte réglementaire*.

The *Conseil Constitutionnel* is also the only court competent to review the constitutionality of legislation and, consequently, to declare an Act of Parliament unconstitutional. In this respect, the powers of the *Conseil* are defined by article 61 of the Constitution. All *lois organiques* and the rules of procedure of both parliamentary assemblies must be submitted to it before promulgation to confirm that they are consistent with the Constitution. Acts of Parliament may also be referred to the *Conseil* for the same purpose by the President of the Republic, the Prime Minister, the President of either parliamentary assembly and, since 1974, by 60 *députés* (M.P.s) or 60 *sénateurs* (Senators).

However, action can only be brought before the *Conseil* prior to an Act of Parliament being promulgated. In such an event, it must deliver its ruling within one month or, in cases of urgency,

---

[18] For reasons of convenience, the Government may leave Parliament to pass an Act on a regulatory matter.

one week. Therefore, except in the specific context of article 37(2) discussed above, *a posteriori* judicial review[19] is not possible. Its ruling is not appealable and is published in the *Journal Officiel* (Official Journal).

According to article 54 of the Constitution, the *Conseil* may scrutinise international treaties, at the request of the President of the Republic, the Prime Minister or the President of either of the parliamentary assemblies, and — since the last amendment — by 60 M.P.s or 60 Senators. In the event that a treaty does not conform with the Constitution, its ratification or approval must be preceded by constitutional amendment.[20]

In addition to these functions, the *Conseil* also adjudicates on the validity of presidential and parliamentary elections as well as referendums.

The advisory functions of the *Conseil Constitutionnel*

First, the *Conseil* plays an important supervisory and advisory role in respect of the organisation of presidential elections and referendums.

Secondly, it is the only authority competent to determine whether the President of the Republic is unable to perform his duties or whether the Presidency has become vacant.[21]

Finally, it must be consulted before the President exercises the emergency powers provided for under article 16 of the Constitution. However, its opinions are not legally binding.

---

[19] Following a public declaration of President Mitterrand on July 14, 1989, a constitutional amendment bill providing for the possibility for any court to raise the issue of constitutionality of Acts of Parliament before the Constitutional Court by way of preliminary rulings, was presented to Parliament in March 1990, but rejected.

[20] In its decision of April 9, 1992, the *Conseil constitutionnel* recommended that the Constitution should be amended before the ratification of the Maastricht Treaties could take place. Following this decision, the Constitution was amended on June 23, 1992.

On the whole process of the constitutional amendment, see F. Luchaire, *L'Union européenne et la constitution*: [1992] R.D.P. 589, 933, 956, 1587 & [1993] R.D.P. 301. On the decision itself, see B. Genevois, *Le Traité sur l'Union européenne et la Constitution. A propos de la décision du Conseil constitutionnel no 92–308 DC du 9 avril 1992*: [1992] R.F.D.A. 373; J.-P. Jacqué, *Commentaire de la décision du Conseil constitutionnel no 92–308 DC du 9 avril 1992. Traité sur l'Union européenne*: [1992] R.T.D.E. 253; and S. Boyron, *The Conseil Constitutionnel and the European Union*: [1993] Public Law 30.

[21] This has happened twice; after the resignation of President de Gaulle ((C.C.), April 28, 1969) and following the death of President Pompidou ((C.C.), April 3, 1974).

Chapter Four
The legal profession

1. THE ROLE OF LEGAL PERSONNEL IN
THE LEGAL FRAMEWORK

The expression "legal profession" must not be understood here by the English reader in its English sense but in a wider one. Although, in English law, this expression covers the separate careers of barristers and solicitors, by contrast, in the French legal system such a concept, according to René David, does not exist:

"(T)here is no general concept of legal profession in France. Many people have a university degree in France, and some elements of law are taught in a great number of schools other than law schools: business schools, or schools established within the various branches of the administration. Anybody can call himself a 'jurist', and exercise the profession of lawyers provided he does not infringe the monopoly given by statute to some categories of lawyer for some purposes (appearing in court, drafting instruments of mortgage, etc.) and provided he does not usurp a title (advocate, notary) to which he is not entitled."[1]

If we translate "legal profession" by "*professions juridiques*", these two expressions, similar in their wording, do not convey exactly the same concept. In French, by *profession*, one means simply employment; therefore, the words *professions juridiques* would cover a wide range of legal careers including not only lawyers,[2] but also legal consultants, judges, judicial personnel

---

[1] See R. David, *English Law and French Law* (Stevens & Sons, London, 1980), p. 49.
[2] The term "lawyer" has also a narrower meaning than the French word *juriste*.

and auxiliary personnel, all of whom could be regarded as being employed in the legal field.

If the term *profession* is understood to mean "an occupation requiring special training," one could use the expression "legal profession" to describe the French *professions juridiques* since the latter do require special training. However, the expression "legal profession", in the English sense, corresponds more closely to the French expression *profession libérale juridique*.

In France, it is usual to classify legal personnel according to their role. On the one hand, there are those who dispense or demand justice: these are called *agents de justice*. These are the *magistrats du siège* (judges of the Bench) and the *magistrats du parquet* or *Ministère Public* (the prosecution service and/or the State Counsel's Office) as well as the *juges administratifs* (administrative judges). On the other hand, one finds the legal personnel who are involved in the operation of the legal public service either by assisting the judge or the parties: these are called *auxiliaires de justice* (court auxiliaries or officers of the court)[3]. This second category of legal personnel includes, *avocats*, *officiers ministériels*, clerks of the courts and police personnel.

What follows is firstly an analysis of the different professions belonging to this second category of legal personnel and then an examination of the role of the judges.

2. THE *AVOCAT*

The profession of *avocat* can be traced back to antiquity. It was abolished under the French Revolution, re-established during the *Consulat* period (1799–1804) and remained unchanged until the legislative reform of December 9, 1971. This reform consisted primarily in the merger of the profession of *avocat* and those of *avoué près le tribunal de grande instance* and *agréé près les tribunaux de commerce*.[4]

---

[3] See M. Weston, *An English Reader's Guide to the French Legal System* (Berg, Oxford, 1991), p. 102.

[4] Unlike *avocats* who are independent lawyers, *avoués* were *officiers ministériels* (see below) whose task was to represent parties in the *tribunal de grande instance*. They were in charge of *postuler*, *i.e.* of signing all the necessary procedural documents, and of *conclure*, *i.e.* of communicating to the Bench the claims of the parties by means of formal *conclusions* (opinions). They were given full powers by their clients.

Agréés près les tribunaux de commerce used to be given an *agrément*, *i.e.* special authorization (hence their name) by a commercial court with the view

—continued on next page

Since the 1971 reform, the role of the avocat has combined
the function of giving advice and assistance with that of representation, the latter previously having been reserved to the
avoués and agréés. The abolition of this professional distinction
between the two functions had a number of advantages:

— it made the legal process simpler for the client;
— it reduced the cost of litigation;
— it harmonised French law with that of other European
  countries where such distinction and separation did not
  exist (for example Belgium, Germany);
— and it restored the balance between the two professions in
  favour of avocats.

This reform had a limited impact however. First, it did not
affect avoués d'appel who remained competent to represent
parties in Courts of Appeal (see below). Secondly, the original
idea of merging the professions of conseillers juridiques (legal
consultants)[5] and avocats was abandoned. The 1971 reform

—continued from previous page
to representing parties before it. They used to carry out both the functions of
avoués and of avocats whose assistance was not required before this court
(under art. 853 N.C.P.C., legal representation is still not necessary nowadays).
Although this profession appeared in the 17th Century, it was only in 1941 and
1945 that it was granted legal status. An agréé could represent and assist
parties before the commercial court in which he was registered only.
[5] Instead of reforming the profession of conseiller juridique, the Act of 1971
merely regulated it with the view to controlling the use of the title of
conseiller juridique (see arts. 54–66 as amended by art. 26 of Act 90–1259 of
December 31, 1990).
     Under the provisions of the 1990 Act, a conseiller juridique who was at the
time of the Act's adoption practising as such, could automatically become an
avocat. Until then, any legal advice or drafting of deeds could be effected by
unqualified people. From 1992 it is the law that, in order to protect clients
from the possible incompetence of these people, legal advice must be
given only by people observing the requirements of morality, possessing a
licence en droit, and of being covered by an insurance policy guaranteeing
their civil liability. On the other hand, the occasional remunerated advice or
drafting of deeds, or the regular but gratuitious advice, can still be carried out
by anyone. Therefore, according to the new provisions, professional lawyers,
such as notaires, huissiers de justice, commissaires-priseurs, etc., are entitled
to provide any legal service. Members of chartered or non-legal professions,
such as accountants, insurance brokers, building societies, banks, etc., can give
legal advice and draft legal documents only as a complementary function to
their main activities. Similarly, an association reconnue d'utilité publique (association officially acknowledged as serving public purposes) and consumer
associations can also provide legal advice in connection with their purposes,
provided that this service is limited to their members. Trade unions and
professional associations are equally entitled to provide legal services in

remained therefore incomplete and inevitably necessitated another reform.

THE MERGER OF THE PROFESSIONS OF AVOCAT AND CONSEIL JURIDIQUE

From January 1, 1992, a new profession, that of *avocat* replaced the two former ones of, respectively *avocat* and *conseil juridique*.[6] The purpose of this legal reform was not to abolish the profession of *conseil juridique* but to draw together the competence of both professions in order to improve them and to strengthen their position in the spheres of representation and advice. *Conseils juridiques* who were practising as such automatically became *avocats*.

The motives for this reform lay in the fact that French professions had to prepare for fiercer European and international competition as a result of the completion of the European internal market in 1993. In 1991, by contrast with other European countries, France had very few lawyers, having a total of 30,000 lawyers (18,000 *avocats*, 7,000 *notaires* and 5,000 *conseils juridiques*) whereas Germany had about 50,000 lawyers, U.K. 60,000 and the United States 750,000.

The merger of the two professions was accompanied by a series of legislative amendments relating to the organisation, recruitment and training of the new profession.

THE ORGANISATION OF THE PROFESSION

Recruitment and training

The system for qualification and entry to the profession of *avocat* can be said to date from 1971. Indeed, after the merger with the profession of *avoué*, a series of centres for professional training for the Bar were created. Under the 1990 Act these were renamed *centres régionaux de formation professionnelle des avocats (CRFPA)*. They are recognised as being established in the public interest and have legal personality. They are attached to Courts of Appeal.

The intending *avocat* must obtain a university law degree, the *maîtrise en droit* or any equivalent degree (article 11 of the

---

connection with their purposes. However, legal advice in newspapers, on the radio and the television may be given only by a member of the legal profession.

[6] See Act 90–1259 of December 31, 1990. It was originally suggested that this "new profession" be called *avocat-conseil* but *avocats* resisted such a proposal.

1971 Act as amended by Act 90–1259 of 1990). Then, in addition, he must pass the *certificat d'aptitude à la profession d'avocat* (*CAPA*). Under the current rules the candidate for the *CAPA* must follow a one year course of both theory and practice which is organised by the *centres de formation professionnelle*. This course is very similar in its aims to the Legal Practice Course and Bar School Finals but, unlike them, entry to the *CAPA* requires the candidate to pass a separate entrance examination.[7]

The preparation for the *CAPA* consists, on the one hand, in core practical courses — on the rules of professional conduct, drafting legal documents, oral argument, proceedings, management of a law firm, and a foreign language — and, on the other hand, in periods of training, either in France or abroad, in a law firm, in an accountant's firm, in the fiscal or legal service of a company or a trade union consisting of at least three laywers, in a court or in a public company (article 58 of *décret* 91–1197 of November 27, 1991 which organises the profession of *avocat*). At the end of this year's course, the candidate will have to pass a final examination.[8]

Once the intending *avocat* has obtained his *CAPA*,[9] he must be entered on the *liste des stagiaires* (register of trainee lawyers), undertake a period of practical training or *stage* — which corresponds to the English traineeship or pupillage — and take up a *domicile professionnel* in the area of the Bar which he has chosen. In other words he has to serve his *stage* in the office of an *avocat* situated in the area of the Bar chosen. He then takes the oath of admission to the Court of Appeal, in the area of which the Bar chosen is located, and becomes an *avocat stagiaire*. His training is no longer supervised by the *Bâtonnier* (the head of the local Bar) but by the centre of professional

---

[7] The jury of examiners consists of two law professors or senior lecturers in law — one of whom is chair — two judges from the civil and administrative courts and three practising *avocats* (art. 53 of *décret* 91–1197 of November 27, 1991).

By way of exception, article 12–1 of the Act of 1971 (as amended by the Act 90–1259), doctors in law, E.C. nationals who fall under the provisions of Directive 89–48 on the mutual recognition of diplomas, those persons who possess certain titles or exercise specific activities (*e.g.*, a *notaire*) have direct access to the examinations for the *CAPA*.

[8] The jury of examiners consists of the same people as above (art. 69 of *décret* 91–1197).

[9] Under article 98 of *décret* 91–1197, a number of practising and academic lawyers and higher civil servants are exempted from taking the *CAPA*.

training. This period of training is usually two years long (article 12 of the 1971 Act as amended).[10]

The *avocat stagiaire* bears the title of *avocat* and is entitled to do any task that a member of the profession may do, such as addressing the court and giving advice in chambers (article 78 of *décret* 91–1197 of November 27, 1991). The only restriction on his work lies in the supervision exercised over him by his principal. At the completion of this period of training, the *avocat stagiaire* receives his *certificat de stage* and is *inscrit au tableau*,[11] *i.e.* entered on the Bar roll. Admission to the Bar is decided by the Bar Council (article 93–96 of the 1991 *décret*).[12]

Traditionally, only French nationals had access to the profession of *avocat*. Following the development of international co-operation, notably the European Union and the European Economic Area, this principle could no longer apply. From January 1, 1994, the profession is accessible to nationals of member States of the European Community or of the European Economic Area, to nationals of States or territories, which grant French nationals the same right, and to refugees and stateless persons (article 11 of the 1971 Act as amended by the Act 93–1420 of December 31, 1993).

The *ordre des avocats*

As previously pointed out, the intending *avocat* who has taken the oath is admitted to the Bar. The *barreau*[13] is a corporation of all the *avocats* attached to a *tribunal de grande instance*.

---

[10] A *stagiaire* must spend at least twelve months in the firm of an *avocat* or of an *avocat* practising in the Court of Cassation or the *Conseil d'Etat*, or that of an *avoué* attached to a Court of Appeal. He may then choose to spend the rest of the training period either in a *notaire*'s office or in an office attached to a foreign Bar, in an accountant's or an auditor's office, in the State Counsel's Office of a Court of Appeal or of a *tribunal de grande instance*, in a public authority, in an international organisation, or in the legal or fiscal service of a company (art. 77 of the 1991 *décret*).

[11] It is referred to as the "*grand tableau*" as opposed to the register of trainees.

[12] Under article 97 of the 1991 *décret*, members or former members of administrative courts, of the Court of Auditors and Regional Courts of Auditors, judges and former judges or ordinary courts, law professors, *avocats* practising in the Court of Cassation or the *Conseil d'Etat*, and former *conseillers juridiques* may become and practise automatically as *avocats*.

Under article 99, EC nationals who fall under the provisions of Directive 89–48 and have successfully passed the aptitude test may register with the French Bar.

[13] The Bar is called *barreau* from the iron or wooden bar separating judges and *avocats* in the court.

Each *barreau* forms an *ordre* or "order" which is an independent body, distinct and separate from other orders.[14] The *ordre des avocats* has legal personality and promotes through its institutions (General Assembly, Bar Council, head of the Bar) the interests of the profession. The General Assembly consists of all the *avocats* having a right to vote, the *avocats inscrits au tableau*, the *avocats stagiaires* and honorary *avocats*. The role of this assembly is to appoint by means of elections the members of the *conseil de l'ordre* (Bar Council).

The *conseil de l'ordre*

The *conseil* has three functions and powers. First, it has administrative powers consisting notably in entering *avocats* on the roll, admitting candidates for the *stage* and in adopting the Rules of Procedure of the Bar. Secondly, under its financial powers, it administers the Bar's assets, determines membership fees and supervises the accountancy of its members. Finally, it has disciplinary powers and can sanction professional faults or infringements of rules of conduct.

The *bâtonnier*

The *bâtonnier*[15] is the head of the local Bar. He is elected for two years (article 15 of the 1971 Act and article 6 of the *décret* of 1991) and is the representative of the *Ordre*, particularly in a court. He chairs the General Assembly and the Bar Council. He has the task of arbitrating disputes arising between members of the Bar or relating to a contract of employment, and of initiating investigations in the case of a complaint against a member of the Bar.

THE ORGANISATION OF THE PRACTICE

Before the 1990 Reform, an *avocat* could practise either in an individual practice or in a *contrat d'association* (partnership) or

---

[14] It must be pointed out that there is no single Bar for the whole of France but a number of separate local Bars, each of which is attached to a *tribunal de grande instance*. The largest and most important Bar is that of Paris. The Bar of Strasbourg is therefore distinct from those of Paris, Lyon or Metz. Co-ordination between these local Bars used to be ensured by the *Conférence des Bâtonniers de France* and, since Act 90–1259 of 1990, by the *Conseil national des barreaux*.

[15] The name "*bâtonnier*" comes historically from the "*bâton*" (stick) of Saint Nicholas, the patron of the profession, which the *bâtonnier* used to carry during ceremonies.

in a *société civile professionnelle*.[16] In the first two situations, the *avocat* had his own clients; in the latter, the clients were those of the company. In principle, the *avocat* was self-employed and his profession was a profession *libérale*. He could not be employed and salaried.

From January 1, 1992 — the date on which the Act 90–1258 of December 31, 1990 came into force — the *avocat* is still able to practise according to one of these three formulas. However the new law also allows him to practise in the framework of a *société pour l'exercise d'une profession libérale* (*SEL*), which may be a *société anonyme* (*SELAFA*) (public limited liability company), or a *société à responsabilité limitée* (*SELARL*) (private limited liability company), or a *société en commandite par actions* (*SELCA*) (partnership limited by shares).[17] The purpose of this innovation is to allow law firms to enlarge in order to be better able to compete with Anglo-American firms. Indeed the old legal structure of law firms was not appropriate for creating large-sized and competitive firms. This explained why there was a preponderance of small-sized *cabinets d'avocats*.

More than half of the capital of the company and half of the votes must be held by professionals practising in the company. The remaining shares may belong to members of the profession practising in other law firms or to members of closely related professions (articles 5 & 6 of the Act 90–1258). Therefore, law firms of this new kind may be created by, and consist of, *avocats*, *notaires* and *experts-comptables* (chartered accountants), etc. This new company can attract external capital of up to 25 per cent of the capital of a *SELAFA* or a *SELARL* or up to 49 per cent if the company is a *société en commandite par actions* (articles 6(1) & (2) of the Act). This permits someone who does not belong to a legal profession to have some interest in these companies.

The Act 90–1259 of 1990 (article 7) also provides that the *avocat* may now practise as an employed and salaried person.

---

[16] See Act 66–879 of November 29, 1966 and *décret* 92–680 of July 20, 1992. A *société civile professionnelle* is a company which has no commercial purpose and the capital of which is shared under certain conditions. Expenses and gains are put together and distributed to its members according to the number of shares each of them holds. However members are liable *in solidum* for the debts of the company and, against their own assets, for their professional action.

[17] See *décret* 93–492 of March 25, 1993 which implements the Act of 1990.

Being employed and salaried was a common practice amongst legal consultants but, as has been indicated, was not previously allowed in the case of *avocats*, although young *avocats* were often employed by a firm as assistants. However this was simply a disguised form of salaried employment since the assistant *avocat* was necessarily subordinate to the *avocat* employing him. Nevertheless, in order to preserve the independence of the salaried *avocat*, article 7(4) of the Act of 1990 provides that a young *avocat* is only subordinate to his employer as regards his conditions of work. The contract of employment must determine the mode of payment of the *avocat*. He is entitled to social security and participates in the *régime de la caisse nationale des barreaux pour l'assurance vieillesse* (national Bar pension scheme) (article 42 of the 1971 Act as amended). The disadvantage of this formula is that the employed and salaried *avocat*, unlike the partner, cannot have his own clients. The law does not however make this system obligatory for the *avocat*, who may therefore choose between being a partner or being employed and salaried.

THE ROLE OF THE *AVOCAT*

Apart from the role of consultant which an *avocat* is normally entitled to exercise, but of which he does not have any monopoly[18], the functions of the *avocat* are of two kinds: assistance and representation.

Assistance consists mainly of the *plaidoiries* (oral argument). In the exercise of this function, *avocats* are not subject to any territorial restrictions (article 5 of the 1971 Act). They can also plead before any court, whatever its nature: civil, criminal, administrative or disciplinary courts, except the *Conseil d'Etat* and the *Cour de cassation* (article 4 of the 1971 Act). In ordinary courts they enjoy an absolute monopoly. Nevertheless, in civil courts, parties need not, under certain conditions, resort to the assistance of an *avocat* and may represent themselves (article 18 *N.C.P.C.*).[19] In special courts — such as the *conseil*

---

[18] Since the Act of 1990, legal consulting is subject to certain conditions (see footnote 5, above). Not only *avocats* but also other auxiliaries are entitled to give legal advice.

[19] The President of the Court may deny this right if the party is overwhelmed by emotion or is incapable of presenting arguments with clarity and decency.

des prud'hommes — parties may be assisted by a counsel for the defence who does not belong to the Bar.

Assistance is not limited to the oral argument — the *avocat* may assist his client throughout the investigation. He is present during the questioning of the witnesses, he takes part in experts' appraisal, and he attends the questioning of the accused by the investigating judge.

The *avocats* also represent the parties. They exercise those functions which, prior to 1971, were attributed to the *avoué* and the *agréé*, attached respectively to the *tribunal de grande instance* and the *tribunaux de commerce*. By virtue of article 4 of the 1971 Act, *avocats* have *mandat ad litem*, *i.e.* authority to appear in court on behalf of their clients. This proxy is implied and general. *Avocats* are the only permitted legal representatives in *tribunaux de grande instance*. In courts of limited jurisdiction however, parties may be represented by legally authorised persons other than *avocats*.[20] The right of audience of *avocats* are territorially restricted as they can exercise it exclusively before the *tribunal de grande instance* in the area in which they had established their *résidence professionnelle*, *i.e.* their office (article 5 of the 1971 Act). This is known as *"territorialité de la postulation"* (territorial exclusivity).[21] However, following the European Court of Justice in the *Klopp* case of July 12, 1984 and that of certain Courts of Appeal (notably at Aix-en-Provence January 13, 1987), the French legislator recognised a wider right of establishment of *avocats* within French territory in Act 89–906 of December 19, 1989.

---

[20] For instance, in the *tribunaux d'instance*, the spouse of the party and relatives in direct or collateral line with the party may act as proxies (art. 828 *N.C.P.C.*). Spouses, trade union representatives, employees or employers may represent a party in a *conseil des prud'hommes* (art. R 516–5 *C.Trav.*). In a *tribunal de commerce*, anyone may act as proxy (art. 853 *N.C.P.C.*). In administrative courts, parties may give mandate either to an *avocat* or to an *avocat au Conseil d'Etat* or *à la Cour de cassation* (art. R 108 *C.T.A.*).

[21] As a result, if a party is free to choose to be represented in a Paris court by a lawyer who is registered with the Bar of Strasbourg, another lawyer who is a member of the Paris Bar — known as an *avocat postulant* — must be appointed as well. This principle of territorial exclusivity, although it is justified in many respects, is increasingly challenged by French lawyers, notably in the light of the decision of the European Court of Justice of July 11, 1991 (case C–294/89, *Commission v. French Republic*: [1991] ECR 3591) in which this principle, when applied to foreign lawyers, was said to be incompatible with articles 59 and 60 of the Treaty of Rome and Directive 77/249).

Firms of *avocats* may establish a second office in the territorial area of a different Bar (new article 8–1 of the 1971 Act).

3. THE *OFFICIERS MINISTÉRIELS*

(A) DEFINITION

Those designated under the general expression of *"officiers ministériels"* [22] are those who have been granted a *charge* (function) for life by the Government over which they enjoy a monopoly. *Officiers ministériels* are not civil servants. They have been granted a charge by a former *officier ministériel*, either gratuitously or for valuable consideration.

An *office ministériel* is a combination of two elements: a title and a financial aspect. The title, which confers a monopoly, is granted after appointment by the *Garde des Sceaux* (Minister of Justice). This appointment ensures that the nominee meets the requirements of nationality, diploma and professional qualifications. The financial aspect corresponds to the patrimonial value of the *charge*. This materialises, during the transfer of the *charge*, into the right to propose (*droit de présentation*) a successor to whom, if approved by the Minister of Justice, the *charge* is sold.

Anyone having a *charge* is fully entitled to be member of the professional corporate bodies created by law. These bodies are, depending on the profession concerned, either an *ordre* (*avocats au Conseil d'Etat et à la Cour de cassation*) or a *chambre* (*avoués, notaires, huissiers*). [23] They are usually of a two- or three-tier hierarchical structure. [24] They lay down the rules of procedure for the profession and exercise disciplinary powers. They give opinions on the creation or suppression of a *charge*. They also organise and supervise professional training, and administer the professions' social schemes. [25]

---

[22] As M. Weston points out: "(t)he term *'officiers ministériels'* is difficult to translate. The adjective *'ministériel'* does not, ... relate to a government ministry but to *'ministèré'* in the older sense of 'duty' or 'function'"; *op. cit.* p. 108. (See *ministère public* discussed below and *le ministère d'un avocat*).

Unlike L.N. Brown (see Office of Notary in France (1953) 2 I.C.L.Q. 60), the term "ministerial official" will not be used but rather *officiers ministériels*.

[23] Before the 1789 Revolution, these professions were organised in *compagnies*. Nowadays this term is still used sometimes as in, for instance, "*compagnie de notaires*".

[24] *e.g. huissiers* are organised in national, regional and local chambers.

[25] As regards the common rules applicable to *officiers ministériels*, see R. Perrot, *Institutions judiciaires* (Montchrestien, Paris, 6th ed., 1994), p. 412; see also J.

The concept of *officiers ministériels* must not be confused with that of *officier public* (public legal officer) although an *officier ministériel* is an *officier public*. For instance, *notaires*, *huissiers* and *greffiers des tribunaux de commerce* are *officiers publics* but so are mayors who officiate at weddings and are responsible for the registration of births, marriages and deaths. The *officiers publics* are those who have powers to authenticate legal acts.

The main examples of *officiers ministériels* are the *notaires*, the *huissiers de justice*, the *avoués près la cour d'appel* and the *avocats aux Conseils*. Each of these professions will be examined in turn.[26]

(B) THE *NOTAIRE*

Notaires[27] may be considered as the second most important group of French lawyers after that of *avocats* due to their number and the importance of their members. This profession employs some 43–44,000 persons including clerks and other employees. Being a monopoly, the *notariat*[28] is, after that of the *avoué*, the most lucrative legal profession.

The *notariat* can be traced back to antiquity and Roman law. Consequently, this institution can be found in countries which have been influenced by Roman law.[29]

Vincent, S. Guinchard, G. Montagnier & A. Varinard, *La justice et les institutions* (Dalloz, Paris, 3rd ed., 1991), p. 386 *et seq.*

[26] Apart from these four professions, one must mention that of the *commisssaires-priseurs*. These are licensed auctioneers. They are in charge of the appraisal and valuation before auction of *meubles corporels* (tangible personal property). They may perform their service either in a *vente à l'amiable* (private sale) or by *vente forcée* (by execution following a distraint). They have a virtual monopoly in the town where they practice. They may exercise their powers in other towns of a *département* concurrently with either their colleagues practising in the same *département* or with other *officiers ministériels* whose legal status permit them to perform a similar service (*notaires, huissiers, greffiers des tribunaux de commerce*).

[27] For a socio-political analysis of this profession, see E.N. Suleiman, *Private power and centralization in France. The notaires and the State* (Princeton University Press, New Jersey, 1987).

[28] This is the generic name of the profession.

[29] This is the case in Italy, Spain, Portugal, Switzerland, Germany, Belgium, Luxembourg, Central and South America, Quebec, Louisiana as well as the French-speaking African, and Middle and Far East countries.

The firm of a *notaire* is called an *étude*, over the street door of which there is a pair of gold painted shields which denote the *notaire's* office.

Recruitment

After passing the *baccalauréat* (the equivalent of "A" Levels), it takes about seven years to qualify as a *notaire*. The entry requirements and training methods of the notarial profession were reformed by *décret* 89–399 of June 20, 1989.

Candidates of French nationality and possessing a *maîtrise en droit* — or any equivalent degree (article 1 of the *arrêté* of June 24, 1991) have to pass an entrance examination (article 10 of the 1989 *décret*) after which they can follow an educational programme provided by universities or by the *centres de formation professionnelle* (article 9). This training lasts 12 months and consists of theoretical and practical teaching on legal consulting and drafting legal documents, as well as the rules of conduct and the management of a firm (article 25). Also included is a two month *stage d'initiation*, half of which may be spent with another profession such as *expert comptable* (chartered accountant), *commissaire aux comptes* (auditor) or in the legal department of a company (article 26). At the end of this training period the intending *notaire* has to pass an examination leading to the *diplôme d'aptitude aux fonctions de notaire* which allows the candidate to register as a *notaire stagiaire*.[30] He must follow a *stage* of up to two years duration and a series of seminars organised by the *centre régional de formation professionnelle notariale* (article 36). In this new system, as set out by the 1989 *décret*, the final examination was replaced by continual assessment and a *rapport de stage* (report on his traineeship). After successfully completing this training, the *notaire stagiaire* is awarded a *certificat de fin de stage* and becomes a *notaire assistant* if he practises in a *notaire's* firm. *Notaires* are appointed by the Minister of Justice when there is a vacant or a newly created post.[31]

---

[30] Those who possess a *DESS de droit notarial* (postgraduate degree) also now have the right to register as a *notaire stagiaire*.

[31] In France, *notaires* may acquire their *charge* either by purchasing it or by means of donation, legacy or succession *ab intestat* (intestate succession). By way of exception, in Alsace and Moselle, where local law of German influence is still applicable in many areas, they register on a waiting list until a charge is made vacant following either the resignation or the death of a *notaire*.

Organisation of a *notaire*'s practice

As with *avocats*, *notaires* may practise either in an individual firm or in a *société civile professionnelle*. Following the Act of 1990 reforming the legal profession, they may also practise in a *société d'exercice libéral* (article 1 *bis of ordonnance* 45–2590 of November 2, 1945 as amended by article 45 of the 1990 Act and *décret* 93–78 of January 13, 1993). They may be employed and salaried by a legal or a natural person running a firm.

They also have the possibility of working in a *groupement d'intérêt économique* (*GIE*) (Economic Interest Group)[32] or in a *groupement européen d'intérêt économique* (*GEIE*) (European Economic Interest Group),[33] or of being a partner in a *société en participation* (an informal association for economic purposes having no separate legal personality) (article 22 of Act 90–1258 of December 31, 1990 and articles 74–79 of the 1993 *décret*).

Role of the *notaire*

Since the *décret* 86–728 of April 29, 1986 on the status of the *notariat*, *notaires* whose competence used to be limited to the area of a *cour d'appel*, can now exercise their functions over the entire national territory, apart from overseas territories (see article 14). *Notaires* are attached to the *service de la justice* (the legal public service) since they must have authorisation from a judge to carry out certain sales such as *ventes immobilières* (sales of real property), *ventes sur saisies* (sales following attachment or distraint), *ventes de biens de mineurs* (sales of goods belonging to minors), *ventes en cas de succession bénéficiaire* (sales resulting from a *beneficio inventarii*),[34] *ventes en cas de succession vacante* (sales resulting from an

---

[32] A *groupement d'intérêt économique* (*GIE*) is a group of businesses with a view to co-ordinating and developing some of their activities (*e.g.* import or export services, research, etc.). This group has legal personality but is different in nature from a company or an association.

[33] Created under E.C. Regulation 2137/85 OJ [1985] L 199/1, an *EEIG* may be constituted by parties in two or more member States of the European Union. It is designed to act as a catalyst to cross-border activity between small and medium-sized firms and help them to co-ordinate and develop activities ancillary to their main business without resorting to a jointly owned company or being forced to operate under an unfamiliar domestic legal system.

[34] Acceptance of an estate without liability beyond the assets left by the deceased.

estate in abeyance), and, in certain cases, *ventes mobilières* (sales of personal property, chattels).

The main function of a *notaire* is to draft, at the request of an individual, legal documents which are regarded as being authentic and enforceable. Owing to their authentic character, their content can be disputed only through an extremely formal procedure called *procédure d'inscription en faux* (a challenge that the document is forged). Because these legal documents are enforceable like any judgment, they may lead to an *exécution forcée* (simple enforcement). These documents are kept by the *notaire* who has drawn them up and parties may ask their *notaire*, at any time, for a *copie exécutoire* (enforceable copy) or a *copie certifiée conforme* (certified true copy).

In addition to this function, *notaires* may also play the role of legal adviser. Their activities may therefore be concerned with businesses (creation and merger of companies, credit transactions, purchase and sale of real property, etc.) as well as with private affairs (wills, *contrats de mariage* [antenuptial settlements], gifts, etc.).

In principle, resorting to a *notaire* is not compulsory except in certain cases. For instance, the law may require that certain legal documents have to be drawn up by a *notaire*: this is the case of *actes solennels* (documents in solemn form) such as enforceable gifts, antenuptial settlements, the creation of mortgages.

Notaires may also be appointed by a judicial authority to draw up documents which are to be approved and sanctioned by a court at a later date: for example following a divorce or a contested succession, a *notaire* may be instructed to settle the financial arrangements between husband and wife, or the rights of succession (*liquidation et partage*). In this case, *notaires* are court auxiliaries.

Of course, *notaires* are held liable for the performance of all these activities. This is why their liability is covered by an insurance scheme, the *caisse de guarantie* (see articles 11–24 of *décret* 55–604 of May 20, 1955).

The *notaires* have a monopoly of practice regarding conveyancing and matters concerning marriage settlements and successions. They are often legal advisers of families and businesses. As has been pointed out:

"... (their) daily work is remarkably like that of a solicitor. There is ... a common territory in which both operate, and on either side a domain special to each. The solicitor has his litigation and the notary his authenticity [*i.e.* the drawing up of authoritative formal documents]."[35]

Functionally, the closest equivalent of *notaire* is solicitor even if the solicitor's work combines parts of the work of a *notaire* and an *avocat*. When the French refer to their *notaire*, the English refer to their solicitor.[36] In other words, most of the work done by a *notaire* in France is done by a solicitor in England. Nevertheless, in some circumstances, the services provided by the *notaire* such as the authentication of documents would be performed in England by a notary.[37]

(C) THE *HUISSIER DE JUSTICE*

Historically, *huissiers* originate from two distinct professions: that of *sergents* whose function was to serve judicial and non-judicial notices, and of *huissiers* who acted as court ushers.[38] It is only after the Revolution of 1789 that these two professions were merged.[39]

Huissiers de justice perform their services at the request of individuals or sometimes at the request of a judge. Therefore their functions are wide ranging.[40]

---

[35] L.N. Brown, *op. cit.* p. 71. Brown uses the common translation "notary" which is the formal equivalent of *notaire*. However, as Weston points out, "...it is equally clearly not remotely equivalent functionally and must usually be rejected"; L.N. Brown *op. cit.* p. 105.

[36] However, *"je dois consulter mon avocat"* may also be translated "I must see my solicitor".

[37] According to Mozley & Whiteley's, *Law Dictionary* (Butterworth, London, 11th ed., 1993), p. 183: a notary or notary public is someone "who attests deeds or writings to make them authentic in another country. He is generally a solicitor."

According to Osborn's, *Concise Law Dictionary* (Sweet & Maxwell, London, 8th ed., 1993), p. 234: it is "A legal practitioner, usually a solicitor, who attests deeds or other documents or makes certified copies of them in order to render the deeds or copies authentic, especially for use abroad."

[38] The name *huissier* originates from the old French word *"huis"* for a door.

[39] Nowadays this profession is governed by *ordonnance* 45–2592 of November 2, 1945 as implemented by *décret* 56–222 of February 29, 1956 and *décret* 94–299 of April 12, 1994.

[40] According to judicial statistics of 1992, there were 3,117 *huissiers* amongst whom 1,223 were practising individually and 1,894 in partnership. See *Ministère de la Justice; Annuaire statistique de la justice 1989–1992 (la Documentation française*, Paris, 1995), p. 217.

The exercise of their functions is confined to the area of the *tribunal d'instance* but may be extended by *décret* to one or more territorial jurisdictions of a court.

Huissiers have a virtual monopoly in three cases. First, they perform *significations judiciaires et extra-judiciaires* (judicial and non-judicial notifications): they send *exploits d'assignation* (serve writs), send *sommations* (summons), and inform litigants about certain procedural acts and courts' decisions. In this respect *huissiers* act as messengers of the parties as well as "postmen" of the courts. As they are *officiers publics*, what they do or see has a character of authenticity, *i.e.* of evidentiary value unless an *inscription en faux* can be proven.

Secondly, they are responsible for the enforcement of *mandements de justice* (court orders), of judgments and of *actes notariés* (acts executed and authenticated by a *notaire*). They perform these services as *officiers publics* particularly with regard to *expulsion* (eviction) and/or *saisie* (attachment or distraint).

Thirdly, some huissiers work in a *Palais de Justice* (Court House). They are then called *huissiers audienciers*.[41] Their tasks consist of introducing the court, *procéder à l'appel des causes* (calling the roll) and maintaining silence and order in the court. In this respect, *huissiers* act principally as court ushers. By contrast, when they perform the two former functions, they act as court bailiffs.

In as far as *huissiers* do not enjoy a monopoly, they act concurrently with other lawyers. Thus, they *procèdent au recouvrement des créances* (collect debts), conduct appraisals before auctions and auction sales when there is no *commissaire-priseur*, and represent parties before the *tribunaux paritaires de baux ruraux* (agricultural land tribunals), the *juge des référés* (judge sitting in chambers), and, since the Act of July 16, 1987, the *tribunal de commerce* (Commercial Court).

Finally, the *ministère* (function or duty) *de l'huissier de justice* is frequently requested, either on instruction by a court or by a private citizen, to make *constats* (sworn statements) which are official reports on a factual situation, excluding opinions of fact or law, which may be used as evidence before a

---

[41] "*Audiencier*" comes from the word "*audience*" which means a sitting or a session of a court.

court (for example, in the case of road accidents, adultery, inventories of premises, etc.).

(D) THE *AVOUÉS PRÈS LA COUR D'APPEL*

As mentioned above, the functions of *avocat* were merged with those of *avoué* attached to a court of first instance (*tribunal de grande instance* and *tribunal d'instance*) by the 1971 Act. This left only the *avoués* who were attached to the Courts of Appeal.

The functions of *avoués près la cour d'appel* (hereafter *avoués*) is to *postuler* on behalf of their clients, *i.e.* to sign all the necessary procedural documents, and *conclure*, *i.e.* to draw up in formal opinions their clients' appeal. In court, they represent their clients but need no proxy. They commit their clients by their acts and declarations. Parties have to be represented by an *avoué* in a Court of Appeal.[42] Their functions are much more specialised and more restricted than those of *avocats*. They simply conduct the procedural stages of litigation in the Court of Appeal but take no part in the oral argument at the appeal, these being reserved for the *avocat*. However, the *avoué* may be allowed to address the court when *avocats* are on strike or when the matter concerned involves very few procedural problems and can be judged summarily. *Avoués* are involved in civil litigation only and in the civil action brought by the victim of a crime.

Their training is also more specialised than that of *avocats*. It is more concentrated on civil procedural matters. This is reflected in the subject matter of the examination of professional competence for the functions of *avoué*, which corresponds to the *CAPA* for *avocats*, and which is taken at the conclusion of a two-year traineeship — one of which must be spent with a practising *avoué*.[43] After successfully completing this examination, the intending *avoué* is enrolled with a Court of Appeal provided he has been admitted by judges of the Bench, convened in assembly, or by the First President of the Court of Appeal concerned, after consulting other judges (*décret 86–997*

---

[42] By way of exception, legal representation by an *avoué* is not compulsory in disputes relating to social security, rent or employment. In these instances, parties may choose either to appear in court without legal representation or to be represented by an *avocat*.

[43] By contrast, the *avocat* takes his *CAPA* before the *stage*.

of August 27, 1986).[44] The profession of *avoué* is organised nationally. It is controlled by the *chambre nationale des avoués*. In addition, in the area of each *cour d'appel*, there is a disciplinary chamber the function of which is to control and oversee the conduct of the *avoués* attached to the court concerned.[45]

(E) The *Avocats Aux Conseils*

Avocats aux conseils are another category of *officiers ministériels* who are attached to the highest courts in France, the *Conseil d'Etat*, the *Cour de Cassation* or the *Tribunal des conflits*. Before these courts, they have complete monopoly over the functions of both *avoués* and *avocats*.[46] *Avocats aux conseils* may practise either individually or in *sociétés civiles professionnelles* or, since Act 90–1258, in a *société d'exercice libéral*.[47] Nowadays their monopoly is losing importance and prestige since recent legislation allows actions to be brought before the highest courts without the need for legal representation: for example, in the case of a *recours pour excès de pouvoir* (judicial review of administrative action) or a *pourvoi en matière sociale* (appeal lodged in the Court of Cassation on social matters).

When they act as *avocats*, they have a right of audience before any court in France. In practice, they hardly use this prerogative except before the *tribunaux administratifs* and the *cours administratives d'appel*.[48]

---

[44] Under *décret* 45–118 of December 19, 1945 as amended by *décret* 90–1210 of December 21, 1990, the profession of *avoué* is accessible not only to French but also European Union nationals.

[45] In 1992, out of 363 *avoués*, 115 exercised their office individually, 248 practised in partnership amongst which 120 were in a *société civile professionnelle*. See *Annuaire statistique, op. cit.* p. 215.

[46] This can be explained by the simplicity of the procedure which consists solely in an *échange de mémoires* (exchange of written submissions); there is therefore no need for a special *ministère*.

[47] In 1992, 36 of them were practising individually, 51 in a partnership and 24 in a *société civile professionnelle*. See *Annuaire statistique, op. cit.* p. 215.

[48] Access conditions are laid down by *décret* 91–1125 of October 28, 1991. These are similar to those required for *avocats*. In addition, the intending *avocat aux conseils* must complete a one-year traineeship in a Bar and pass a special examination followed by two years training organised by the profession. *Avocats aux conseils* are organised in an *ordre* headed by a President appointed for three years by the Minister of Justice on a proposal from the *Conseil de l'ordre*.

4. THE *AUXILIAIRES DU JUGE*

Whilst the task of the two categories of lawyers examined above is to assist clients, that of the *auxiliaires du juge* is to assist judges. [49] Some of them, without whose assistance the work of the courts could not be accomplished, are employed permanently: these are the *greffiers* [50] and the personnel of the *police judiciaire*. Others are employed intermittently by courts when their assistance is requested: these are the *experts judiciaires* (experts appointed by a court) and the *administrateurs et liquidateurs de biens*. [51] These two professions will not be examined here.

(A) THE *GREFFIERS*

No court can work without a *greffe*, a body of administrative staff headed by a *greffier en chef* assisted by *greffiers*. [52] All administrative and ordinary courts have a service of *greffiers*. [53] This service is called *secrétariat-greffe* in civil courts as opposed to *greffe* in *tribunaux de commerce*.

Since the application of the Act of November 30, 1965, *greffiers* have been civil servants. However, *greffiers des tribunaux de commerce* remained *officiers ministériels et publics* and therefore own their *charge*. [54]

---

[49] The *auxiliaires du juge* must not be confused with the *auxiliaires de justice* (see introduction to this chapter) but constitute one category of the latter.

[50] The word *greffier* could be translated by "registrar" but this would not be sufficiently accurate as they exercise no judicial powers and are civil servants. On this point, see M. Weston, *op. cit.* p. 107.

[51] An *administrateur de biens* can be either a receiver (in the case of bankruptcy) or an executor or administrator (in the case of succession). The *liquidateur de biens* is a liquidator in bankruptcy.

[52] These are two categories of *greffiers* listed respectively in categories A and B under article 29 of the Act of January 11, 1984. These are assisted by assistants, technical office clerks, secretaries and auxiliaries. Altogether they are quite numerous. The *greffe* is similar in size to a company, and, for instance, the *greffe* of the *tribunal de grande instance* of Paris has more than 320 employees. In 1992, there were 6,996 *greffiers* and *secrétaires-greffes*, and 11,661 civil servants and clerks.

[53] Before the 1965 reform, besides the *greffe*, there was a separate and distinct service called *secrétariat du parquet* (which assisted the State Counsels' Office). Nowadays, the *secrétariats-greffes* bring together the administrative services of *le siège* and *le parquet*, except for certain courts whose list is drawn by the *Garde des Sceaux* and which have a separate *secrétariat du parquet* (e.g. Lyon).

[54] In 1992, 267 *greffiers* owned their office. See Act 87–550 of July 16, 1987 (art. 5 deals with duties), and *décret* 87–601 of July 27, 1987 on recruitment of
—continued on next page

The organisation of the *greffes* and the status of *greffiers* are governed by a number of Acts. The most important ones can be found under articles L 811-1 to L 831-1 and R 811-1 to R 841-2 of the *Code de l'organisation judiciaire* (*C.O.J.*) and in articles R 25 *et seq.* of the *Codes des tribunaux administratifs et des cours d'appel* (*C.T.A.*).

The function of a *greffier* is to assist the judges. He must be present to authenticate the judges' acts. During hearings, he keeps the *plumitif* or *registre d'audience* (the minutes book) in which he reports all incidents which occurred during the hearing, the decision taken, the judgment ruled, etc.

The *greffier* is present throughout the proceedings: he registers the case on the roll, and opens a *dossier* (file) in which all relevant documents will be inserted. The *greffier en chef* keeps the minutes of which he sends, on request, copies or *copies exécutoires* (enforceable copies). The *greffier* also takes part in the drafting of the court's budget and the administration thereof, and has a number of tasks related to the documentation, furniture and equipment of the court.

Apart from these functions which are common to all *greffiers*, they have more specific tasks related to the particular type of court. In *tribunaux de grande instance*, the *greffier en chef* keeps a copy of the *registre de l'état civil* (register of births, marriages and deaths); he updates *casiers judiciaires* (criminal records); he keeps the *répertoire civil*, *i.e.* the register in which are reported acts and judgments relating to the capacity of persons following any changes affecting their legal status or their *régime matrimonial*[55] (for example *mise en tutelle* [tutelage or guardianship], *retrait de pouvoirs entre époux* [redistribution of matrimonial powers], *rejet de demande de séparation de biens* [rejection of a claim for the separation of property]). In *tribunaux d'instance*, a *greffier en chef* keeps the *registre du commerce et des sociétés* (trade register) and is in charge of publicising a number of legal acts such as *vente de fonds de commerce* (sales of businesses), *opérations de leasing* (leasing transactions), etc. In *tribunaux administratifs*, *greffiers* accomplish the tasks carried out by *huissiers* in proceedings

---

—*continued from previous page*
  greffiers (diploma, traineeship, examination, oath) and *décret* 88-38 of January 13, 1988 organising the disciplinary procedure before the *tribunal de grande instance*.

[55] In order for third persons to be informed.

brought before any ordinary courts. They keep a record of *requêtes* (applications lodged with the court), transmit to the opposing party the *mémoire en défense* (opinion of the defendant), *mémoire en réplique* (the plaintiff's replication) and the *mémoire en duplique* (defendant's rejoinder). They also inform parties of the *mesures d'instruction* (investigation measures by the judge(s)); communicate to the parties the date of the hearing and, finally, notify them of the decision of the court.[56]

(B)   THE *POLICE JUDICIAIRE*

In France, the police play an important role in the conduct of investigations under the supervision of the investigating judge or the public prosecutor.

In French law however, a major distinction is made between *police judiciaire* and *police administrative*.[57] Therefore, before describing the organisation of police services and their personnel, some explanations about this distinction must be provided.

The distinction between *police judiciaire* and *police administrative*

The *police administrative* act mainly preventively in order to maintain or restore law and order: for example they break up unauthorised demonstrations, etc. By contrast, the *police judiciaire* operate when the action of the former police has proved to be inefficient, *i.e.* after a criminal offence has been committed. They then have to record criminal offences, to assemble evidence, to search perpetrator(s) of crimes and to carry out instructions from investigating judges (article 14 *C.P.P.*). Therefore, the two police have separate and distinct spheres of operation:[58] the *police judiciaire* intervene after an

---

[56] *Greffes* of *tribunaux administratifs* have their headquarters in the court itself and annexes in each of the *préfectures* (public authorities under the central government which administers each of the *départements* of France) which are located within the territorial jurisdiction of the court.

[57] On the *police administrative*, see G. Vedel & P. Delvolvé, *Droit administratif*, Vol. 2 (PUF, Paris, 12th ed., 1992), p. 678; M. Rougevin-Baville, R. Denoix de Saint Marc & D. Lateboulle, *Leçons de droit administratif* (Collection PES, Hachette Supérieur, Paris, 1990), p. 289; and E. Picard, *La notion de police administrative* (L.G.D.J.), Paris, 1984).

[58] The powers of the police are examined below in Chapter Five.

offence has been perpetrated whereas the *police administrative* try to prevent their perpetration.[59]

The *police administrative* are subordinate and accountable to administrative authorities or administrative courts whilst the *police judiciaire* are answerable to the prosecution department and investigating judges.

The difficulty in clearly distinguishing between the two police forces is due to the fact that they may share personnel[60] and that certain police operations may fall between the two jurisdictions.[61]

General organisation of police services

For a long time, the French police was organised at local level. Small towns and parishes used to have a *garde champêtre* (rural policeman) while larger towns and cities had police services. Since the 1941 and, more importantly, the 1966 reforms, police forces have been centralised. Nowadays, the police consist of two main bodies: the *Police Nationale* and the *Gendarmerie*.

(a) The *Police Nationale*

This body was created under the Reform Act of July 9, 1966, which merged the former services of *Sûreté Nationale* and *Préfecture de Police*.

The *Police Nationale* is subordinate to the *Ministère de l'Intérieur* (Home Office) and is under the authority of the *Directeur Général de la Police Nationale*.

Basically, the *Police Nationale* is organised in central and local services. Central services consist of:

---

[59] The criteria for distinguishing the activities of either police force have been formulated by diverse decisions of the courts (see in particular, C.E. May 11, 1951, *Baud;* (T.C.), June 7, 1951, *Noualek*: [1951] Rec. Lebon 636; ((T.C.), June 27, 1955, *Dame Barnier*: [1955] D.).

[60] For instance, *commissaires de police*, *inspecteurs de police*, *gendarmes* and *agents de police* act either as personnel of the *police judiciaire* or as members of the *police administrative*.

When a police officer takes part in police *cordon* during a demonstration, he will act as a member of the *police administrative* but will perform an act of the *police judiciaire* if he arrests an offending demonstrator. Similarly, when a *gendarme* is on traffic duty and records an offence against the highway code, he performs an act of *police administrative* and *police judiciaire* respectively. However this may not be the case of a prosecutor or an investigating judge, who have powers of *police judiciaire* only.

[61] *e.g.* by breaking up an unauthorised demonstration, policemen may arrest demonstrators who have committed offences.

— the *direction centrale des polices urbaines*, the role of which is to maintain public order and combat petty and major crime;

— the *direction centrale des renseignements généraux* (*RG*), which collects and centralises information of a political, economic and social nature, and controls horse racing and gambling. *RG* are also organised at the level of *régions* and *départements*;

— the *direction centrale de la police judiciaire* (*PJ*), responsible for combatting serious crime. It is itself divided into services specialising in different categories of crime (organized crime, trade of people, theft of objects and works of art, drug trafficking, arms smuggling, money counterfeiting and financial crime). It has authority over the 19 regional services of the *police judiciaire* (*SRPJ*) and the *police judiciaire* service of the *Préfecture de Police* based in Paris;

— the *direction de la surveillance du territoire* (*DST*) is the counterintelligence agency, equivalent to the British MI5;

— the *service central de la police de l'air et des frontières*, which is in charge of controlling borders; and

— the *service central des compagnies républicaines de sécurité* (*CRS*), which are special riot forces. There are 63 of these which are split into 10 regional groups.

Even though the *Préfecture de Police* (the police services of Paris and its region) and the *Police Nationale* share the same personnel, the former has maintained, probably for historical reasons[62], its complex structure under the authority of a *Préfet de Police*.

(b) The *Gendarmerie Nationale*

The *Gendarmerie Nationale* is a military institution which originates from the *maréchaussée* (mounted police force) created in the twelfth century and the main functions of which are those of the police. As it is a military force, it is subordinate to the Ministry of Defence.

Besides specialised units such as the *Garde Républicaine* (Republican Guard used on ceremonial occasions in Paris), the *Gendarmerie de l'Air* (Air police force), the *Gendarmerie des*

---

[62] The origins of the *Préfecture de Police* can be traced back to the *Ancien Régime* (prior to the 1789 Revolution). Its role was to maintain law and order in Paris and its surrounding area.

Transports Aériens (Air transport police force), the *Gendarmerie Maritime* (Coastguard), and the *Groupe d'Intervention de la Gendarmerie Nationale*, known as *GIGN* (anti-terrorist force), the *Gendarmerie Nationale* consists of two main forces: the *Gendarmerie Départementale* — which fulfil the tasks of *police administrative* and *judiciaire* — and the *Gendarmerie Mobile*, an anti-riot force.

The personnel of the *police judiciaire*

The *police judiciaire* has no independent personnel. These are drawn mostly from the *Gendarmerie* and the *Police Nationale*. The personnel of the *police judiciaire* can be divided into three categories (article 15 *C.P.P.*).

(a) *Officiers de police judiciaire* (police officers):
Under article 16 of the Code of Criminal Procedure, these are:

— mayors and their deputies: these may exercise their police powers only within the boundaries of their town or city and if there are no police stations;
— officers of the *Gendarmerie nationale* and *gendarmes* having served for four years;
— some members of the *Police Nationale* such as *inspecteurs généraux de police, contrôleurs généraux, commissaires de police* (equivalent to the English detective superintendents or the American police captain), and *inspecteurs de la police nationale* having tenure (equivalent to the British police inspectors or the American lieutenant), heads and deputy heads of the *police judiciaire* and heads and deputy heads of the *Gendarmerie*. [63]

(b) *Agents de police judiciaire*:
Besides the *officiers*, the *police judiciaire* include *agents de police judiciaire* (*APJ*) (articles 20 and 21 *C.P.P.*). Since Act

---

[63] *Commandants* and *officiers de paix* have also been granted the title of *officiers de police judiciaire* by the Act of July 28, 1978. Their territorial jurisdiction is limited to a *département*. They are personally appointed by the Ministry of Justice and the Home Office after the assent of a commission (art. 16(1)–3 *C.P.P.*). Their powers are limited to a certain category of offences (traffic offences, homicide or unintentional battery resulting from a road accident). They are forbidden from exercising powers in connection with *garde-à-vue* (custody) or *visites de véhicules* (vehicle searches) (art. L 23–1(2) of the *Code de la route* (traffic rules)).

78–788 of July 28, 1978, these are divided into two categories: *agents de police judiciaire* and *agents de police judiciaire adjoints*.

Under article 20 *C.P.P.*, *gendarmes* and *inspecteurs de police* who do not meet the requirements for being *officiers*, together with certain *chefs enquêteurs* (chief investigators), *enquêteurs de première et deuxième classe* (investigators grade I and II) belong to the first category. Act 87–1130 of December 31, 1987 also includes in this category a number of members of the *personnel en tenue* (staff in uniform).[64] With respect to the second category, that of *agents adjoints*, article 21 *C.P.P.* includes in it both civil servants of *police nationale* who are not *OPJ* nor *APJ* — including certain *inspecteurs de police* — and *enquêteurs de police* (in particular trainees), and members of the *police municipale* (municipal police).

(c) *Fonctionnaires et agents investis de pouvoirs de police judiciaire*:

The category of *agents de police* must not be confused with that of *fonctionnaires et agents investis de pouvoirs de police* (civil servants vested with police powers). The personnel of this latter category do not belong to the *police judiciaire* but have police powers conferred upon them by special statutes. These powers are restricted to their administrative tasks.[65] *Ingénieurs des eaux et forêts* (waterways and forestry officials), *garde champêtres* (rural policemen), *inspecteurs du travail* (factory inspectors), certain servants and members of public services (such as the railways, the mail service, the Paris public transport services, the tax administration, etc.) are some examples of the kind of personnel who are vested with such police powers. Under article 29 *C.P.P.*, *gardes particuliers assermentés* (special sworn officials) also belong to this category.[66] These are entitled to report breaches of rules governing fishing and hunting, and to order the payment of fines.

---

[64] These are the *commandants*, the *officiers de paix principaux*, the *officiers de paix titulaires*, *brigadiers-chefs* and *brigadiers de la police nationale* and certain *gardiens de la paix* who meet the conditions of qualifications and experience (art. 20(3) *C.P.P.*).

[65] Notably they may impose fines on offenders.

[66] These are the *garde-chasse* and *garde-pêche* (game keepers). They used to be regarded as members of the *police judiciaire*.

It is essential to understand the distinction made in French law between *officiers de police judiciaire* and *agents de police judiciaire*. The powers of the latter are much more limited than those of the former. *Agents* mainly operate in the field of *enquête préliminaire* (ordinary investigation)[67] and generally assist *officiers* in carrying out their tasks (articles 20(3) & 21(2) C.P.P.). Unlike *officiers*, they may not, in the case of a flagrant offence, carry out investigations under the instructions of an investigating judge. They cannot make an order to hold someone in custody (article 20(6) C.P.P.). However, they are entitled to record by means of *procès verbal* (policeman's report) all offences that have been committed, record statements (article 20(4) & (5) C.P.P.) and, under the instructions of *officiers*, carry out identity controls (article 78(2) C.P.P.). *Agents de police adjoints* have even less powers as their role is, by complying with their superiors' instructions, merely to record breaches of the law and collect information leading to the arrest of offenders (article 21(4) C.P.P.).

5. *MAGISTRATS* AND *JUGES*

In France, there are two categories of judges: those of the ordinary courts and those of the administrative courts.

The French use the word *magistrats*[68] or the collective noun *"la magistrature"* to designate those lawyers who are members of ordinary courts or the State Counsels' Office and the Prosecution Department.[69] With the exception of judges of the *Cour des comptes*, members of administrative courts are not referred to as *magistrats* but as *juges*.

---

[67] As opposed to an *enquête de flagrant délit*, *i.e.* an investigation following the commission of a flagrant offence. see Chapter Five, below.

[68] On judges in France, see G. Boyer Chammard, *Les magistrats* (Coll. Que-sais-je? PUF, Paris, 1985); Bodigel, *Qui sont les magistrats français? Esquisse d'une sociologie* in *La justice* (Revue Pouvoirs, PUF, Paris, 1981).

[69] The word *magistrat* may therefore not be translated by "magistrates" but by "judge". Note however that, if members of the State Counsels' Office or the Prosecution Department are *magistrats*, they are not *juges* as they do not deliver judgments. The term *juges* must be reserved for judges of the Bench.

Diagram 4.1 **The Main French Legal Professions (Recruitment and Training)**

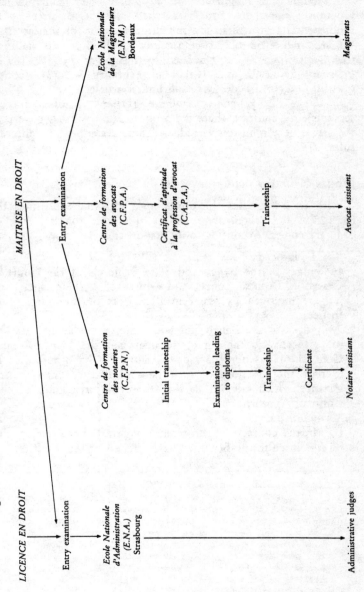

Although both *magistrats* and *juges* carry out similar judicial functions, they do not have the same legal status. The fundamental text which governs the profession of *magistrats* is the *ordonnance* 58–1270 of December 22, 1958 on the status of the *magistrature* — as amended by *lois organiques* 92–189 of February 25, 1992 and 94–101 of February 5, 1994. Consequently, *magistrats* do not fall under article 1 of the *Statut général de la fonction publique* (general status of civil servants). By contrast, there is no one single legal text governing the status of administrative judges. These are subject to different rules.

JUDGES OF ORDINARY COURTS

With its 84 articles the *ordonnance* of 1958 constitutes the charter of the *magistrature* and is applicable to all judges of ordinary courts. According to its first article:

"I. The judiciary consists of:
1. judges of the Bench and State Counsels of the Court of Cassation, Appeal courts and courts of first instance, and judges employed by the central services of the Ministry of Justice;
2. judges of the Bench and State counsels, who are attached to, respectively, the First President and the Principal State Counsel of a Court of Appeal, and who have authority to exercise the functions of their rank in all the courts of first instance which fall within the territorial jurisdiction of that Court of Appeal;
3. junior judges.
II. In the course of their career, *magistrats* have the right to be appointed to the Bench or to the State Counsels' Office." [70]

---

[70] "I. *Le corps judiciaire comprend:*
1. *les magistrats du siège et du parquet de la Cour de cassation, des cours d'appel et des tribunaux de première instance ainsi que les magistrats du cadre de l'administration centrale du ministère de la justice;*
2. *les magistrats du siège et du parquet placés respectivement auprès du premier président et du procureur général d'une cour d'appel et ayant qualité pour exercer les fonctions du grade auquel ils appartiennent dans l'ensemble des tribunaux de première instance du ressort de la cour d'appel à laquelle ils sont rattachés;*
3. *les auditeurs de justice;*
II. *Tout magistrat a vocation à être nommé, au cours de sa carrière, à des fonctions du siège et du parquet.*"

Whilst this lays down the principle of unity of the profession, this provision established a fundamental distinction between *magistrats du siège* and *magistrats du parquet*.[71]

Before examining their respective roles, the method of recruitment and training of *magistrats* will be analysed as well as their duties and privileges.

Recruitment and training

Probably, one of the main differences between the English and French judicial systems lies in the method of training and recruiting judges. Both judges of the Bench and prosecutors are usually recruited from among those who pass out successfully from the *Ecole Nationale de la Magistrature* (National Legal Service College)[72] in Bordeaux.

Entry to the College is by open competitive examination amongst French law graduates possessing a *maîtrise en droit*; candidates having five years experience in the civil service; or practitioners having a *licence en droit* such as *avocats*, *avoués*, *greffiers*, *officiers*, and assistant law lecturers (article 22 of the 1958 *ordonnance*).

Successful candidates are appointed *auditeurs de justice*. These belong to the *corps judiciaire*, *i.e.* the personnel of the judiciary, entry to which confers a salary. They follow a 31-month course combining taught courses[73] and traineeships. At the end of the training, the intending judge is appointed to an ordinary court in the provinces as a judge of the *premier groupe*, second grade.[74]

---

[71] In 1990, there were 6,796 judges: 169 in the *Cour de cassation*, 1,164 in the *cours d'appel* and 4,463 in the *tribunaux de grande instance* and *tribunaux d'instance*. 25 per cent of them belong to the *ministère public* (see *Annuaire statistique de la justice*, 1989–1990 (*la Documentation française*, Paris, 1992) p. 49).

[72] Translation suggested by M. Weston, *op. cit.* p. 109.

[73] Subjects taught include topics on the organisation of the courts, practice and procedure, legal ethics and penology.

[74] See article 2 of the *décret* 58–1277 of December 22, 1958 as amended by *décret* 86–463 of March 14, 1986. Apart from a special rank (*position hors hiérarchie*), the judges' career is divided into two *grades* (ranks), each of them being sub-divided into two groups:
— *Second grade, premier groupe* (lowest level):
  Judges of the *tribunal de grande instance*, investigating judges, *auditeurs* of the Court of Cassation.
— *Second grade, deuxième groupe*:
  President of a *tribunal de grande instance* having one single division, *premier juge*, *conseiller référendaire* in the Court of Cassation.
—continued on next page

Under article 26 of the 1958 *ordonnance*, judges of the Bench are appointed by *décret* of the President of the Republic following a proposal from the Minister of Justice. The powers of the President are limited however by those of the *Conseil supérieur de la magistrature* (Superior Council of Judges of the Bench and State Counsels), the *avis conforme* (assent) of which is required under article 65(5). The *Conseil* also makes proposals for the highest appointments: those of the Court of Cassation and the first Presidencies of the Courts of Appeal and *tribunaux de grande instance*.

Privileges and duties

In order to guarantee the impartial administration of justice, the independence of judges *vis-à-vis* the executive and legislative powers must be ensured. The independence of judges is guaranteed by two principles: irremovability and non-liability.

Judges are said to be irremovable, *i.e.* they cannot be moved, suspended from office, dismissed or prematurely pensioned off except under specific conditions laid down by law. The principle of irremovability is provided for by article 64 of the 1958 Constitution:

"The President of the Republic guarantees the independence of the judiciary. In this, he is assisted by the *Conseil supérieur de la magistrature*. An 'organic law' establishes the status of *magistrats*. Judges of the Bench are irremovable."[75]

This general provision is further clarified by article 4 of the 1958 *ordonnance*:

—continued from previous page
— *Premier grade, premier groupe*:
   President of a *tribunal de grande instance* with two divisions, *conseillers* in a Court of Appeal.
— *Premier grade, second groupe*:
   President of a Court of Appeal, *premier juge* in Paris.
— *Hors hiérarchie*:
   Conseiller in the Court of Cassation, First President of a Court of Appeal, President of a Division of the Court of Appeal of Paris.

[75] "*Le Président de la République est garant de l'indépendance de l'autorité judiciaire. Il est assisté par le Conseil supérieur de la magistrature.*
   Une loi organique porte statut des magistrats. Les magistrats du siège sont innamovibles."

"Consequently, judges of the Bench cannot be appointed to a new post without their consent, even if such an appointment is a promotion."[76]

The principle of irremovability cannot be affected by disciplinary rules.[77] When an action is brought by the Minister of Justice against a judge before the *Conseil supérieur de la magistrature*, the latter sits in the Court of Cassation under the chairmanship of the First President of the Court and not in the *Elysée Palace* under the chairmanship of the President of the Republic. The judge's right to a defence is guaranteed. The decision taken by the *Conseil* is binding upon the Minister of Justice who cannot reverse it. There are seven sanctions ranging from the *réprimande* (reprimand) which is reported in the file of the judge concerned, to the *révocation* (dismissal) with or without suspension of pension benefits.[78]

The principle of irremovability is an important guarantee. In fact, what used to be a customary practice was elevated to a rule of law during the French Revolution. This principle permits one to distinguish between judges and civil servants. Indeed, it forms a real and essential element of the independence of French judges from citizens and other judges, as well as from public authorities. This principle is intended to guarantee the impartiality of justice and not necessarily the efficient operation of the public legal service. As G. Boyer Chammard pointed out:

"Popular opinion doubts the independence of the judiciary. Such wide-spread scepticism is unjustified. In fact, in France, the judiciary is far more independent than one imagines."[79]

With respect to carrying out their functions, judges enjoy immunity from liability except in the case of abusive conduct. The Court of Cassation reiterated this principle in a decision of June 23, 1980. Judges are vested by the law with powers to judge the behaviour of those brought before them without any limitations except those dictated by their conscience. Indeed, the

---

[76] "*En conséquence, le magistrat du siège ne peut recevoir, sans son consentement, une affectation nouvelle même en avancement.*"

[77] Breaches of discipline are defined by article 43 of the *ordonnance* of 1958 as being: "Any deviation by a judge which undermines the duties, honour, estimation or dignity of his office" ("*Tout manquement par un magistrat aux devoirs de son état, à l'honneur, à la délicatesse ou à la dignité*").

[78] These sanctions are set out in article 45 of the 1958 *ordonnance*.

[79] "*L'opinion doute de l'indépendance des juges. Ce scepticisme généralisé est injustifié. En fait, en France, les magistrats sont beaucoup plus indépendants qu'on ne le pense*"; G. Boyer Charmand, *op. cit.* p. 49.

independence of judges could be undermined if they were subject to actions for damages by dissatisfied litigants. The fact that judicial decisions are taken collectively makes them anonymous. Therefore it is impossible for a litigant to find out which judge has not fulfilled his duties. Besides, appeals are more efficient than any action for damages based on article 1382 of the Civil Code.[80]

Nevertheless, the question of liability of judges may be raised in connection with the malfunctioning of the public legal service as a result of practices which, without being subject to disciplinary rules, may distort the normal course of justice. In the case of serious error it may be necessary for a litigant to challenge a judge or a court and claim damages.

The ancient *Code de procédure civile* of 1806 (Code of Civil Procedure) provided for an action against judges called the *prise à partie*.[81] This action was implicitly abolished[82] by the *loi organique* of January 18, 1979 which incorporated into the *ordonnance* of 1958 a new article 11–1. This article provides that:

> "Judges may be liable for their wrongful acts while acting in their judicial capacity. Such offences may be brought to the attention of the court only by means of an *action récursoire* of the State. Such an action is only brought before the Civil Division of the Court of Cassation."[83]

Therefore, individuals cannot sue judges directly but must bring an action against the State through the ordinary court proceedings with a view to showing that the public legal service is malfunctioning due to a wrongful act of a judge.

---

[80] Article 1382 provides: "Every individual who causes another person harm as a result of conduct for which he is to blame must compensate the victim" ("*Tout fait quelconque de l'homme, qui cause à autrui un dommage, oblige celui par la faute duquel il est arrivé, à le réparer*").

[81] This action could be brought against a judge or a court only in the cases of *déni de justice* (miscarriage of justice), *dol* (deceit), *concussion* (extortion) or *faute lourde* (serious error). The damage caused to the litigant could be remedied by an award of damages, or by the annulment of the decision of the judge or the court concerned. The *prise à partie* is different from other appeals since it is used more against judges than judgments.

[82] But it is still applicable to lay judges, such as members of the *tribunaux de commerce* and the *conseils des prud'hommes*.

[83] "*La responsabilité des magistrats qui ont commis une faute personnelle se rattachant au service public de la justice ne peut être engagée que sur l'action récursoire de l'Etat. Cette action récursoire est exercée devant la chambre civile de la Cour de cassation.*"

This reform was extremely important as the State could be held liable more easily for the malfunctioning of the public legal service. However, the rules governing the liability of judges have been modelled on those governing the liability of civil servants. Thus, this reform, although it is technically sound, has placed judges in the same position as ordinary civil servants.

Apart from these two principles which guarantee the independence of judges and the impartiality of justice, a number of legislative acts protect judges from actions which might undermine their dignity[84] or the authority of the judiciary.[85]

As judges enjoy great respect and authority, it is necessary to impose on them professional duties. Apart from being subject to the obligation of adjudicating a case,[86] of keeping the proceedings secret, of residing where the court has its seat, and of not leaving the area without authorisation, judges are also subject to certain prohibitions, incompatibilities or incapacities.

Judges are prohibited from exercising certain activities due to the disruptive effect these may have on the sound operation of the public legal service. These activities are listed in article 10 of the *ordonnance* of 1958 and concern political activities and the right to strike. As regards politics, judges have an *obligation de réserve* (duty of confidence). The law strictly forbids them from undertaking activities which are incompatible with the nature of their functions.[87] However, judges are not citizens with fewer rights than others: for instance, it would not be realistic to prohibit judges from having the right to join a trade union.

---

[84] See articles 222, 223, 224 and 228 of the *Code pénal* (Code of Criminal Law) concerning violence and contempt of court.

[85] See articles 226 and 227 *C.P.* concerning actions undermining the credit of judicial decisions and comments intended to exercise pressure.

[86] See article 4 *C.Civ.*: "The judge who refuses to adjudicate a case on the grounds that the existing law is silent, unclear, or insufficient can be held guilty of a miscarriage of justice" ("*Le juge qui refusera de juger, sous prétexte du silence, de l'obscurité ou de l'insuffisance de la loi, pourra être poursuivi comme coupable de déni de justice*").

[87] Article 10 of the 1958 *ordonnance* provides that: "The judiciary is forbidden to participate in political debates. Similarly judges are prohibited from expressing opposition to the principles or form of government of the Republic and from taking part in all political demonstrations which are incompatible with their office" ("*Toute délibération politique est interdite au corps judiciaire. Toute manifestation d'hostilité au principe ou à la forme du gouvernement de la République est interdite aux magistrats de même que toute démonstration de nature politique incompatible avec la réserve que leur impose leur fonctions*").

Judges have a right of expression but they must use it with caution and moderation in order not to obstruct or hinder the operation of the public legal service.

As regards the right to strike, article 10(3) of the 1958 *ordonnance* provides that judges are prohibited from undertaking "any concerted action which is directed at preventing or hindering the operation of the courts."[88]

Other activities are not prohibited but their exercise is restricted because of their incompatibility with the performance of judicial functions. If a judge has no choice but to exercise such activities he must immediately cease his judicial functions, at least temporarily, and request a *détachement* (secondment) or a *mise en disponibilité* (leave of absence on half-pay). The functions of a judge are incompatible with those of any other public service and any other salaried or professional activities. For instance, a judge cannot be a *commissaire de la République*,[89] an *avocat* or a trader. However, he may be appointed as an expert, or undertake works of an artistic, literary or scientific nature. He may also teach, after receiving authorisation from his superiors.

The function of judge is also said to be incompatible with political functions (for example M.P.s, county and town councillors, etc.). This incompatibility also applies to the spouse of a judge: a judge whose wife or husband is elected M.P. is temporarily relieved from duty.

In order to avoid challenges concerning the impartiality of a judgment, the law has provided that judges may not adjudicate in certain circumstances. These are called *incapacités* (incapacities). Some of these incapacities are applicable *ipso jure*: for instance, a judge cannot adjudicate a case if the lawyer of one of the parties is a relative of his. Apart from these situations, it may happen that one of the litigants has some reason for suspecting the impartiality and the independence of a judge. In such a case, if the judge is aware of this suspicion, he has the

---

[88] "*Toute action concertée de nature à arrêter ou à entraver le fonctionnement des juridictions.*"

[89] The function of *commissaire de la République* was created in 1982 by the Decentralisation Act. The *commissaire de la République* replaced the *préfets* (prefects) and is the official of the central authorities (Prime Minister and ministers) in the *département*. He administers the services of the State in the *département* and is in charge of supervising the administration of local government.

duty to withdraw: the judge *s'abstient* (he refrains from adjudicating a case) or *se déporte* (he withdraws). If the judge does not withdraw, the litigant can use the *récusation* (challenge of the judge's authority) by which he will request the judge not to adjudicate the case. As a civil action, this is examined by the court itself; as a criminal matter, it is examined by the First President of the court. If the action is successful the judge concerned is replaced; if it is not, the litigant is fined. Because a judge whose authority is questioned would withdraw automatically, an action *récursoire* is often employed. A litigant may also request that the case be transferred to another court: this is called *renvoi d'un tribunal à un autre*. This claim can be used in two situations:

— where the litigant suspects the whole court: this is then a *renvoi pour cause de suspicion légitime* (transfer for reasons of legitimate suspicion); or,
— where the administration of justice might be disturbed by public unrest, demonstrations or riots: this is *renvoi pour cause de sûreté publique* (transfer for reasons of public order).

Magistrats du siège

Magistrats du siège have the authority and the task of passing judgments after having examined the case and/or heard the parties' and their lawyers' opinions. They perform their functions whilst being seated. This explains why they are called *magistrats du siège*[90] or *magistrature assise*. *Magistrats du siège* may, at the same time or successively, carry out any of the following diverse functions, each of which requires particular and different qualities.

(a)   The *juge du siège* in civil matters:

Usually, the *magistrature assise* hearing civil matters consists of three judges (one of them acting as President) and one *greffier* (in exceptional cases, as indicated in Chapter Three, the court may consist of a single judge). They hear cases concerning *droit des personnes* (family law, obligations) and *droit des biens* (property law and succession). Therefore, they adjudicate on

---

[90] In French, *siège* means a seat.

cases relating to divorce and judicial separation, execution of contracts, torts, succession, etc.

(b) The *juge des référés*:

Articles 808 to 811 of the *nouveau Code de procedure civile* (New Code of Civil Procedure) provide that the President of the *tribunal de grande instance* is in principle *juge des référés* who orders urgent and provisional measures in chambers (see Chapter Three, above). The role of this judge has increased considerably during the past twenty years. The *tribunal de grande instance* of Paris makes judgments by means of this procedure in around 3,000 cases per month and renders around 30,000 orders per year.[91]

(c) The *juge du siège* in criminal matters:

These deal with criminal matters, in particular with *délits correctionnels* (major offences). During the proceedings before a *tribunal correctionnel* judges may deal with a number of situations: for example an accused who is on bail or in custody, an accused committed for trial, breach of confidence, fraud, slander and libel, indecent offences, etc.

(d) Other functions of a *juge du siège*:

Juges du siège can also be appointed to a *tribunal d'instance*. As such, they try minor cases in civil as well as criminal matters. *Juges d'instance* supervise the administration of the property of minors under tutelage and guarantee the protection of adults who are mentally incapable. In a *tribunal de grande instance*, judges may be appointed as *juges des affaires familiales* (*JAF*) (judges for family matters)[92] or as *juges d'instruction* (investigating judge) for at least three years. They may also be *juges de l'application des peines* (*JAP*) (judges in charge of the execution of sentences) whose role is to determine the mode of enforcing penalties. The latter may grant or refuse a *réduction des peines* (reduction of sentences), a *libération conditionnelle* (release on probation), or *semi-liberté* (semi-imprisonment), or *permission*

---

[91] The procedure of *référé* was established by the *Edit de Louis XIV* of January 1685 and was intended to provide swift, economical and permanent justice. Limited first to the region of Paris, it was extended throughout France by the *Code de procédure civile* of 1806. Nowadays, any matter can be the object of this procedure. (See Chapter Five, below.)

[92] Family law constitutes more than 57 per cent of the litigation in a *tribunal de grande instance*; this is due in particular to the increase in divorce cases.

de sortir (authorisation for temporary leave). They also supervise the application of *mesures de sursis avec mise à l'épreuve* or *sursis probatoire* (suspended sentence supervision order).

Within the territorial jurisdiction of each *tribunal de grande instance* there is also a *tribunal des enfants* (Youth Court) and a *juge des enfants* (judge specialising in young offenders). Finally, the *juge foncier* or *juge de l'expropriation* (judge dealing with expropriation cases) is responsible for awarding damages to individuals whose property has been subjected to an expropriation order.

Magistrats du parquet

Courts do not only consist of *magistrats du siège* in charge of settling disputes, but also of officials of the State called *magistrats du parquet*.[93] The formal name for *parquet* is *ministère public*.[94] It is very difficult to find an equivalent in English law.[95] The *ministère public* is not only responsible for the conduct of all criminal proceedings as regards serious offences, but also plays an important role in civil proceedings by representing the interests of society. With respect to criminal proceedings, the nearest equivalent institution in English law was the office of the Director of Public Prosecutions (although the great majority of prosecutions were conducted by the police), and since 1986, the Crown Prosecution Service headed by the Director of Public Prosecutions which has taken over the conduct of most criminal offences.

---

[93] This expression comes from the fact that the prosecutor used to stand in the *parquet* (well) of the court opposite the Bench which was sitting on a platform. As they were standing up, they were called *magistrature debout*. Nowadays, they stand on the same platform as the judges of the Bench but their desk is separate and distinct from that of the Bench.

[94] This most distinctive legal institution has its roots in the *droit ancien*. The King used to entrust lawyers with the task of dealing with his affairs. Since the affairs of the King were confused with those of the State these royal agents were exercising a *ministère public*, *i.e.* a task of general interest. This expression remained.

[95] The term *ministère public* is also difficult to translate. Indeed, it cannot be rendered as "public ministry" which is meaningless in English nor by "Crown Office" which is inappropriate for a Republic. M. Weston suggests therefore the term "State Counsel's Office" (M. Weston *op. cit.* p. 113 *et seq.*). However, as he also indicates, the more common translations, *i.e.* "Public Prosecution Department" for *"parquet"* "Public Prosecutor" for *"procureur de la République"* and "Principal Public Prosecutor" for *"procureur général"* may be used when applied to criminal proceedings.

Unlike *magistrats du siège, magistrats du parquet* are:

" ... under the leadership and the supervision of their superiors
in rank and under the authority of the Keeper of the Seals, the
Minister of Justice." [96]

The *ministère public* is decentralised and organised according
to a national hierarchy. This is a fundamental feature of the
organisation of this institution. As a result each member of the
parquet is answerable to the Government. The Minister of
Justice has direct authority over the *procureurs généraux*
(Principal State Counsels) [97] who are attached to the Court of
Cassation [98] and to the Courts of Appeal (article 36 *C.P.P.*). Those
of the latter preside over the members of the *parquet* of their
Court of Appeal and have, under article 37 *C.P.P.*, authority over
the *procureur de la République* (State Counsel or Public
Prosecutor) who heads the *parquet* in a *tribunal de grande
instance*. [99]

Each member of the *parquet* must keep their immediate
superior informed by reporting to him on the state of current
cases being dealt with in their respective areas (article 35(2)
C.P.P.) and carry out his instructions. This principle of
accountability is nevertheless mitigated by two fundamental
rules. First, members of the *parquet* are answerable to their
superiors only in so far as their written submissions addressed to
the court are concerned. They are free to put the contrary case
orally according to their own convictions. This follows from the
maxim: "*La plume est serve mais la parole est libre.*" [1] Secondly,
each head of the *parquet* is vested with independent powers
(article 41 *C.P.P.*). For instance, the head of the *parquet* may
undertake a prosecution in criminal proceedings without instructions or even contrary to the instructions given to him. Such
disobedience may be subject to disciplinary sanctions only.

---

[96] "*... placés sous la direction et le controle de leurs chefs hiérarchiques et sous
l'autorité du Garde des Sceaux, ministre de la justice.*"(art. 5 of the 1958
ordonnance).

[97] See M. Weston who explains why *procureur général* cannot be rendered in
English as Attorney-General or as Director of Public Prosecutions, *op. cit.*
p. 114.

[98] It has to be noted that the *procureur général* of the Court of Cassation no
longer has authority over the members of the *parquet*.

[99] According to article 44 *C.P.P.*, the *procureur de la République* also presides
over the *ministère public* of a Police Court.

[1] "The quill is in serfdom but the word is free." See also article 5, second
sentence of the 1958 *ordonnance*.

Moreover the Minister of Justice cannot act as a substitute for the head of the *parquet* when the latter does not follow his instructions.

If the *ministère public* is answerable to the Government, it is independent of judges of the Bench according to the principle of separation of judicial functions (see Chapter Five, below). It submits opinions to the court with complete freedom.

As indicated above, the general rules governing the *magistrature*, notably those relating to recruitment, career, duties and liability, also apply to members of the *ministère public*. *Magistrats du parquet* belong to the *corps judiciaire*. These are appointed by a *décret* of the President of the Republic following a proposal from the Minister of Justice (article 26 of the 1958 *ordonnance*) and after the *Conseil supérieur de la magistrature* has been consulted in compliance with article 65(7) of the Constitution. The only exception is those appointments made by *décret en conseil des ministres* (*décret* adopted in Cabinet after deliberation). Members of *the ministère public* who are *hors-hiérarchie* (above and beyond the hierarchy),[2] such as the *procureurs généraux* attached to the Court of Cassation and to the Court of Appeal of Paris, are appointed by *décret* of the President of the Republic after consultation with the *Conseil supérieur de la magistrature*, unless they are appointed by *décret en conseil des ministres*.

Unlike their colleagues from the Bench, *magistrats du parquet* do not enjoy irremovability. However, because this could lead to arbitrary decisions of the Minister of Justice, who could dismiss any member of the *parquet* without justification, the 1958 *ordonnance* — as amended by the *loi organique* 94–101 of

---

[2] The hierarchy is organised as follows:
1. *Second grade, premier groupe*:
substitut du procureur de la République.
2. *Second grade, second groupe*:
Procureur de la République in a *tribunal de grande instance* with one division, *premier substitut*.
3. *Premier grade, premier groupe*:
Procureur de la République in a *tribunal de grande instance* with two divisions, *substitut général* in a Court of Appeal.
4. *Premier grade, second groupe*:
Procureur in a *tribunal de grande instance hors-classe*, *avocat général* of a Court of Appeal.
5. *Hors-hiérarchie*:
Procureur général in the Court of Cassation, *procureurs généraux* in a Court of Appeal.

February 5, 1994 — provides that the *Conseil supérieur de la magistrature* is to be consulted prior to any sanctions being imposed.[3] The *Conseil* only has advisory powers and its decisions are not binding on the Minister of Justice. Nevertheless, if the Minister of Justice wants to impose a more serious sanction than that suggested by the *Conseil*, he must request a new opinion (article 66 of the *ordonnance*).

The *ministère public* has a number of diverse functions which are both judicial and non-judicial and are allocated to its members according to their rank. Since the judicial functions are the most important, the latter will simply be mentioned. These are functions such as supervising and instructing the *officiers de police judiciaire*, controlling the register of birth, marriages and deaths, examining claims for legal aid, granting waiver of the age limit for marriages, etc.

Judicial functions are those related to proceedings before the court and include certain functions of an administrative nature. While the role of the *ministère public* is important in civil proceedings, it is essential in criminal proceedings.

The *ministère public* may intervene either as a *partie principale* (original party) or *partie jointe* (joined party). When it is *partie principale* it intervenes by means of *voie d'action*, *i.e.* it brings an action as plaintiff, or acts as a defendant, on behalf of society. When it is a *partie jointe* it intervenes by means of *voie de réquisition* (address to the court), *i.e.* it intervenes only for the purpose of addressing an opinion to the court concerning the applicable law without being plaintiff or defendant. As a *partie principale* the *ministère public* is free to bring any claim. As a *partie jointe* it cannot contradict the opinions of the *parties* and can only put forward new arguments, addressing the court after the lawyers have closed their case. The *ministère public* may lodge an appeal against a decision of the court only if it acts as *partie principale*.

In civil proceedings, the *ministère public* usually acts as a *partie jointe*. It only has the obligation to submit opinions in a limited number of cases namely:

— at the request of the court, which wishes to have more information on a complex case or;

---

[3] On the composition of the *Conseil supérieur de la magistrature* acting as a disciplinary court, see Chapter Three, above.

— when the law requires it for certain subject matters (for example filiation, tutelage or guardianship, liquidation of an insolvent debtor's property, etc.) or;

— before the Court of Cassation on any case.

In these situations, the case is said to be *communicable* (referable) to the *ministère public*.

In exceptional circumstances, the *ministère public* may act as *partie principale*. This is necessary when it represents the State or a local government authority (for example in the case of a refusal to recognise the jurisdiction of a court). In other cases, mentioned by the law, the *ministère public* may intervene if it wishes to do so (for example nullity of marriages, parental authority, nullity of patents, etc.). Apart from these cases, the *ministère public* may, under article 423 *N.C.P.C.*, generally intervene to protect public policy.

In criminal proceedings, the *ministère public* usually acts as *partie principale*. It is responsible for the conduct of criminal proceedings as regards serious offences. It brings the prosecution as it represents the interests of society against the offender. It acts therefore as a *plaideur*. When such an action is initiated the *ministère public* plays a role at each stage of the proceedings (see Chapter Five, below).

JUDGES OF ADMINISTRATIVE COURTS

Administrative judges do not have the same legal status as judges of ordinary courts. As mentioned above, because administrative judges do not belong to a single judicial body, they are covered by no single general legislation but by specific provisions which concern each administrative court separately. However, where specific legislation does not apply, administrative judges are automatically covered by the Act 83–634 of July 13, 1983 on the rights and duties of civil servants.

Only recruitment and status which are common to the different categories of administrative judges will be examined here.

Recruitment

There is no special judicial training similar to that provided by the *Ecole Nationale de la Magistrature*. There is a dual method of recruitment: ordinary and external recruitment.

(a) Ordinary recruitment

Administrative judges are recruited from the *Ecole Nationale de l'Administration* (National Civil Service College).[4] Selection for admission to the College is normally by means of two competitive examinations — the *concours externe*, which is open to graduates and the *concours interne* which is open to certain civil servants. Students of this College are trained to be civil servants in general and not administrative judges in particular. Moreover, the choice of an administrative function is linked to the final mark obtained by the student at the end of the period of training. The best students generally choose the most prestigious administrative functions in the *Conseil d'Etat* and the *Cour des comptes*. The other students are appointed to the *tribunaux administratifs*, the *cours administratives d'appel* or the *chambres régionales des comptes*. As the first two courts attract most of the students, provision has been made for the lowest ranked positions — those of *auditeurs* — to be exclusively allocated to students from the *ENA*. This is not the case with the other courts, where additional recruitment has been externally organised for the same category of posts.

(b) External recruitment

In the *Conseil d'Etat*, *maître des requêtes* (junior members) are mainly recruited from amongst the *auditeurs de première classe* (Legal assistants Grade I).[5] Twenty-five per cent of the former are recruited from civil servants who are over 30 with 10 years experience in the civil service. Two-thirds of the *conseillers d'Etat*[6] have previously been *maîtres des requêtes*. The others are recruited externally and discretionally by the Government which may appoint anyone over 45.[7]

---

[4] See M. Weston, *op. cit.* p. 110.

[5] On the composition of the *Conseil d'Etat*, see Chapter Three, above.

[6] There are two categories of *conseillers d'Etat*: the permanent ones, *i.e.* the *conseillers en service ordinaire* and those on secondment, *i.e.* the *conseillers en service extraordinaire* who are appointed by the Government, for periods of four years from civil servants, distinguished lawyers, etc., and who participate only in the advisory functions of the *Conseil*.

[7] However, in order to avoid political favouritism, article 2 of the Act 94–530 of June 28, 1994 provides that these appointments may be made after consulting the Vice-President of the *Conseil d'Etat* only. Some of these posts of *conseillers d'Etat* are reserved for members of the *tribunaux administratifs* (according to the first article of the *décret* of November 29, 1985). This was extended to members of the *cours administratives d'appel* by the Act of December 31, 1987 which created these courts.

In the *Cour des comptes*, the method of recruitment is very similar to that discussed above. Three-quarters of the *conseillers référendaires* (senior members) have previously been *auditeurs* (junior members) while the rest of them are externally recruited by the Government from people over the age of 36 with 10 years experience in the civil service or in a service controlled by the *Cour des comptes*. Two-thirds of the *conseillers-maîtres* (senior members) are selected from the *conseillers référendaires*, while one-third are over 40 and have 15 years previous experience in the civil service.

In a *tribunal administratif*, one *conseiller de deuxième classe* (junior member Grade II) in three is admitted after an external examination open to civil servants with 10 years experience, judges of ordinary courts and candidates who have passed the written part of the *aggrégation de droit public*.[8] This ratio is one in seven as regards the *conseillers de première classe*.

Finally as regards the *cours administratives d'appel*, article 6 of the Act of December 31, 1987 provides that national civil servants of category A (the highest category), local civil servants of the same category, *avocats* and *avocats aux Conseils* with 10 years' experience are eligible for the functions of *conseillers de première classe* or of *conseillers hors classe*. Only a third of the members of the *cours administratives d'appel* can be recruited externally. Therefore, the law favours heterogeneity rather than corporatism. Higher civil servants have to work and co-operate with academics, lawyers and judges. However this method of recruitment is meant to be temporary only and is intended to supply these newly created courts with the first cohort of staff members. The recruitment procedure also guarantees a high quality staff.

Status

There is no general provision which states clearly whether administrative judges are *magistrats* or not. The *ordonnance* of 1958 applies only to members of ordinary courts. The *Conseil d'Etat* has ruled that the term *magistrat* as mentioned in articles 34 and 64 of the 1958 Constitution applies only to judges of

---

[8] This is a national competitive examination held every two years for professorships in public law. Similar examinations exist in private law and legal history.

ordinary courts,[9] whilst the *Cour de Cassation* has considered that this same term, as mentioned in the Act of June 26, 1941 (which has been repealed) on the profession of *avocats*, could apply to *conseillers* of *tribunaux administratifs*.[10] There is no doubt however that article 64 of the Constitution, which guarantees the independence and irremovability of judges of the Bench, excludes administrative judges from its scope of application. Furthermore, apart from article 2 of Act 67–483 of June 22, 1967 on the *Cour des comptes*, no one provision applying to the different administrative courts, expressly lays down the principle of irremovability of their members. This does not necessarily mean that these are not independent. Although members of the *Conseil d'Etat* do not enjoy this guarantee because they are *conseillers*, *i.e.* advisers of the Government, in practice they are irremovable. The principle of irremovability has been extended to the *conseillers* of the *chambres régionales des comptes* (Regional Courts of Auditors) by article 11 of the Act of January 11, 1984, to members of the *tribunaux administratifs* as a result of the Act 86–14 of January 6, 1986,[11] and *counseillers* of the *cours administratives d'appel* by the Act 87–1127 of December 31, 1987.

As far as their professional duties are concerned, there is no general legislation describing these but only a few specific provisions concerning the members of each court separately. For example, *décret* 63–767 of July 30, 1963 imposes on the members of the *Conseil d'Etat* an *obligation de réserve* (duty of confidence). Similarly, according to article 23 of the *décret* of May 5, 1987, judges of the *chambres régionales des comptes* are subject to the obligation of keeping their deliberations secret. Article 12 of the Act of January 6, 1986 provides that members of *tribunaux administratifs* and *cours administratives d'appel* must reside within the area of their respective court. Article 5 of

---

[9] See (CE Ass.), February 2, 1962, *Bausse*: [1962] A.J.D.A. 189.

[10] See (Cass. Civ.), April 25, 1958: [1958] D. 430.

[11] The first article provides that: "When they carry out a judicial activity, in an administrative court, (members of administrative courts) cannot be appointed to a new post without their consent, even if such appointment is a promotion" ("*Lorsqu'ils exercent leurs fonctions de magistrats dans une juridiction administrative, (les membres du corps des tribunaux administratifs) ne peuvent recevoir, sans leur consentement, une affectation nouvelle même en avancement*").

See the similar wording of article 4 of the *ordonnance* of 1958, footnote 76, above. Note however that the term "irremovability" does not expressly appear.

this Act also provides that no one can be appointed a member of a *tribunal administratif* if they have been elected or have been a national or local civil servant during the previous three years in the same area as that of the court concerned. When these special provisions do not apply, the principle is that administrative judges are subject to the general status of civil servants provided this is compatible with their judicial functions.[12]

Although the general administrative courts are subordinate to the *Ministère de l'Intérieur* (Home Office) and not to the Ministry of Justice, there is no reason why administrative judges should be regarded as civil servants and not as *magistrats*.[13] One should not adopt a too narrow definition of the term *"magistrat"*. In a series of decisions, the *Conseil Constitutionnel* clearly established the principle of independence of the members of the administrative courts and that of a separate administrative justice system.[14] Furthermore, the reform of the administrative courts system of 1987 has confirmed the principle of independence of judges of *tribunaux administratifs* and *cours administrative d'appel* whilst maintaining them within the general status of civil servants. Finally, under the Act 82–595 of July 10, 1982, members of *chambres régionales des comptes* are, like those of the *Cour des comptes*, said to be *magistrats*. The Act of 1987 even provides that members of *tribunaux administratifs* and *cours administratives d'appel* may be sent on secondment to a regional court of auditors. This would not be conceivable if they did not have similar status. The mode of recruitment of members of administrative courts certainly assimilate them to civil servants but, even if they are not *magistrats* within the meaning of the Constitution and the 1958 *ordonnance*, there is no doubt that they carry out the functions of *magistrats* in an administrative court.

---

[12] For instance, the duty of obedience cannot apply since they are, as judges, independent of the Government.

[13] However, during the Senate debates on the Act of December 31, 1987, the Home Secretary at that time refused to regard administrative judges as magistrats. *"Il n'est pas concevable de parler de l'ordre administratif, les membres des tribunaux administratifs n'étant pas des magistrats mais des fonctionnaires."* (*Sénat Débats*, session of November 10, 1987: [1987] JORF 3801).

[14] See decision 80–119 of July 22, 1980; and also decisions of January 23, 1987 and July 28, 1989. See the introduction to Chapter Three, above.

Chapter Five
Judicial proceedings

1. GENERAL CHARACTERISTICS

It is commonly accepted that one of the major differences between Common law systems and Civil law systems lies in the opposition between accusatorial and inquisitorial procedures, the latter being the main feature of French procedural law.

In inquisitorial procedures, judges are given a greater role as it is believed that it will be easier for them to arrive at the truth. They have, therefore, the power to conduct investigations, to discover evidence and to conduct the proceedings. The parties do not control the action (principle of *indisponibilité du procès*). This procedure is secret, written and is not *contradictoire* (adversarial).

However, this distinction is not as clear-cut as it first appears. Indeed, a close examination of French procedures shows that they contain elements of the accusatorial system.

The administrative procedure is mainly inquisitorial since it involves the administration, against which the citizen is regarded as being weak and unprotected. It therefore depends on the judge to re-establish the balance between the two parties and to conduct the proceedings. He also has extensive powers to order disclosure of evidence. However, the plaintiff, who is free to institute proceedings, may stop them at any time. Besides, the procedure is truly *contradictoire* as the parties have the right to be heard and to present their defence.

The criminal procedure, on the other hand, is hybrid. Its pre-trial stage is clearly inquisitorial: initiated by the prosecution, the proceedings are conducted by the investigating judge who has full powers to order the disclosure of evidence. The procedure is written and, to a large extent, secretive. However, the rights of the defence have been strengthened in recent years. The trial stage is more accusatorial and is oral, public and *contradictoire*.[1]

By contrast, the civil procedure is traditionally accusatorial and based on the classical, individual and liberal conception of an action as a private affair between two parties brought before a judge. It follows that the parties initiate and control the proceedings, and may determine the form of the action, its object and cause. However, the civil action has been given an inquisitorial dimension particularly with the creation of the *juge de la mise en état* (preparatory judge) in 1965. As a result, the French system appears to be a mixed system where the parties and the judge share the directing role and where the procedure remains *contradictoire*, oral and public.

2. GENERAL PRINCIPLES

THE *PRINCIPE DU CONTRADICTOIRE*

Enshrined in all western systems of law, this principle is a basic principle embodied in the maxim *audiatur et altera pars*. In French law it is of particular importance since it is laid down in articles 14–17 of the *nouveau Code de procédure civile* (*N.C.P.C.*) and is regarded as a general principle of law.[2]

It follows that a judgment cannot be delivered by a court before a fair opportunity has been given to both parties to be heard (article 14 *N.C.P.C.*) and each party has had the right to examine and discuss the claim, arguments, considerations and evidence put forward by the other party (article 15 *N.C.P.C.*).

This principle not only applies to the parties but also to the judge who:

> "must in all situations ensure that the principle that both sides must be heard is observed and must himself observe it" (article 16(1) *N.C.P.C.*).[3]

---

[1] Act No. 93–2 of January 4, 1993 on the reform of the Code of Criminal Procedure (January 5, 1993: [1993] *JORF* 215) extended this accusatorial dimension of the trial stage (see arts. 83 to 101 and, in particular, arts. 86 & 88). This innovation was short-lived however as it never came into force following the repeal of the above mentioned provisions by article 28 of Act 93–1013 of August 24, 1993.

[2] See (C.E.), October 12, 1979, *Rassemblement des nouveaux avocats de France*: [1979] Rec. Lebon 370.

[3] "*Le juge doit, en toutes circonstances, faire observer et observer lui-même le principe de la contradiction.*"

The judge may not base his decision on legal considerations observed *ex officio* without previously having invited the parties to submit their views thereon (article 16(3) *N.C.P.C.*).

This principle is observed in all procedures in civil, criminal, administrative and disciplinary courts.

The Formal Aspects of Procedure

Procedure is always characterised by formality which is meant to guarantee justice and protect the rights of the defence against arbitrary decisions of the judge.

However, the formalities are not as rigorous as they used to be. In civil procedure, as a result of reform, formal irregularities no longer lead to the invalidity of an act unless annulment is expressly provided for by legislation ("no nullity without a text"),[4] or an essential or mandatory formality (*formalité d'ordre public*) has been omitted (article 114 *N.C.P.C.*). Moreover, the annulment of an act depends on proof of the existence of a prejudice, even in the case of an essential or mandatory formality, according to the principle *"pas de nullité sans grief"* ("no nullity without prejudice") (article 114(2) *N.C.P.C.*). French law also allows the subsequent regularisation of an annulled act if no time-limit has expired in the interim and provided that the regularisation remedies any prejudice caused (article 115 *N.C.P.C.*). Finally, French civil procedure is influenced by international legislation such as the European Convention on Human Rights (in particular, article 6(1)), the 1968 Convention of Brussels and the 1988 Convention of Lugano on Jurisdiction and the Enforcement of Judgments in Civil and Commercial Matters, and the 1965 Hague Convention on Notification Abroad of Judicial and Extrajudicial Acts in Civil and Commercial Matters, etc.[5]

In criminal procedure the rule "no nullity without prejudice" applies, whereas in administrative procedure irregular acts regarding minor formal requirements may be subsequently regularised.

The principle of public hearings, which is considered to have resulted from the French Revolution and is now confirmed by several international conventions, is a general principle of French

---

[4] *"Pas de nullité sans texte."*
[5] On the incorporation of international law into French law, see above, Chapter Two.

law (articles 22 *N.C.P.C.*; 306, 400 & 601 *C.P.P.*; R 195 *C.T.A.*
and article 66, *ordonnance* of July 3, 1945). However, this
principle is not absolute and some hearings may be held *en
chambre du conseil* (in camera) (articles 433–436 *N.C.P.C.*), in
particular for reasons of public security or morality (article 435
N.C.P.C.). Failure to observe the principle of public hearings
carries no sanction and can be remedied at once by the judge
(article 437 *N.C.P.C.*) unless the principle is invoked before the
conclusion of the trial (article 446(2) *N.C.P.C.*) in which case the
proceedings are declared invalid.

Finally, it should be appreciated that both civil and criminal
procedures are written and oral whilst administrative procedure
is mainly written.

3.   PRINCIPLES ON LEGAL AID

The Act of January 3, 1972 on legal aid laid down the
principle of a right of access to justice by creating a
comprehensive legal aid scheme for the poorest and partial legal
aid for those with insufficient income. It was for the State to bear
the cost of legal aid and to determine conditions for eligibility.[6]

However, this system of aid has been subject to a number of
criticisms from beneficiaries, lawyers and the State institutions
themselves. Following a report of a working group of the *Conseil
d'Etat*, presided over by Paul Bouchet, the reform of the 1972
legal aid system was completed by the Act of July 10, 1991
which came into force on January 1, 1992.

This reform was based on two main principles: the extension
of the scope of application of legal aid, and the creation of
politico-administrative structures.

Legal aid has been extended by enlarging the group of eligible
beneficiaries of *aide juridictionnelle* (access to courts) —
replacing the former *aide judiciaire* — and by introducing the
concept of *accès au droit* (access to legal information), *i.e.* aid
for legal consultation and assistance in procedures operating
outside the courts.

Aide juridictionnelle is made available in all civil, criminal and
administrative litigation, to plaintiffs as well as defendants, who
cannot afford to pay for the cost of the proceedings. The income

---

[6] In 1990, 341,500 cases benefited from legal aid and the State spent 384 million
FF.

limit is reassessed every year in the Government budget. Furthermore, the Act declared the objective of the State to increase its financial contribution to legal aid, raising it from 414 million FF to 1.5 billion FF. Finally, the Act provided for a decentralised system for the remuneration of lawyers, which is now the responsibility of the Bar associations.

The second innovation, *accès au droit*, was intended to encourage legal consultation and assistance without litigation in court (for example *conciliation*, *médiation*, etc.), and to develop, at a local level, better access to legal information.

In order to fulfil these purposes, the 1991 Act created two types of bodies. The first, established in each *département*, are the *conseils départementaux de l'aide juridique*. These are *groupements d'intérêt public* (public interest groups) which bring together the State authorities, those of the *départements* and the concerned legal professions, etc., and are responsible for determining and implementing a policy of aid to facilitate access to the law, to assess the quality of the service offered, and to locate and collect funds for the implementation of their policy. The second is the *Conseil national de l'aide juridique* which is responsible for collating information on access to the courts and to legal information and for making proposals to public authorities.

4. Civil procedure

(A) Definition of Civil Procedure

In French law, the term *procédure* has two meanings. In its wider sense, procedural law includes not only the rules governing the proceedings in a court but also the rules governing judicial organisation, *i.e.* the composition, the jurisdiction and operation of the various courts. In this sense, *procédure civile* is also referred to as *droit judiciaire privé*. In its narrower sense, procedural law deals with the rules governing the judicial process from its commencement to the judgment and the enforcement of judgments.[7] Procedural law also includes part of the law of evidence, *i.e.* the rules relating to the administering of

---

[7] However, methods of enforcement and, in particular attachment, are dealt with separately. See M. Donnier, *Voies d'exécution et procédures de distribution* (Litec, Paris, 2nd ed., 1990).

proof, the rules on admissibility of proof remaining part of civil substantive law.

It is in its narrow sense that procedural law will be examined here, excluding the rules of evidence.

(B) SOURCES OF CIVIL PROCEDURE

According to article 34 of the 1958 Constitution, rules of criminal procedure, the status of judges and the creation of new courts fall within the domain of statutory law. Therefore, for instance, rules governing the organisation of all civil and criminal courts are to be found in the legislative part of the *Code de l'organisation judiciaire*. On the other hand, those which concern civil procedure in the narrower sense, fall within the domain of *règlements*. All the reforms of procedural law occurred in 1958, 1965, 1971, 1972 and 1973 and were implemented by means of *décrets*. Even the *nouveau Code de procédure civile* is the creation of a *décret*. As a result, the conformity of rules of procedure with legislation and, in particular, with general principles of law is examined by the *Conseil d'Etat*.

The original Code of Civil Procedure of 1806 was severely criticised in France for being too similar to the *ordonnance* of 1667 and for implementing a long, complex and expensive procedure. Despite a few specific reforms after 1935, the code was substantially untouched until the 1965 reform which created in certain Courts of Appeal and courts of first instance, on a experimental basis, a *procédure des mises en état des causes* (preparatory stage) and reinforced the powers of the judge.

In 1969, a Law Commission presided over by the Minister of Justice, J. Foyer, was set up to work on the reform of the Code of Civil Procedure. Its proposals materialised in four *décrets* which came into force between 1971 and 1973 and which were codified and supplemented by the *décret* of September 5, 1975 into the *nouveau Code de procédure civile*. However, this new Code remains incomplete. Procedures for the enforcement of a judgment are still unreformed as are parts of the original Code which remains in force.[8]

The new Code is an example of rationality. Its first Title contains the general rules applicable to all courts, while Title II

---

[8] This is why it is necessary to indicate whether a text is part of the new Code (*N.C.P.C.*) or the original one (*C.P.C.*).

relates to rules which are specific to each court. Title III contains the provisions which are specific to certain matters (persons, goods, matrimonial property regimes, succession and gifts, obligations and contract). Title IV governs domestic and international arbitration, whereas Title V on measures of *exécution* remains an empty shell. However, it is regrettable that certain rules of procedure are not incorporated in the Code of Procedure, such as those governing the procedure in Social Security Courts (which are to be found in the *Code de la sécurité sociale*) as well as the rules applied by the *conseils de prud'hommes* which are contained in the *Code du travail*.

(C) CIVIL PROCEEDINGS

(1) Commencement of the proceedings: the *action en justice*

Action en justice is defined by article 30 *N.C.P.C.* as being:

"... the right, for the claimant, to be heard on the merits of his claim so that the judge may declare it well or ill-founded.

For the defendant, the *action* is the right to dispute the validity of this claim."[9]

From this definition, it follows that there is no strict corollary between an *action en justice* and a right itself.[10] On the one hand, a right may not give rise to a right of action. This is the case of an *obligation naturelle*, the non-performance of which cannot be legally sanctioned.[11] On the other hand, when the

---

[9] *"L'action est le droit, pour l'auteur d'une prétention, d'être entendu sur le fond de celle-ci afin que le juge l'a dise bien ou mal fondée.*
    Pour l'adversaire, l'action est le droit de discuter le bien-fondé de cette prétention."

[10] This is not the view of authors in the past who considered that there was no right without an action and no action without a right.

[11] Compared to the *obligation civile*, the *obligation naturelle* is only recognised in rare cases by a text, expressly or implicitly, or in the case-law. For instance, articles 205 & 206 *C.Civ.* deal with the civil obligation of maintenance between descendants and parents. By contrast, the court has only admitted the existence of a natural obligation of maintenance between brothers and sisters. More explicitly, although article 1965 *C.Civ.* provides that a gambling debt cannot give rise to an action in court, under article 1967 *C.Civ.* a voluntary payment is valid and therefore its recovery by the debtor (the gambling loser) is inadmissible.

procureur de la République institutes criminal proceedings or, in civil matters, brings a *pourvoi dans l'intérêt de la loi* (action to protect the interests of the law), no individual right is involved.

The *action en justice* also has to be distinguished from the *demande en justice* which initiates the former in a specific case (see below).

(a) *Locus standi*

According to article 31 *N.C.P.C.*:

"An action may be brought by anyone who has a legitimate interest in a claim being successful or rejected, except for those cases in which the law grants a right of action only to those qualified to support or contest a claim, or to defend a given interest."[12]

Therefore, a person who has an *intérêt à agir* and *qualité à agir* has *locus standi*.

Article 31 applies the maxim *"pas d'intérêt, pas d'action"*. Having an interest seems to be the first requirement in order to institute proceedings. However, this interest must have certain specific features. First, it must be an existing interest, *i.e. né et actuel*. This means that an action is inadmissible if the damage may only occur hypothetically. On these grounds, courts have always declared inadmissible *in futurum* actions such as the *actions interrogatoires*[13] or the *actions provocatoires* (or *action de jactance*).[14] On the other hand, some actions may be brought before the court even though there is no dispute. These are called *actions déclaratoires* by which a person may request a court to decide on the regularity of a given legal situation.[15] However, a preventive action is admissible in the case of a right

---

[12] *"L'action est ouverte à tous ceux qui ont un intérêt légitime au succès ou au rejet d'une prétention, sous réserve des cas dans lesquels la loi attribue le droit d'agir aux seules personnes qu'elle qualifie pour élever ou combattre une prétention, ou pour défendre un intérêt déterminé."*

[13] Such an action is intended to force a person to make an immediate legal decision where normally a time-limit is allowed by the law. For instance, an heir has three months and 40 days to draw up the inventory and choose the most appropriate option offered to him by law (i.e. renunciation or acceptance, or acceptance without liability beyond the assets inherited).

[14] Such action is used against someone who publicly pretends to have a right in order to force the claimant to prove it.

[15] For instance, anyone has the right to have his nationality confirmed by a court decision (art. 129 of the *Code de la nationalité* (*C.Nat.*)).

being threatened and before the occurrence of any harm, such as in the case of an *action de nouvel oeuvre* (action for disturbance of possession following the erection of new structures), provided that possession is simply threatened.[16] Also some *mesures d'instruction* (measures for investigation) may be taken before the litigation is initiated, "if there is a legitimate reason to protect or establish before a trial factual evidence upon which the solution of a dispute depends ..."[17]

Secondly, the plaintiff must have a legitimate interest protected by law. For instance, until a decision of the Court of Cassation in 1970, an action for damages brought by a *concubine* against the person responsible for the accidental death of her partner had been declared inadmissible on the grounds of a lack of legitimate interest.

Thirdly, the plaintiff must be individually and directly concerned. This raises the question of whether organisations such as trade unions, professional associations or associations defending a collective interest have *locus standi*. French law has acknowledged that trade unions have the right to go to court to defend the collective interest of the professional category they represent (article L 411–11 *C.Trav.*), as do professional associations and a number of associations such as consumer associations, anti-racism associations, etc.

Article 31 *N.C.P.C.* stipulates a second requirement for an action to be admissible: *qualité pour agir*. Those who have *qualité pour agir* have the right to bring an action. In practice, those who are individually and directly concerned have *qualité pour agir*. *Intérêt à agir* and *qualité à agir* are therefore two different concepts which, in practice, may be difficult to distinguish. Indeed, in principle, the law grants *qualité à agir* to those who have an interest, such as, for instance, the person having the right, his creditor(s) or his heir(s). However, as article 31 *N.C.P.C.* suggests, *qualité à agir* can be reserved expressly by the law for specific persons in specific situations: for example divorce suits or actions for judicial separation can

---

[16] Another example is given by article 326 *C.Civ.* which gives a husband the right to contest the paternity of the child of his wife within six months from the day he was informed of the child's birth. Also, as a principal issue, one can request a judge to proceed to the identification of handwriting (art. 296 *N.C.P.C.*).

[17] "*S'il existe un motif légitime de conserver ou d'établir avant tout procès la preuve de faits dont pourrait dépendre la solution d'un litige, ...*"

only be brought by the spouses; actions for repudiating a child are reserved for the husband of the mother; actions for avoidance of contract are reserved for the parties to the contract, etc.

(b) Forms of the *action en justice*

As article 30 *N.C.P.C.* suggests, an *action en justice* is initiated by a plaintiff through a *demande en justice* (articles 53 to 70 *N.C.P.C.*) which is then contested by the defendant through the *défense* (defence) (articles 71 to 126 *N.C.P.C.*). Therefore, *demande en justice* and *defense* are the two elements of an *action en justice*.[18]

The demande en justice

According to article 53 *N.C.P.C.*, the claim by which a civil action is initiated is called *demande d'instance* or *demande introductive d'instance* (writ of summons). All other claims occurring during the process are *incidentes* (incidental). These are listed in article 63 *N.C.P.C.* The applicant may amend, by restricting or extending, the original statement of claim by means of a *demande additionnelle* (amendments) (article 65 *N.C.P.C.*). The defendant may wish not only to submit a defence, but also to make a counterclaim or *demande reconventionnelle* (article 64 *N.C.P.C.*). A third party may also intervene in the lawsuit, either by making a claim (*intervention volontaire*) or by being the object of a claim made by the plaintiff or the defendant (*intervention forcée*) (article 66 *N.C.P.C.*).

The *demande d'instance* and the intervention are called *demandes principales* (original claims) since their purpose is to challenge someone in court for the first time. However, a claim may also be called *principale* (principal claim), as opposed to the *demandes accessoires* which are of secondary importance (minor claims), or to the *demandes subsidiaires* (subsidiary claims) made alternatively in case the principal claim is rejected.

A *demande en justice* has consequences both for the judge and the parties. It gives rise to the judge's obligation to

---

[18] This generally accepted view is however contested by H. Croze and C. Morel who consider that the concept of the right of the defence is self-sufficient and need not be incorporated in that of the *action en justice*. Moreover, in the case of a counterclaim, the defendant would become a plaintiff within the meaning of article 30(1) *N.C.P.C.*. See *Procédure civile* (PUF, Paris, 1988), pp. 131, 140.

adjudicate.[19] The judge may neither make a decision on points which have not been raised by the parties (*extra petita*) nor award a remedy other than that requested by a party (*ultra petita*). With regard to the parties, the claim has the effect of suspending the running of time-limits of actions, even in case of an application *en référé*. A *demande en justice* has the same effects on the merits as a *mise en demeure* (court order), and any interest on overdue payment or *intérêts moratoires* are calculated from the day the claim or counterclaim was made.

The défenses

According to article 59 of the *N.C.P.C.*, the defendant must first provide the court with information regarding his identity.[20] Then, he can submit his defence in four different ways.

First, the defendant may submit that the claim is unjustified and ill-founded. This is the *défense au fond* (plea on the merits) (article 71 *N.C.P.C.*). Such a plea is available at any stage of the proceedings, *i.e.* in the court of first instance, before the Court of Appeal or the Court of Cassation provided that this does not give rise to new arguments (article 72 *N.C.P.C.*).

Secondly, the defendant may also raise an objection concerning the regularity of the procedure before challenging the claim on the merits. This plea of defence is called *exception de procédure* (procedural plea). The New Code of Procedure provides four *exceptions de procédure*. The defendant may plead by means of *exception d'incompétence* (plea of lack of competence) (article 73) that the court is incompetent. He may also allege by means of *exception de litispendance et de connexité* (*lis alibi pendens*) that the suit is already pending before another competent and similar court (article 100). Through an *exception dilatoire* (dilatory plea) (article 108), the defendant may ask the court for more time — for example if he is an heir, to proceed to the inventory and make the appropriate decision[21]. Finally, the

---

[19] Unless the law suit is terminated before a judgment is pronounced following a *désistement d'instance* (waiver of claim) or a *péremption d'instance* (extinction of the action since no step has been taken).

[20] Name, surname, profession, address, date and place of birth for natural persons; form, name, registered office, representative for "legal" persons.

[21] The proceedings may also be suspended in two other cases: namely, when one of the parties invokes a decision which is subject to an *action en opposition* by a third person, to *révision* or to an appeal in *cassation* (art. 110); and, in the case of an *exception de garantie* when the defendant, a guarantee, challenges his guarantor by way of *intervention forcée* (art. 109).

defendant may resort to an *exception de nullité* whereby the nullity of procedural acts can be invoked provided that there is a prejudice (articles 112–121).

Fins de non-recevoir (dismissals) are other pleas available to the defence (articles 122–126). The aim of these pleas is to have the claim declared inadmissible, without examination of the merits, on the grounds that the applicant has no right to sue (*défault de droit d'agir*) (article 122).[22]

Finally, instead of submitting a defence properly so-called, the defendant may wish to make a counterclaim against the plaintiff which is admissible only if there is a sufficient connection with the original claim. An exception to this is the case of a *compensation* (debt set off against another) (article 70 *N.C.P.C.*). Counterclaims are also admissible in an appeal (article 567 *N.C.P.C.*). Logically, a counterclaim will be examined only if the original claim is admissible. In principle, according to the maxim *"reconvention sur reconvention ne vaut"* ("counterclaim over counterclaim is void"), the plaintiff may not make a counterclaim against the defendant's counterclaim.

(2) Conduct of the proceedings: the *instance*

Different procedures are available to the plaintiff: the *procédure contentieuse* (litigious procedure), the *procédure gracieuse* (non-litigious procedure) or the procedure of *référé* (procedure in matters of special urgency). If the defendant (or, in certain circumstances, the plaintiff) fails to appear in court, the *procédure par défault* (procedure in default) is used. All these procedures will be examined in turn. However particular emphasis will be put on the most important one, *i.e.* the ordinary litigious procedure, distinguishing between that of the *tribunal de grande instance* and that of the courts of limited jurisdiction.

(a) The ordinary procedure before the *tribunal de grande instance*

The procedure in the *tribunal de grande instance* is, in many respects, a model of civil procedure which is more or less copied in the Courts of Appeal and courts of limited jurisdiction.

---

[22] Either as a result of lack of *intérêt à agir* or *qualité à agir* or of *prescription* of the action, or of the expiry of the *délai préfix* (time-limit set by law), or simply because the case has already been adjudicated (*chose jugée*).

Nowadays the establishment of different procedures adapted to the complexity of each dispute and the institution of the *juge de la mise en état* (preparatory judge) constitute the basic techniques and elements of civil procedure gradually being adopted by other French courts.

Commencement of the proceedings

Article 750 *N.C.P.C.* provides that, in the ordinary procedure, an action may be brought either by *assignation* or, more rarely, by *requête conjointe*.

The *assignation* (writ of summons), set out in an *exploit d'huissier* (bailiff's document), must contain certain information such as, *inter alia*: name, surname, domicile or residence of the plaintiff and defendant, and of the bailiff serving the writ (article 648 *N.C.P.C.*) as well as the court before which the defendant is summoned, the object and the legal points supporting the action (article 56 *N.C.P.C.*), and finally, the *constitution d'avocat* (appointment of a lawyer)[23] by the plaintiff and the time-limit within which the defendant must appear in court through the representation by a lawyer (article 752 *N.C.P.C.*).[24] This time-limit is normally 15 days (article 755 *N.C.P.C.*) from the date of the summons but can be extended for up to two months if the defendant resides abroad (article 643 *N.C.P.C.*).[25] Failure to include these details results in the nullity of the *assignation*.

Proceedings are deemed to be instituted only after a copy of the *assignation* has been delivered to the *secrétariat-greffe*. The case is then *mis au rôle* (entered on the roll). This copy must be delivered within four months of the assignation being served otherwise it is declared *caduque* (lapsed) by order of the President of the court or the judge in charge of the case (article 757 *N.C.P.C.*). The "*assignation vaut conclusions*", *i.e.* it constitutes the plaintiff's pleadings (article 56 *N.C.P.C.*).

---

[23] Representation by a lawyer is compulsory for both plaintiff and defendant as well as for third parties (arts. 751 & 814). Each party is obliged to be represented by only one lawyer (art. 414).

[24] The defendant's lawyer must serve notice of his appointment on the plaintiff's lawyer (arts. 756 & 814). A copy of this notification must be delivered to the *secrétariat-greffe* of the court (arts. 756 & 816).

[25] Failure to appear within this time-limit, called *délai de comparution* (*comparaître* meaning accepting to appear to court through a lawyer, personal appearance of the defendant being unnecessary), does not automatically deprive the defendant of the right to appoint a lawyer. Indeed, the time-limit can be implicitly extended to allow the defendant time to organise his defence.

If the matter is urgent, the plaintiff may be authorised by the President of the court to summon the defendant to appear on a fixed date. This is the *assignation à jour fixe* (article 646 *N.C.P.C.*). The plaintiff's request must be justified and contain the *conclusions* (pleadings), demonstrate that there is urgency, and incorporate the documents supporting the allegations (article 788 *N.C.P.C.*). A copy of the request and of the documents must be filed (articles 788(3) & 824 *N.C.P.C.*). Subject to the sanction of nullity, the date and time of the hearing and, if relevant, the name of the division of the court dealing with the case, must be mentioned in the *assignation*. This informs the defendant that the documents produced by the plaintiff are available for examination and that defence documents must be disclosed before the date of the hearing. A copy of the petition is served together with the *assignation* on the defendant (article 789 *N.C.P.C.*). The case will be heard as soon as the defendant has appointed a lawyer, even if no pleadings have been submitted.[26] However, if the case proves to be more complex than it first appeared, it is referred to the *juge de mise en état* for examination (article 792(3) *N.C.P.C.*).

The parties may also bring an action by *requête conjointe* (combined petition) (articles 793–796 *N.C.P.C.*) signed by both parties and in which their respective claims, the litigious points of law and facts, the respective grounds supporting their allegations and the documents produced by each party are presented. As with the *assignation*, the *requête conjointe* constitutes the parties' pleadings (article 57 *N.C.P.C.*). Where the parties have rights which they may exercise freely, they may agree that the judge act as a *compositeur amiable* (friendly conciliator) only, or that the hearing be limited to a mere clarification of certain points of law (article 58 *N.C.P.C.*). There is no time-limit for appearance once the parties have agreed to bring their case to court.[27]

Preparation of the case

Since 1958 successive procedural reforms, and in particular the institution of the *mise en état* (preparatory stage of a case), have

---

[26] However, the President of the court must make sure that the defendant has had sufficient time to prepare his defence (art. 792(1)). If the defendant does not appear, a judgment in default is given (art. 792(4)).

[27] The parties may agree to have their case heard by a single judge or renounce the right to have it referred to a Bench of judges (art. 794).

reinforced the powers of the judge and given civil procedure an inquisitorial character. Nowadays, even if the parties retain control of the cause and the object of their action, the conduct of the proceedings lies mostly with the judge.

At an initial hearing, the *audience d'appel des causes*, the President of the court decides whether the case can be dealt with without preparation or whether it must be referred to the *juge de la mise en état* (article 759 N.C.P.C.). In the case of proceedings initiated by *assignation*, the President may send simple cases for trial either immediately after the exchange of pleadings and documents (ultra-short route) (article 760(1) N.C.P.C.), or after a further exchange of pleadings and documents (short route) (article 761 N.C.P.C.). The case is then deemed to be *en état*, *i.e.* in a state permitting a decision. All other cases are referred to the *juge de mise en état* for examination and preparation (long route).[28]

The preparatory judge is a judge of a Division of the court to which the case has been brought. The role of this judge is first to supervise the proceedings by fixing *ad hoc* time-limits for the performance of procedural acts by the parties according to the nature, complexity and urgency of the litigation (article 764 N.C.P.C.).[29] Secondly, he conducts the enquiry. For this purpose he may order that originals or copies of those documents mentioned in the proceedings be produced (article 765(3) N.C.P.C.). He has full powers to order either party or a third person to produce documents (article 770 N.C.P.C.) and may also hear the parties on his own initiative (article 767 N.C.P.C.). Thirdly, the judge may award provisional remedies which can be modified or revoked (article 771(4) N.C.P.C.). Fourthly, he may influence the course of the proceedings either by inviting the

---

[28] In the event of *requête conjointe*, only the latter two routes may be used. If the procedure of *assignation à jour fixe* is used, the trial takes place immediately unless the President considers that further exchange of pleadings (short route) or further preparation of the case (long route) is necessary.

[29] If one of the lawyers fails to perform the necessary procedural acts within the set time-limit the judge may, on his own motion or at the request of the other party, close the preparatory stage by means of a reasoned and unappealable order and send the case for trial (art. 780). Moreover, if none of the lawyers perform the procedural acts within the time-limit, the judge, after giving notice to them, may on his own motion order the case to be struck out (art. 781).

parties to call on third persons whose participation is deemed to be necessary for the solution of the dispute (article 768 *N.C.P.C.*) or by ordering that the claims be separated or combined (article 766 *N.C.P.C.*).[30] He may also accept the settlement of the parties (article 768 *N.C.P.C.*). Finally he decides on the costs (article 772 *N.C.P.C.*). In principle, the decisions of the preparatory judge take the form of a simple endorsement on the record but in a number of cases he is required to make decisions by means of a reasoned order (article 773 *N.C.P.C.*). Such orders have no *autorité de chose jugée* (*res judicata*) with respect to the main proceedings (article 775 *N.C.P.C.*) and, in principle, may only be appealed against together with the judgment on the merits (article 776 *N.C.P.C.*).[31] These powers and functions enable the preparatory judge to acquire the full details of a case before it is sent for trial.

When the judge considers that the case is ready for trial, he issues an *ordonnance de clôture* (closing order) and sends the case to the court for a trial date to be fixed (article 779 *N.C.P.C.*). In principle, after the closing order no further pleadings or documents may be submitted (article 783 *N.C.P.C.*).

The trial

Once the preparatory phase is finished the date of the trial is fixed, either by the President of the court or by the preparatory judge (article 779 *N.C.P.C.*). As a general rule the trial takes place in public, unless otherwise provided for by law (article 433 *N.C.P.C.*) or unless the judge decides that the trial should take place *en chambre du conseil* (*in camera*) for reasons of public decency or public policy (article 435 *N.C.P.C.*).

The President of the court keeps order at the trial and conducts the proceedings (articles 438 & 440 *N.C.P.C.*). He may request the preparatory judge or another judge to submit an objective written report to the court presenting the object of the

---

[30] Those actions are called respectively *disjonction* and *jonction de l'instance*.
[31] However, decisions ordering an expert's report can be appealed against independently if there are serious and legitimate reasons. Orders putting an end to the proceedings or those relating to provisional remedies in divorce and separation cases may be appealed against within 15 days of the order being made.

claim, the parties' arguments and the factual and legal issues raised by the case (article 785 N.C.P.C.).

The parties' lawyers are then heard (*audience des plaidoiries*), the plaintiff's lawyer being heard first (unless a third party intervenes in the proceedings as main party). Each side has the opportunity to reply to the other (*duplique* and *réplique* respectively). If the President considers that the court has sufficient information he may order the parties to close their arguments (article 440 N.C.P.C.). Alternatively, under article 442 N.C.P.C., the court may invite the parties to provide further factual and legal explanations.

When the member of the *ministère public* intervenes in the proceedings as a *partie jointe*, he delivers an opinion either after the arguments of the parties or at a subsequent hearing (article 443 N.C.P.C.).

After the parties have expressed their arguments the President declares the argument closed.

(b) The ordinary procedure in specialised courts

The procedure in specialised courts is intended to be swift, simple (no preparatory judge is involved in the proceedings), cheap (the parties need not be represented by a lawyer) and less formal (it is mainly oral).

The tribunal d'instance

A claim before the *tribunal d'instance* is usually commenced by means of an *assignation à toutes fins*, directed at either conciliation or judgment (article 829 N.C.P.C.). Apart from the usual details the summons must state the time, date and place of the hearing at which the attempt at conciliation is to be made or the case tried, as well as whether the defendant will be assisted or not (article 836 N.C.P.C.). This must be delivered at least 15 days before the date of the hearing and deposited at the court office (articles 837 & 838 N.C.P.C.).[32]

If conciliation fails the case is tried at once or is adjourned to a later hearing if it is not ready for trial (article 840 N.C.P.C).

---

[32] Under article 839 N.C.P.C. this time-limit may be reduced in urgent cases.

Before issuing an *assignation*, an attempt at conciliation may be made either orally or by letter deposited at the court office. Both parties must be present in person. If conciliation fails, the judge notifies the plaintiff of this by means of a *bulletin de non-conciliation* unless the parties have agreed that the case be tried immediately (articles 830–835 *N.C.P.C.*).

The parties may also institute an action by *requête conjointe* or by *présentation volontaire* (voluntary appearance). In both cases, the judge will attempt to reconcile the parties or, if he fails, to settle their dispute (articles 845–847 *N.C.P.C.*).

The tribunal de commerce

An action is brought before the *tribunal de commerce* either by means of an *assignation* or by a *requête conjointe*, or by *présentation volontaire* (article 854 *N.C.P.C.*). When a case proves to be too complex, it can be allocated for preparation to a *juge rapporteur* whose function and powers are quite similar to those of the *juge de la mise en état* (articles 862–869 *N.C.P.C.*). If the parties consent, he may conduct the hearings on his own and report to the court during the deliberations. Otherwise, he refers the case for trial to the court.

The conseil de prud'hommes

In the *conseil de prud'hommes* the procedure, which is entirely oral, starts before the conciliation panel (since attempt at conciliation is compulsory) and, if conciliation fails, finishes before the adjudication panel.

The proceedings are initiated by a claim deposited at the court office or by registered letter. In principle, the presence of the parties at the hearing is required but they can be represented if they have legitimate reasons for absence (article R 516-4 *C.Trav.*).[33] Hearings of the conciliation panel are not public. Partial or total conciliation is recorded and is enforceable. If conciliation fails or if the defendant fails to appear, the case is referred to the adjudication panel. However, if the case is not ready for trial, one or two *conseillers rapporteurs* may be appointed to prepare the case. Their decisions are not binding

---

[33] Those persons who may assist or represent the parties are: other employees or employers working in the same area, trade union representatives, the party's spouse and lawyers. Before the Court of Appeal, they can be represented by an *avoué* (art. R 516-5 *C.Trav.*).

on the adjudication panel and are appealable, together with the final decision, on the merits. The parties are summoned to appear before the adjudication panel orally or by registered letter. After listening to the parties the panel deliberates and delivers its judgment immediately or at a later hearing. Decisions are taken by an overall majority.

(c) Specific procedures

The procédure par défaut

The *procédure par défaut* may result either because of the parties failing to appear in court or failing to perform the necessary procedural acts within the time-limits.

In the first situation, if the plaintiff fails to appear in court without a legitimate reason, the defendant has the right to request a judgment on the merits — which is then said to be *contradictoire* — unless the judge decides to adjourn the case to a subsequent hearing (article 468(1) *N.C.P.C.*). The judge himself may also consider that the claim has lapsed unless the plaintiff is able to prove within 15 days that he had a legitimate reason for not appearing (article 468(2) *N.C.P.C.*). Where the defendant fails to appear, he may be informed by letter from the judge of the consequences of his absence, or he may be summoned to appear again (article 471 *N.C.P.C.*). A judgment may be entered in the absence of the defendant once the judge has ensured that the claim is admissible and well founded (article 472 *N.C.P.C.*). This judgment is *réputé contradictoire* (considered as having been contested) if it is appealable or if the defendant has been personally served with the writ. It is *par défaut* (a default judgment) when it is *en dernier ressort* (not open to appeal in a Court of Appeal) or if the writ has not been served personally on the defendant (article 473 *N.C.P.C.*), in which case a particular form of appeal, the *opposition*, is available. Under article 474 *N.C.P.C.*, certain special rules apply where there are several defendants to the same action or where the court's decision is not appealable.

It may also happen that one or both parties fail to perform the procedural acts in due time. Where one party fails to do this, the court may deliver a *jugement contradictoire* unless the defendant requests the court to declare the summons lapsed (article 469 *N.C.P.C.*). If both parties default, the court may strike the case off the roll (article 470 *N.C.P.C.*).

The *procédure gracieuse*

In French procedural law the judge may be required by law to intervene even where there is no litigation between two or more parties (article 25 *N.C.P.C.*). The intervention of the court may be necessary in order, for instance, to authenticate a legal act (*e.g.* the emancipation of a minor) or to protect incapable minors and adults. The court may also be requested to take a decision intended to protect the family (for example divorce by mutual consent, legitimation, adoption, etc.) or to protect individuals (for example appointment of an official receiver, a liquidator, etc.).

The absence of litigation is a characteristic of this procedure which can be distinguished from the *procédure contentieuse*.

This non-litigious procedure is also characterised by a lack of formalism, a *requête* in the form of a registered letter being deposited at the court office (article 60 *N.C.P.C.*). The case is not necessarily entered on the general list nor is it filed.

A *juge rapporteur* in charge of the preparation of the case is appointed by the President of the Division of the *tribunal de grande instance* dealing with the case (article 799 *N.C.P.C.*). The hearing takes place *en chambre du conseil* (*in camera*) (article 434 *N.C.P.C.*) and therefore is not public (article 436 *N.C.P.C.*). All cases must also be transmitted to the *ministère public* (article 798 *N.C.P.C.*).

The *procédure de référé*

As mentioned previously in Chapter Four, Presidents of ordinary courts enjoy specific powers, in particular those of making *ordonnances de référé* by which the *juge* may order urgent, interim or provisional measures.

Application for a *référé* is made by *assignation*. Hearings take place at fixed intervals (article 485 *N.C.P.C.*) or, in the case of extreme urgency, immediately at a fixed time, in court or at the residence of the judge, even on a public holiday (article 485(2) *N.C.P.C.*).

Before the judge delivers a judgment once the parties have expressed their views, it is necessary to ensure that the defendant has had sufficient time to prepare his defence (article 486 *N.C.P.C.*). He may also refer the case to the court for a subsequent hearing (article 487 *N.C.P.C.*). The judge may only take temporary measures. Along with a condemnation, he may impose an *astreinte* (daily fine for delay in the performance of a contract or payment of a debt) and rule on the costs (article 491 *N.C.P.C.*).

The *ordonnances de référé* are enforceable as soon as they are served or, if necessary, immediately on presentation of the original draft (*exécution sur minute*) (article 489 *N.C.P.C.*). They have no *autorité de chose jugée* in the main proceedings (article 488 *N.C.P.C.*).

These *ordonnances* are appealable to the same court within 15 days after they have been served unless they have been made by the President of a Court of Appeal or made *en dernier ressort*. Where an *ordonnance* has been made by default and is not appealable, the *opposition* is the only available way in which it can be challenged (article 490 *N.C.P.C.*).

(3) The phase of the judgment

In French the term *"jugement"* has two meanings. In the broad sense, this is a judicial or non-judicial decision delivered by a court during or at the end of proceedings. In the narrow sense, this is a decision of a court of first instance as opposed to the *arrêt* which is a decision of the Courts of Appeal and the Court of Cassation. Throughout this section, the term *jugement* will be used in its wider meaning. After explaining how they are made, the service and enforcement of judgments will be examined.

(a) The making of judgments
Before a judgment is delivered, it is discussed, adopted, and then drafted.

Judges who have heard the oral arguments will consult on the case (article 447 *N.C.P.C.*). This is known as *délibérations*. However, an exception is made in the case where the *juge de la mise en état* or the *juge rapporteur*, who have heard oral arguments sitting alone, must report to the court during the *délibérations* (article 786 *N.C.P.C.*). *Délibérations* take place behind closed doors (article 448 *N.C.P.C.*) and, because decisions can only be adopted by a majority (article 449 *N.C.P.C.*), an uneven number of judges convene (article 448 *N.C.P.C.*).[34]

The drafting of the judgment is of course subject to formal rules. The *minute*, the original and authentic draft of the judgment, is drawn up by the *greffier* under the dictation of the

---

[34] Except in the *conseil de prud'hommes* and the Court of Cassation.

judge or on the basis of the judge's notes. Under article 454 *N.C.P.C.*, the judgment, which is delivered "*au nom du peuple français*" must contain a series of indications which are essential for its validity, namely: the court concerned, the names of the judges who took part in the *déliberations*, the date of the judgment, the name of the representative of the *ministère public*, the name of the *greffier*, the names of the parties and their counsels, their domicile or registered office. The judgment must also sum up the allegations and arguments of the parties (article 455(1) *N.C.P.C.*). It consists of two parts: the *motifs* in which the judges indicate the reasons for their decision[35] and the *dispositif* which is the ruling of the court (article 455(2) *N.C.P.C.*). Finally, the judgment must bear the signatures of the President of the court and of the *greffier* (article 456 *N.C.P.C.*).

In ordinary litigious proceedings, judgments (or ruling only) are given in open court whereas decisions taken in non-litigious proceedings are delivered *in camera* (article 451 *N.C.P.C.*). In the simplest cases, the court delivers its judgment either *sur le champ* (immediately) at the hearing without retiring to consult (*délibéré sur le siège, i.e.* a consultation *sotto voce* during the sitting) or after retiring for only a short while (*délibéré en chambre du conseil*). In other cases, judgments are given at a subsequent hearing and are *mis en délibéré* (reserved or adjourned for further consultation).

(b) Service and enforcement of judgments

Under articles 500 & 501 of the *N.C.P.C.*, judgments are enforceable only after they have been given *force de chose jugée*,[36] *i.e.* where they are not subject to appeals which suspend their enforcement, or where appeals have not been made within the time-limits.

In principle, judgments cannot be enforced until an *expédition* or *copie exécutoire*[37] (first authentic copy of the judgment) — which contains the *formule exécutoire* (enforcement order) — is delivered to the successful party. The judgment must then be

---

[35] The obligation to motivate decisions was introduced by the Act of August 16–24, 1790. However, decisions may not indicate all the grounds for reasons of circumspection (*e.g.* decision on child adoption) or where the judges have exercised their discretionary powers (*e.g.* decision to suspend judgment), etc.

[36] Note, on the other hand, that judgments have *autorité de chose jugée* as soon as they are passed.

[37] This was formerly called "*la grosse du jugement.*"

served on the defendant unless this is an *exécution sur minute*, *i.e.* enforcement without service and on presentation of the original copy of the judgment.

However, the date of the enforcement of a judgment may be either brought forward or postponed. In the first case, there is an *exécution provisoire* (provisional enforcement)[38] which permits a judgment to be enforced soon after it has been served despite the suspensive effect of an appeal. It is a characteristic of *ordonnances de référé* or *sur requête*, provisional remedies, etc., that they can be enforced in this way. In other cases, provisional enforcement can be ordered by the judge, either on his own motion or at the request of the parties provided this is necessary and compatible with the nature of the case, and it is not prohibited by law (article 515 *N.C.P.C.*). In the second case, under article 510 *N.C.P.C.*, the judge may postpone the enforcement of a judgment by granting, in a reasoned decision, an extra period of time for enforcement (*délai de grâce*). This does not however prevent *mesures conservatoires* (provisional remedy intended to preserve a right or a thing) from being taken (article 513 *N.C.P.C.*).

(c) Remedies

In French law, civil remedies can be classified into four categories: enforcement, money remedies, pecuniary sanctions and the modification of legal transactions.

Enforcement

Where a party does not fulfill his obligation(s), the other party may have no other remedy than the *exécution forcée* (enforced execution). In the case of a claim in debt (for example repayment of a loan), the movable property of the debtor may be subject to *saisie* (attachment and/or distraint), and then sold in a public auction with a view to reimbursing the creditor(s). However, in the case of fraudulent insolvency, article 1167 *C.Civ.* provides that an action called the *action paulienne* may be initiated by the creditors, permitting them to challenge transactions made by their debtor in order to deliberately cause his insolvency with the purpose of defrauding the creditors of their rights.

---

[38] Note that this is to be distinguished from the *exécution minute*.

Where the obligation is an obligation to do a particular thing, such as supplying a service or carrying out a deed, or an obligation to refrain from doing a particular thing, the creditor will first seek an order of specific performance before requesting damages in the event of the obligation not being performed. For this purpose the *juge des référés* has been vested by law with the power to order specific performance (article 809 *N.C.P.C.*), and the judge of a *tribunal d'instance* has the power to use an *injonction de faire* (mandatory injunction) against the debtor where not all the contracting parties are *commerçants* (traders) and where the monetary value of the obligation is small (articles 1425–1 *et seq. N.C.P.C.*).

Also, article 1144 *C.Civ.* provides that a creditor may, in the case of non-performance, be authorised to perform the obligation at the expense of the debtor. For instance, where someone undertakes to sell something by a *promesse de vente* but refuses to sign the necessary deed, the promisee may request the judge to declare the contract binding and the judgment as constituting the *acte authentique*, *i.e.* the necessary formal document. A mandatory obligation can also be performed *manu militari*, *i.e.* by force, such as the removal of furniture of an illegal occupier, or the demolition of a non-authorised building extension ordered by the judge at the request of a neighbouring owner. However, there are cases where such remedies prove inefficient because non-performance has created an irremediable situation (*e.g.*, failure to deliver goods in due time). In such an event, besides ordering the debtor to pay damages (article 1142 *C.Civ.*), the judge may impose on him the payment of an *astreinte*, *i.e.* a daily fine for delay in the performance of an obligation, the only purpose of which is to exercise psychological pressure on the debtor.[39]

Money remedies

Where there is civil liability, the usual remedy will be *dommages et intérêts* (damages) whereas *restitution* (restitution) may be ordered where liability is not established.

---

[39] First created by judges, the *astreinte* was then incorporated into legislation by the Act of July 5, 1972 with respect to relationships between private individuals. The Act of July 16, 1980 applied it to the enforcement of judicial decisions by administrative authorities, and since the Act of July 30, 1987 it has been available against those "legal" persons in private law who administer a public service.

Damages are usually awarded for the purpose of compensating material loss or moral suffering. Under article 1149 *C.Civ.*, "damages due to a creditor are, in general, for the loss which he incurred and for the gain of which he was deprived...."[40]

Such damages are called *dommages et intérêts compensatoires*, but they are said to be "*moratoires*" where they result from a delay in performance, in which case the rate of damages is fixed by law (article 1153 *C.Civ.*).

Sometimes, instead of claiming damages, a person may claim restitution of money which was inadvertently or wrongly paid to another person. Under article 1235 *C.Civ.*, "any payment supposes a debt; that which has been paid without being due is subject to restitution."[41] This is known as *répétition de l'indu* (return of a payment made in error). For instance, if the debtor pays his debt to a person other than the real creditor, the recipient must then return the money.

Pecuniary sanctions

Remedies may also consist of a sanction for an offence or a wrong, which is directed solely at benefiting the victim, and which consists of a pecuniary loss or deprivation for the offender.

In succession, for instance, the heir who has diverted or concealed assets loses his right to claim any share in the things diverted or concealed though he remains an unconditional heir (article 792 *C.Civ.*). Similarly, killing or attempting to kill the deceased, or accusing the deceased, in a defamatory manner, deprives the offender of his succession rights (article 727 *C.Civ.*).

In divorce cases which are based on the exclusive fault of one of the spouses, the latter is deprived of any legal rights to any gifts and all the matrimonial advantages which were granted by the other spouse, whether at the time of the marriage or afterwards (article 267 *C.Civ.*).

With respect to guardianship, if the guardian makes a false inventory of the assets of the minor, the minor may prove the

---

[40] "*Les dommages et intérêts dus au créancier sont, en général, de la perte qu'il a faite et du gain dont il a été privé...*"

[41] "*Tout paiement suppose une dette: ce qui a été payé sans être dû est sujet à répétition.*"

value and composition of the assets by any means (article 451(3) *C.Civ.*). The defaulting guardian is then likely to be forced to pay for assets which may not have originally been part of the minor's estate.

Under article 955 *C.Civ.*, *inter vivos* gifts may be revoked because of ingratitude if the donee makes an attempt on the life of the donor, or is guilty of serious cruelties, wrongs and injuries towards him, or refuses sustenance to him. In such event, the donee will be ordered to restore the value of the gifts (article 958 *C.Civ.*).

Modification of legal transactions or proceedings

Where legal transactions or court proceedings are tainted with procedural error, they may either be modified or annulled.

Nullity may be the remedy available where the legal transaction does not comply with specific requirements for its validity (for example those relating to capacity, form of the act, consent).

Where the legal transaction cannot come into effect, although it has been regularly formed, it will be declared *caduc*, *i.e.* lapsed. For instance, a legacy would lapse if the subject-matter of the bequest was destroyed.

However, where only part of the contract breaches the law, nullity will affect only this part and not the whole contract. The illegal provision(s) is said to be *réputée non écrite* (considered as unexpressed).

As the exercise of a right is always subject to time-limits, a court action initiated after the set time-limit leads to the *prescription extinctive* of the right, *i.e.* to the extinction of the right. Similarly, where a plaintiff has not proceeded with the claim for at least two years after having initiated proceedings, these will be subject to *péremption*, *i.e.* they will be concluded and will have to be initiated again. However the *péremption* does not extinguish the right in question.

Where a party to a contract does not perform his obligation(s), the other party may resort to the procedure of *résolution* (*annulment ex tunc*) by which he will be released retrospectively from his own obligations. However in the case of *contrats successifs*, *i.e.* contracts for periodically renewable performance or service (for example lease, employment), the procedure of *résolution* cannot operate retrospectively, and therefore the contract will be terminated for the future by means of *résiliation* (*annulment ex nunc*).

Finally, a legal transaction may be regarded as being *inopposable* as regards third parties, *i.e.* as having no legal force or effect on them where the legal requirements for publicity of the transaction have not been met. For instance in property law, if transfers of property, mortgage contracts, servitudes, etc., are not publicised in the *registre des conservation des hypothèques*, they may be regarded by third persons as having no legal effect on them although such transactions are valid with respect to the parties thereto.

(4) *Voies de recours*

Any party or third party has the right to have his case re-examined by means of *voie de recours* (appeal).[42] In French law the distinction is made between *voies de rétractation* (appeals intended to set aside a judgment), where the case is re-examined by the same court (*opposition* and *recours en révision*), and *voies de réformation* (appeals intended to reverse a judgment), where the case is referred to a higher court (*appel*). A further distinction is made between *recours ordinaires* (ordinary appeals), which are available to any party (*appel* and *opposition*) and *recours extraordinaires* (extraordinary appeals), which are available only when provided by law (*tierce opposition*, *révision* and *pourvoi en cassation*).

The *appel*

Apart from judgments passed *en dernier ressort* (in last resort), any *jugement définitif* (judgment on the merits),[43] in litigious or non-litigious proceedings, may be subject to an *appel* before a Court of Appeal (article 543 *N.C.P.C.*). This is a general and systematic right[44] of those parties who appeared in the lower

---

[42] This convenient translation is however not accurate since the term "*voie de recours*" covers more situations than the English appeal.

[43] This excludes the *jugements avant dire droit* which are interim judgments passed in the course of proceedings and before the final resolution of the litigation. Such judgments are passed either to facilitate measures of investigation or to provide provisional remedies.

[44] Unlike in English law, there is no need to seek leave of appeal.

court and, in non-litigious proceedings, of those against whom the judgment has been served. The parties against whom the appeal lies are called *intimés* (respondents) (article 547 *N.C.P.C.*). They, in turn, may bring a counter-appeal, the *appel incident*, against the original appeal, the *appel principal* (article 548 *N.C.P.C.*). Moreover, parties who are not *intimées* but who were parties at first instance may also bring an appeal against the *appelant*, the *appel provoqué* (article 549 *N.C.P.C.*). Finally, third persons who have not been parties at first instance may intervene, under article 554, at the appeal stage if they have an interest in doing so (*intervention volontaire*), or they may be challenged under article 555 by the parties to the case (*intervention forcée*). Unlike the English appeal, the *appel* has a suspensive effect on the original judgment except in the case of *exécution provisoire*. The *appel* also has another effect called *effet dévolutif* whereby the authority of the judgment of the lower court is challenged, thus permitting a re-examination of the factual and legal issues (article 561 *N.C.P.C.*).

In general, time-limits to *interjeter appel* (to lodge an appeal) are rather short. In civil, commercial and social proceedings, an appeal must be brought within one month from the judgment being served (article 528 & 538 *N.C.P.C.*) or within 15 days as, for instance, in the case of a *référé* or in non-litigious proceedings.

The *opposition*

The *opposition* is the only appeal available to those parties against whom a default judgment has been passed (article 571 *N.C.P.C.*). *Opposition* must be lodged before the court which passed the challenged judgment. It is then quite similar to the English application to set aside a decision. The application is in the same form as the original action in court and must contain the arguments of the defaulting party. The factual and legal issues of the case are re-examined. The execution of the challenged judgment is suspended as a result of the *opposition* but remains valid until a new decision is made. This decision may either confirm the previous judgment — the confirming decision having retrospective effect from the day of the original judgment — or consist in a new judgment setting aside the previous one — in which case the original judgment is retrospectively made ineffective by the second one.

An appeal by means of *opposition* must be lodged within a month after the default judgment has been served (article 538 *N.C.P.C.*) and according to the rules and procedure applicable to the original action brought before the court which delivered that judgment (article 573 *N.C.P.C.*).

The *tierce opposition*

A third person, who has been affected by a judgment but has not been a party to it, or has not been represented in the litigation, may challenge it before the same[45] or another court[46] by means of *tierce opposition*. Such an appeal can be brought against judgments passed in litigious as well as non-litigious proceedings (articles 582 & 583 *N.C.P.C.*).[47] Being an *appel extraordinaire*, the *tierce opposition* has no suspensive effect unless this is stipulated by the judge (article 590 *N.C.P.C.*). The challenged judgment is either confirmed with legal effects on the challenging party, or those parts of it which have caused prejudice are reversed or set aside. In the latter case, the whole of the original judgment will continue to have effect between the original parties (article 591 *N.C.P.C.*).

Tierce opposition may be lodged within a period of 30 years from the date of the judgment unless the law provides otherwise (article 586 N.C.P.C.).[48]

The *recours en révision*

In certain situations an aggrieved party may appeal against a decision by means of *recours en révision* in order to have it set

---

[45] This is the case when the appeal is lodged *par voie principale*, *i.e.* as a main action (art. 587 *N.C.P.C.*).

[46] This is the case where the appeal is lodged *par voie incidente*, *i.e.* as an incidental action, by a party who is affected by a judgment while involved in other litigation. In such a case, the party concerned may lodge a *tierce opposition* before the court dealing with his current litigation provided that the court is superior to that which has passed the challenged judgment (art. 588 *N.C.P.C.*).

[47] However, this cannot be used against decisions of the Court of Cassation or against divorce judgments.

[48] The reason for this long time-limit is quite simple: it is clear that third persons may remain unaware of a judgment until its enforcement since this is not served on them. As the period of enforcement of a judgment is 30 years, third parties must be allowed to challenge it, within that same period of time, if this has adverse effects on them.

aside and have the case retried. Article 595 *N.C.P.C.* provides that the *révision* is available in four cases only:

— where the successful party has acted fraudulently; or
— where, since the judgment, vital documents were discovered which had been withheld by another party; or
— the decision has been based on false documents; or
— where it has been given on the basis of false attestations (statements in writing by a third person), false testimony or false oaths.

The *recours en révision* may be brought only against judgments which are *en force de chose jugée, i.e.* no longer subject to an appeal having a suspensive effect. Such an appeal lies to the court which passed the challenged decision and is admissible unless the *appelant* can demonstrate, before the judgment has been granted *force de chose jugée*, that the other party acted fraudulently (article 595 *N.C.P.C.*). The *recours en révision* has no suspensive effect. A judgment passed following a *révision* can be challenged by means of *appel* or *opposition* but not by means of *révision* (article 603(1) *N.C.P.C.*).

This appeal must be lodged within two months from the day when the appellant has established a ground for *révision* (article 596 *N.C.P.C.*).

The *pourvoi en cassation*

The Court of Cassation is not strictly speaking an Appeal court or, as a French lawyer would call it, a *juridiction du troisième degré*. This is because it only re-examines the points of law of a case and also because it does not readjudicate the case referred to it as a Court of Appeal would. When, within two months (article 612 *N.C.P.C.*), a *pourvoi en cassation* is lodged with the Court, there are only two alternatives:

— either the Court considers that the challenged decision of the lower court was based on a proper application of the law, in which case the *pourvoi* is rejected and the decision of the lower court is final;[49] or

---

[49] A new application is inadmissible, even if based on new grounds (art. 621 *N.C.P.C.*). The *arrêt de rejet* (decision of rejection) cannot be challenged by way of *opposition* or *tierce opposition*.

— it considers that the challenged decision was ill-founded and then partially or totally quashes it, and remits it to another court of a similar rank or to the same court differently constituted. However, this *juridiction de renvoi* is not bound by the decision of the Court of Cassation. Indeed, the case is re-examined as regards both the facts and the law and a new decision is rendered. As a result, two situations may occur: either this new decision complies with that of the Court of Cassation and the case is concluded, or the lower court declines to follow the Court of Cassation, in which case the new decision might in turn be challenged before the Court of Cassation on the same legal grounds as before. In the latter situation the case is referred to the *assemblée plénière*, *i.e.* the Full Court (article L 131–2(2) C.O.J.). This may reject the second *cassation* appeal (and therefore disagree with one of its own divisions). Alternatively it may quash the lower court's decision and remit the case to a third lower court, which is then bound by the law expressed by the *assemblée plénière* (article 131–4(2) C.O.J.). In such a case, the Court of Cassation has the last word.

There is also a third situation in which the Court of Cassation may quash a lower court's decision without remitting it. This is called "*cassation sans renvoi*" (article L 131–5 C.O.J.). The Court of Cassation may do this when there is no need to pronounce a judgment on the merits again (for example when an appeal was declared admissible by the Court of Appeal although it was not, etc.) or when "… the facts, which have been definitely established and considered by the judges (of the lower courts), allow (the Court of Cassation) to apply the appropriate rule of law" (article L131–(2) C.O.J.).[50]

This third possibility may occur in all six divisions of the Court of Cassation, the *chambre mixte* and the *assemblée plénière*, which may decide the case and fix the cost incurred before the lower courts (article L 131–5(3) C.O.J.). A decision of *cassation sans renvoi* is enforceable (article 131–5(4) C.O.J.). In this situation, the Court of Cassation appears to act as a real Appeal Court.

---

[50] "… *les faits, tels qu'ils ont été souverainement constatés et appréciés par les juges du fond, lui permettent d' appliquer la règle de droit appropriée.*"

Diagram 5.1 **The Pourvoi en Cassation**

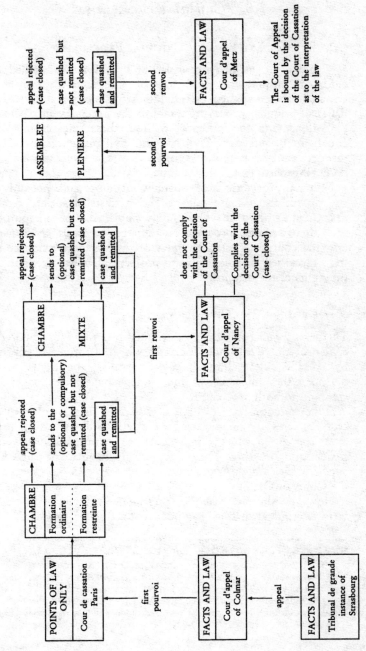

5. CRIMINAL PROCEDURE

(A) PURPOSE AND ROLE OF CRIMINAL PROCEDURE

Whereas the majority of rules of civil law are applied and enforced without the need for the intervention of a court, criminal law is applied essentially through criminal procedure. Rules of criminal procedure establish the necessary link between the offence and the sentence. Without these rules criminal law could not be effective. Civil law and civil procedure are clearly distinct and separate areas of law whilst criminal law and criminal procedure are closely inter-related.

Criminal procedure is of a paramount importance not only for society but also for individuals. The interests of society demand that offences are swiftly and surely punished. For this purpose, the role of criminal procedure is therefore to create and organise criminal courts, to establish rules of investigation, evidence and trial. However, its role is also to protect individual freedoms and the rights of the defence.[51]

(B) CRIMINAL AND CIVIL PROCEDURE

The gravity and complexity of criminal procedure, as opposed to civil procedure, explain sufficiently why the former is governed by specific rules, although rules regarding the rights of the defence, the impartiality and independence of judges are common to both procedures.

Some common features have already been mentioned: civil and criminal cases are adjudicated by the same ordinary courts (apart from specialised courts); judgments are in principle made by a Bench of more than one judge; judgments may be subject to appeal before a higher court; judgments may also be reviewed by the Court of Cassation.

However, the fact that the same judges adjudicate on civil as well as criminal matters has not led to a single procedure. The

---

[51] This explains why article 34 of the 1958 Constitution provides that, unlike the rules of civil procedure, those of criminal procedure are created only by Acts of Parliament. For instance, the Code of Criminal Procedure was recently reformed by Act 93-2 of January 4, 1993 (hereafter the Reform Act) which was intended, in particular, to reinforce the rights of the defence. Soon after its coming into force, it was partially amended, under the new right-wing Cabinet, by Act 93–1013 of August 24, 1993.

criminal procedure has specific characteristics in many respects. First, evidence is governed by rules which are different from those of civil procedure, not only as regards the assembling of evidence but also the general principles governing its admissibility. Secondly, in the criminal trial, like the civil trial, it is always presupposed that the defendant is identified. However, this trial may start with an *information contre X* (a judicial investigation against an unknown person), the purpose of which is to identify the perpetrator of an offence. Moreover, unlike in a civil trial, the defendant must be personally present at his trial before a criminal court (articles 410, 544 & 317 *C.P.P.*)[52] and cannot be simply represented as in civil proceedings. Thirdly, apart from the *pourvoi en révision* (appeal for reconsideration of a case on the basis of new facts), all appeals, including the *pourvoi en cassation*, have suspensive effect with regard to the enforcement of criminal judgments (articles 506 & 569 *C.P.P.*). Fourthly, as regards the enforcement of judgments, in the criminal procedure, *contrainte par corps* (imprisonment in default — of payment of a fine or of payment to the Treasury) may still be used against the defaulting person whereas, in civil and commercial procedures, this was abolished in 1867 (article 749 *C.P.P.*). Finally, the criminal proceedure is more complex than the civil procedure: it is characterised by a series of distinct and separate stages (prosecution, investigation and trial) which are carried out by different authorities (police and public prosecutors, investigating judges, adjudicating judges).

(C) SOURCES OF CRIMINAL PROCEDURE

Unlike civil procedure, criminal procedure falls within the domain of *loi* and not that of *règlements*, as provided for in article 34 of the present Constitution (see Chapter Two, above). Therefore, reforms of the criminal procedure may not be undertaken by means of *décrets*, as is the case for civil procedure (see above), but only by means of Acts of Parliament. This clearly shows how important the role and the place of criminal procedure are in the French legal system, compared to civil procedure.

---

[52] However, if the accused has escaped, he may be tried in his absence before the *cour d'assises*, by the procedure of *contumace* (described below) (art. 627 *C.P.P.*).

The *Code de procédure pénale* (*C.P.P.*) replaced the original 1808 *Code d'instruction criminelle* in 1958. It is organised in a chronological way. The preliminary title is concerned with the two available criminal actions, the *action publique* and the *action civile* (articles 1–10). Book One relates to the respective role of the police, the prosecution and the investigating bodies in the preliminary stage of criminal proceedings (articles 11–230). Book Two is concerned with the trial stage (articles 231–566). Book Three deals with two special appeals (the *pourvoi en cassation* and the *pourvoi en révision*) (articles 567–626). Book Four relates to specific procedures (articles 627–706) and Book Five to procedures for the enforcement of judgments (articles 707–802). The Code of Criminal Procedure is also divided into a first part for legislation and three parts for *règlements* (*décrets en Conseil d'Etat*, *décrets simples* and *arrêtés*).[53]

(D)   CLASSIFICATION OF OFFENCES

The classification of offences is not strictly part of criminal procedure. References to categories of offences are found not in the *Code de procédure pénale* but in article 1 of the *Code pénal*. However this classification has some influence on criminal procedure since it determines the competence of criminal courts.

Unlike in English and other continental criminal legal systems, in French criminal law a distinction is made between three, rather than two, categories of offences. Under article 1 of the Criminal Code, these are, in ascending order of gravity: *contraventions* (minor offences) — these being divided into five classes — which are tried by *tribunaux de police*; *délits* (major offences), which are tried by *tribunaux correctionnels*; and *crimes* (serious crimes), which are tried by *cours d'assises*.

(E)   CRIMINAL PROCEEDINGS

Criminal proceedings consist of several stages, *i.e.* from the moment the offence is committed to the final judgment. Of course these stages are different according to the gravity of the offence, thus influencing the length of the whole proceedings. However, following the chronological order, these proceedings

---

[53] Articles from these three parts are preceded respectively by the letters R, D and A, whereas articles from the legislative part are quoted without a letter.

are usually preceded by police enquiries and are commenced by an action by the prosecution department or by the victim himself. Then, after going through the stage of the judicial investigation,[54] they are concluded by a judgment.

(1) Prelude to the proceedings: police investigations

The police play an important role in the stage prior to when the case is referred to a court for trial. They usually intervene either before or during the judicial investigation. In the former case, their task is to provide the prosecutor with sufficient information to enable him to consider whether a prosecution should be brought or the proceedings discontinued. In the latter case, the police simply assist the investigating judge and act under his supervision (article 14 C.P.P.). Only the first case, that of the police investigation phase, will be examined here, the judicial investigation stage being considered later on.

When an offence has been reported to the police, they will carry out an *enquête* (investigation), reporting the offence, assembling evidence and searching the offender(s). In order primarily to determine the scope of police powers, a distinction is made in the Code of Criminal Procedure between two types of investigation: the *enquête préliminaire* (ordinary police investigation) and the *enquête sur infraction flagrante* (investigation in the case of a flagrant offence).

The *enquête sur infraction flagrante*
The police investigation may be an *enquête sur infraction flagrante* only where a serious crime or a major offence, punishable by imprisonment, has been committed. Under article 53 C.P.P., the offence will be considered as *flagrant* where it is being or has just been committed (*crime* or *délit flagrant*); or where, shortly after the perpetration of the offence (in practice within 36 hours), a suspect is followed by hue and cry or is found in possession of various articles, or bears traces of evidence connecting him with the offence (*crime ou délit réputé flagrant*); or, finally, where the occupier of a house, in which an offence has been committed, reports the offence to the police or

---

[54] On these pre-trial phases, see L.H. Leigh & L. Zedner, *A Report on the Administration of Criminal Justice in the Pre-trial Phase in France and Germany* (The Royal Commission on Criminal Justice, HMSO, London, 1992), pp. 3–24.

the prosecutor (*crime ou délit assimilé au crime ou délit flagrant*).

When such an offence is committed it is essential for the police to take action swiftly in order to preserve fresh evidence. For this purpose the police are granted a wide range of powers and consequently individual freedoms are less protected.

After a flagrant offence has been reported to the police, the prosecutor must be informed of it and a police officer must be sent to the scene of the crime. The role of this officer is to establish the facts and to ensure that evidence is not destroyed or tampered with. He will also seize weapons and instruments which are connected with the offence (article 54 *C.P.P.*). At this stage of the investigation the prosecutor may come to the scene of the crime and take over from the police officer unless the latter is assigned to carry on the investigation (article 68 *C.P.P.*). Under article 72 *C.P.P.*, the investigating judge, once informed, could also be present at the scene and carry out all police measures, thus relieving the police officer or the prosecutor of their responsibility. However, article 14 of the 1993 Reform Act has abolished this prerogative.

The police may proceed with all necessary *perquisitions* (searches) and *saisies* (seizures). There is no equivalent in France to the Anglo-American search warrant. However these powers are limited by rules guaranteeing individuals' rights.[55] If it is necessary to conduct technical or scientific tests, the police may call upon any expert witnesses (article 60 *C.P.P.*). Also, for the purpose of questioning witnesses, the police officer may prohibit any person from leaving the scene of the offence and call and hear any person capable of supplying information relating to the facts or objects and documents seized (article 61 *C.P.P.*).

---

[55] In the absence of demand from the occupier of the house, searches may only be undertaken between 6 a.m. and 9 p.m. except in certain public places, or in drug or terrorist cases (art. 59 *C.P.P.*). Searches must also be made in the presence of the person at whose domicile they are made, or in the presence of a representative chosen by this person, or two witnesses chosen by the police (art. 57 *C.P.P.*). Furthermore, searches effected in the firm of an *avocat* or his domicile must be led by a judge and take place in the presence of the head of the local Bar or his representative (art. 56–1 *C.P.P.*). This provision has been extended by the Reform Act to include medical practitioners, *notaires*, *avoués* and *huissiers*. Searches effected on their premises must take place in the presence of a member heading their respective professional body (art. 7 of the Act).

Persons summoned by the police are bound to appear (article 62 *C.P.P.*).[56] Finally, the range of police powers includes *garde-à-vue* (police custody) and *arrestation* (arrest). The *garde-à-vue* allows the police to hold a suspect or other persons at the police station for the purposes of their investigation. Nevertheless, the police do not have unlimited powers. Under article 41 *C.P.P.* (as amended by article 5 of the 1993 Reform Act), measures relating to custody can only be taken under the supervision of the prosecutor. Custody may also only be ordered by an *officier de police* and is limited to 24 hours (except in terrorism and drug cases where it can be extended to 48 hours).[57] The 1993 Reform Act strengthened the rights of the detainee (see articles 5–16). Under the new article 63 *C.P.P.*, the police officer must inform the prosecutor that he intends to keep someone in custody.[58] Where there is insufficient information to justify a prosecution the detainee may only be kept in custody for the period of time necessary to take his statement, not exceeding 24 hours. Where sufficient evidence may justify a prosecution procedure, the detainee must be brought, within the 24-hour period, to the prosecutor who may authorise the extension of the custody for a further 24 hours, in writing. Exceptionally this extension may be authorised by the prosecutor in a written and reasoned decision without the detainee being brought before him (article 9 of the Act). Furthermore, anyone placed in custody must be informed, in a language he understands, of his rights such as those relating to

---

[56] Under article 62(2) *C.P.P.*, witnesses were also bound to "*déposer*" (make statements). This obligation has been abolished by article 8 of the Reform Act.

[57] In 1990, 347,107 persons were held in custody (26 per cent more than in 1981) (see *Le Monde*, February 27, 1992, p. 12).

[58] It was ruled by the Court of Paris that the public prosecutor should be informed within 12 hours of the beginning of the custody, otherwise it would be declared unlawful (Trib. Paris, March 12, 1993: [1993] Gaz. Pal. 72).

The Act of August 24, 1993 abolished the obligation imposed on the police officer by the Reform Act to inform the prosecutor "immediately" of custody decisions. It simply provides that this information may be communicated "*dans les meilleurs délais*" ("in the shortest period of time"). In its decision of August 8, 1993, the Constitutional Court stressed that individual freedoms were guaranteed by the judiciary and that it was highly important that police officers should inform the public prosecutor when they place someone in custody. It ruled that if the prosecutor is not to be informed immediately for objective reasons, he must be informed "*dans les plus brefs*" ("the soonest possible") so that the rights of the person in custody are safeguarded.

The approach of the French legislator is rather regrettable and the decision of the Constitutional Court should be welcomed.

the duration of the custody; the right to request that a member of his family be informed by telephone of his custody (new article 63–2(1);[59] and the right to request a medical test (new article 63–2(3) *C.P.P.*).[60] Even more importantly, the new article 63–4 of the *C.P.P.* provides that the detainee may request to speak to a lawyer. If the detainee cannot appoint a lawyer or if the appointed lawyer cannot be contacted, the detainee may request that a lawyer be nominated by the head of the local Bar.[61]

It is the right and the duty of the police to arrest the perpetrator of a flagrant offence immediately. The latter can even be apprehended and handed over to the police by anyone (article 73 *C.P.P.*). In principle, when there is sufficient and weighty evidence, the police need do no more than bring the suspect before the prosecutor who may then request a *mandat de dépôt* (committal order) from the President of the court (article 396 *C.P.P.* as amended by article 204 of the Reform Act).

---

[59] If the police officer considers that the circumstances of the investigation require that such a right should not be granted, he must immediately refer to the prosecutor who will decide whether or not the detainee's request should be satisfied (new art. 63–2(2) *C.P.P.*).

[60] A second medical test may be requested in the case of an extension of the custody (new art. 63–3(2) *C.P.P.*), or requested by a member of the detainee's family if the detainee himself fails to do so (new art. 63–3(3) *C.P.P.*). The medical certificate shall be then added to the file (new art. 63–3(4) *C.P.P.*).

[61] This was an innovation compared to the original proposal for article 4 of the Reform Bill which did not include the right to a lawyer. This was also strongly criticised, notably amongst police forces. In the first semester of 1993, senators and members of the National Assembly agreed on the decision to deny this right from the beginning of the custody, in contrast to the situation proposed under the Reform Act — the provision of which should have come into force on January 1, 1994. From now on, a lawyer may be available only after the first 20 hours of detention, and after 36 hours in the case of *association de malfaiteurs* (conspiracy), *vol* (theft or robbery), destruction by explosives, *proxénétisme aggravé* (procuring) and *extortion de fond* (extortion).

In its decision of August 8, 1993, the Constitutional Court regarded the new Act as complying with the Constitution in all but two of its provisions regarding custody. It notably held that this right is the "... right of the defence which is exercised during the investigatory stage of the criminal procedure". As the rights of the defence have been regarded since 1976 as being a *principe fondamental reconnu par les lois de la République*, this means that this right to a lawyer during custody may no longer be questioned. The legislator is free however to limit its exercise and therefore, as is the case in the Act, permit the assistance of a lawyer only after a given period of time.

The lawyer may only interview the detainee for a limited period of time, which may not exceed 30 minutes (new art. 63–4(4) *C.P.P.*).

The *enquête préliminaire*

In the absence of a *flagrant* offence the police will, either on their own initiative or, more often, under the instructions and direction of the prosecutor, carry out an *enquête préliminaire*. This investigation has the same purpose as that previously examined, *i.e.* to provide the prosecutor with sufficient information to decide whether or not to prosecute.

In this ordinary investigation, the powers of the police include only searches and seizures, questioning and the custody of witnesses.

Searches and seizures are subject to the same rules as those previously examined. However, they may not be carried out without the express and written consent of the person on whose property the operation takes place (article 76 *C.P.P.*). Under article 77 *C.P.P.*, for the purpose of the investigation, the police may hold anyone[62] in custody for questioning.[63] The police may detain this person for more than 24 hours if there is sufficient evidence supporting a prosecution. Before the end of the period of custody the detainee must then be referred to the prosecutor who may authorise in writing[64] an extension of the custody for a further period, not exceeding 24 hours (new article 77(3) & (4) *C.P.P.* as added by article 15 of the Reform Act). The detainee also has the same rights to inform a member of his family, to a lawyer and to medical tests as in the case of *enquête sur infraction flagrante* (article 15 *in fine* of the Reform Act).

(2) Commencement of the proceedings: the *action publique* and the *action civile*

Once the police investigation has been completed the results are sent to the prosecutor who will then decide what action to take. If he decides to prosecute he will bring an *action publique*. Moreover, since in most cases an offence causes harm, the victim may join the proceedings as a civil party to seek damages by

---

[62] Even witnesses could be held in custody. The Reform Act provided that this would no longer be the case, except in the case of a *flagrant* offence. No one may be held in custody unless there are grounds for suspecting that they have committed or attempted to commit an offence (art. 15).

[63] The Reform Act provided that the prosecutor or the investigating judge should be informed immediately of any decision to hold someone in custody (*ibid.*).

[64] Previously, it was the usual policy for the prosecutor to give their authorisation after a telephone conversation with the police.

means of an *action civile*. Such a procedure being called a *constitution de partie civile*.

As will emerge from the following, both actions are considered independently since they have different grounds, purposes, parties and regimes although they are examined jointly by the same criminal court and not separately by a criminal and a civil court.

The *action publique*

According to the principle of *opportunité des poursuites* the prosecutor has considerable discretion as to whether to prosecute or not (article 40(1) *C.P.P.*). If prosecution is inappropriate or there are insufficient grounds, the prosecutor may opt to discontinue it by means of *classement sans suite*. However the prosecutor's discretion is not unlimited. Indeed, the prosecutor may be forced to initiate the prosecution by the victim, who may summon the offender to court by means of *citation directe* or may lodge a complaint with the investigating judge together with an application to join the proceedings by means of a *plainte avec constitution de partie civile*, thus, in either case, bringing a private prosecution. The prosecutor may also be ordered to bring a prosecution by his superior, the Principal Public Prosecutor of the Court of Appeal. In other exceptional cases and if the offence concerns them, the prosecution may be brought by administrative authorities such as Customs, Inland Revenue, Waterways and Forestry authorities and the Civil Engineering Department. Finally, the prosecutor cannot prosecute in cases where the privacy of the victim is at stake (for example illegal telephone tapping cases, slander or libel cases and certain family cases), until the victim has made a formal complaint.

In order to institute proceedings, the prosecutor may use two procedures: the *citation directe* and the *réquisitoire à fin d'informer* (application for judicial investigation). Where a minor or a major offence has been committed, the former allows the prosecutor to summon the accused directly to court whereas the latter is used, where a serious crime or a major offence committed in complex circumstances has been perpetrated, to transfer a case to the investigating judge. Therefore, where a judicial investigation is compulsory or necessary, the prosecutor may only use the *réquisitoire à fin d'informer*.

The public prosecution is brought in the interest of society and public policy. As a result, once the case has been referred to the court or the investigating judge by the prosecutor it cannot be dropped even if the prosecutor wishes to terminate the prosecution. Indeed article 1 *C.P.P.* entrusts the prosecutor with the task of bringing the prosecution but gives him no right to use the *action publique* as he wishes. In particular he may not plea bargain with the offender or terminate the proceedings at any time.

Under article 6 *C.P.P.*, the public prosecution may be terminated by the death of the accused, amnesty, or repeal of the criminal legislation. In such an event the *action civile* may still continue and, in the case of the death of the accused, be brought against his heirs. Where the prosecution is initiated by public services (see above), the latter may end it by agreement with the accused.[65] Moreover, where the public prosecution is instigated by the victim's formal complaint, as seen above, it may be terminated by the withdrawal of this. More usually a public prosecution is terminated either by the court's final judgment with *autorité de chose jugée* (*res judicata*) or by *prescription*,[66] *i.e.* the time-limit at the expiry of which the prosecution is barred. Unlike English law where a prosecution of an offence can begin at any time after its commission, French law provides that the offender can no longer be prosecuted once the community and the State have failed to do so within the time-limits set by law.[67]

The *action civile*

The purpose of the *action civile* (civil action) is to remedy the harm caused by the offence by awarding *dommages et intérêts* (damages), *restitutions* (restitution) and refund of the legal costs incurred by the victim.

This civil action has a dual and mixed character. As an action for damages, it is governed by the rules of civil liability,[68] but, as

---

[65] This is an important exception to the principle laid down by article 1 *C.P.P.* Unlike the prosecutor, these services may negotiate with the accused.

[66] This term has a totally different meaning from that in English law. Note that the *prescription de l'action publique* should not be confused with the *prescription des peines*, which is the time-limit for the enforceability of sentences (respectively 20, five and two years).

[67] These time-limits are 10 years for serious crimes, three years for major offences and one year for minor offences (respectively arts. 7, 8 & 9 *C.P.P.*).

[68] To be considered as a civil action in criminal proceedings, this must be an action for damages. Therefore, divorce proceedings, even if they result from assault and battery, cannot be dealt with by a criminal court.

the consequence of an offence, it may be brought before a criminal court.[69]

By definition a civil action is reserved for the victim, *i.e.* the person who has "personally suffered the harm directly caused by the offence" (article 2 *C.P.P.*). However, since the prejudice creates a pecuniary asset, which becomes part of the victim's estate, the right to sue may be transferred to the *ayants droit* (interested parties) such as the *héritiers* (heirs), the *créanciers* (creditors), the *cessionnaires* (assignees) and the *subrogés*[70] of the victim. Moreover, civil action by certain associations is admissible where provided for by law. For instance, consumer associations (Act of January 5, 1988), anti-racism, anti-sexual violence and protection of children associations (articles 2(1) to 2(12) *C.P.P.* as amended by article 1 of the Reform Act & articles 1 to 6 of the Act of December 16, 1992) have the right to sue in respect of certain offences. Trade unions also have this right (article L 411–11 *C.Trav.*).

As the *action publique* is the main action, the victim may either join the proceedings before the same criminal court, or bring a separate and distinct action before a civil court. Indeed, although the *action civile* is usually initiated in a civil court, articles 3(1) & 4(1) *C.P.P.* give the victims the option. Victims do not have unlimited choice however since, in accordance with the principle *electa una via, non datur recursus ad alteram*, under article 5 *C.P.P.* they are prohibited from bringing an action before a criminal court once they have brought one before a competent civil court, unless the public prosecution has commenced before the judgment on the merits has been delivered by the civil court. Nonetheless, they may drop the proceedings before the criminal court and institute them before the civil court. The purpose of this principle is to protect the accused who may invoke its violation at the outset of the proceedings.

If an action has been brought to the competent civil court by the victim, the decision of the court is suspended until after the conclusion of the prosecution (*le criminel tient le civil en état*) (article 4(2) *C.P.P.*) and this civil court is bound by the criminal

---

[69] Although an action for unfair competition is an action for damages, it is not regarded as a civil action in criminal proceedings since it is not the consequence of an offence.

[70] *e.g.* the right to sue the offender in place of the victim may be assigned to Social Security authorities or insurance companies which have indemnified the loss suffered by the insured victim.

decision (*autorité au civil de la chose jugée au criminel*). On the other hand, the civil court's decision is not binding on the criminal court if it has been delivered before the start of the criminal prosecution (*pas d'autorité au criminel de la chose jugée au civil*).

The *partie civile* may always terminate the civil action either by means of *transaction*, *i.e.* by coming to an agreement with the offender or by waiving the claim before (*désistement*), or after (*renonciation*) the prosecution is initiated. In such an event only the *action publique* remains. Moreover, the *action civile* may also come to an end as a result of the criminal decision or due to its own *prescription*.[71]

(3) Preparatory stage of the proceedings: the *instruction préparatoire*

The *instruction préparatoire* (judicial investigation) is the phase during which the investigatory courts, *i.e.* the *juge d'instruction* (investigating judge) and the *chambre d'accusation* (Indictment Division) have the task of assembling evidence and examining whether there are sufficient charges to commit the accused for trial. This phase may only commence after the prosecution has been initiated.

The judicial investigation is only optional where a minor offence or major offence has been committed. It is compulsory in the case of serious crime.

The investigation by the *juge d'instruction*

As provided for in article 81 *C.P.P.*, the role of the investigating judge[72] is to undertake any investigation which he deems useful for establishing the truth, whether or not this leads to a judgment as to the guilt or the innocence of the accused.

---

[71] Article 10 of the *C.P.P.* provides that a civil action shall be barred according to the rules of the Civil Code, the time-limit being 30 years. Since the Act of December 23, 1980, the *prescription* of the civil action is no longer dependent on that of the prosecution and in the event of the prosecution being barred, the civil action may only be brought before a civil court.

[72] For a critical assessment of judicial supervision in French criminal procedure, see A.S. Goldstein & M. Marcus, *The Myth of Judicial Supervision in Three "Inquisitorial" Systems*: France, Italy, Germany, (1977) Yale Law Journal 242 *et seq.*, esp. pp. 250–256; and J.H. Langbein & L.L. Weinreb, *Continental Criminal Procedure: "Myth" and Reality* (1978) Yale Law Journal 549 *et seq.*, esp. pp. 1551–1559.

The scope of his investigation is determined by the matters set out in the prosecutor's application, the *réquisitoire à fin d'informer*, but may be extended to include other matters by requesting, from the prosecutor, a *réquisitoire supplétif* (a supplementary application from the prosecutor).

The investigating judge is vested with wide powers which allow him to assemble evidence but which may also affect individual freedoms. First, he may go to the scene of the crime (*descente sur les lieux*) in order to make relevant examinations. He can also conduct searches in any place where objects and documents, which may be useful for revealing the truth, may be found (articles 92 & 94 *C.P.P.*).[73] Such objects may consequently be seized and immediately inventoried and placed under seal (article 97 *C.P.P.*).

Secondly, the investigating judge may question all persons who are likely to provide information, *i.e.* suspects, witnesses, civil parties and other persons. Witnesses and others are interviewed by means of an *audition* (articles 101–113 *C.P.P.*) for which they have to take an oath. Although, in principle, they are interviewed separately and not in the presence of the accused, the judge may wish to organise *confrontations* (confrontations) with the latter or other witnesses. However, once a suspect is *inculpé* (charged), he is interviewed by means of *interrogatoires* which are subject to more formal rules than the *auditions* so that the rights of the defence are safeguarded. Before the 1993 reform of criminal procedure, it was only from this point that a suspect could be assisted by a lawyer. Therefore a suspect had to be charged as soon as there was sufficient prima facie evidence against him and could no longer be interviewed as a witness.

In order to guarantee the presumption of innocence, the Reform Act replaced *"inculpation"* (which etymologically carries a connotation of guilt) with a procedure which separates the exercise of the rights of the defence from the notification of the charges. Where there are *"indices graves et concordants"* (weighty and concordant evidence) (new article 80–1 as added by article 23 of the Act), the suspect is *"mis en examen"* (placed under judicial investigation) and may not be heard as a witness (new article 80–2 *C.P.P.*). It is from the start of the *mise en examen* stage that the suspect may use his full defence rights,

---

[73] These searches are subject to the same safeguards as those which apply to police investigations in the case of flagrant offences (see above).

in particular, that of legal assistance.[74] It is only when the investigating judge considers that the investigation has come to an end that he will inform the *"personne mise en examen"*, in the presence of his lawyer, of the *"présomptions de charges constitutives d'infractions pénales"* (alleged charges relating to a criminal offence) against him, at which point the person charged may make comments which will be recorded (new article 80–3(1) *C.P.P.*). Under previous articles 114 & 115 *C.P.P.*, during the first interview, known as *interrogatoire de première comparution* (first examination),[75] the suspect would be told of the charges against him and informed of his right to remain silent and to be assisted by a lawyer, the latter then being notified in advance of all subsequent interviews that he should attend. Under the amended article 114, parties may not be *"entendues, interrogées ou confrontées"* (heard, questioned or confronted) without their lawyer being present unless they have expressly renounced this right. During the *première comparution* the investigating judge will establish the identity of the prosecuted person and inform him of the facts to be investigated[76] (article 116 *C.P.P.* as amended by article 34 of the Reform Act). At this point, the judge will start the *interrogatoire*. The lawyers for the defence and those of the civil parties will have constant access to the file, at least within the four working days preceding the *première comparution* or *première audition* (article 114(3) *C.P.P.* as amended by article 32 of the Reform Act). Previously, under article 118 *C.P.P.* (abolished by article 37 of the Act) this was only possible within two days before the *interrogatoire*. The legislator has also prohibited the handcuffing of an arrested person unless this person is regarded as being dangerous to others or himself, or is likely to escape (new article 803 *C.P.P.* added by article 60 of the Act).

Thirdly, in cases which raise an issue of a technical nature, such as medical, ballistic and handwriting aspects of a case, the judge may order an *expertise* (expert's report) (articles 156–167 *C.P.P.*).

---

[74] One can no longer talk of *"inculpé"* but of a *"personne mise en examen"*.

[75] This term is misleading since the person has been interviewed previously as a suspect. It must be understood as being his first interview as an accused.

[76] Note again the change of the vocabulary used: *"chacun des faits dont il est saisi"* ("the facts to be investigated") now replaces *"chacun des faits qui lui sont imputés"* ("the facts which implicate him [the person charged]"), thereby emphasising the presumption of innocence of the prosecuted person.

As is evident from the above, the investigating judge has a serious and complex task. This is facilitated however by powers which directly affect individual freedoms. For example, by issuing a variety of *mandats* (warrants) he may secure the attendance of the person charged or those persons he wishes to interview (articles 122 *et seq. C.P.P.* as amended by article 59 of the Reform Act). First, by means of a *mandat de comparution* (summons to appear, or warrant for appearance) which is issued in the simple form of a letter and served by a *huissier* or a police constable, he may require the addressee to appear before him at a specified place and time. As such a warrant is not enforceable, it might prove ineffective, in which case the police will be ordered, by means of *mandat d'amener*, to bring the person concerned before the judge. Secondly, the investigating judge may consider it necessary to deprive the accused of his liberty and order his *détention provisoire* (pre-trial detention), in which case he will issue a *mandat de dépôt* (committal or confinement warrant) ordering the prison governor to keep the person concerned in custody (article 122(4) *C.P.P.*). Where the *inculpé* or, according to the new terminology, the *"personne à l'encontre de laquelle le mandat est décerné"* ("the person against whom the warrant is issued") (article 122 *C.P.P.* as amended by article 59(II) of the Reform Act) cannot be found, or lives abroad, a *mandat d'arrêt* (warrant of arrest) ordering the police to seek him out, arrest him and produce him at a specified jail (article 122(5) *C.P.P.*) may be used, thus combining the effects of the *mandat d'amener* and the *mandat de dépôt*. Although it results from one of these two warrants, the *détention provisoire* may only be ordered after an *ordonnance de mise en détention provisoire* (detention order), stating the reasons for the detention, has been issued. Moreover, before placing the accused in pre-trial detention, the investigating judge must hold an *audience de cabinet* (session in his chambers) in order to hear the arguments of the prosecution and the accused. Due to its gravity, such detention may only be ordered in the case of serious crimes and major offences punishable by at least two years imprisonment (article 144 *C.P.P.*), and may not exceed one year with respect to the former offences and four months in respect of the latter (articles 145–1 & 145–2 *C.P.P.*).[77] This

---

[77] However, although this detention is supposed to be *provisoire* (temporary), the period of detention may be unlimited in respect of serious crimes and over a year in respect of major offences, as a result of successive extensions.

power of pre-trial detention is considerable and is used extensively by French judges.[78]

In 1970 the procedure of *contrôle judiciaire* (judicial or pre-trial supervision) was created to limit the number of pre-trial detentions by restricting, rather than removing, a person's liberty. Such measures, which may be ordered only if the accused faces imprisonment, require him to comply with a number of conditions laid down in article 138 *C.P.P.* (*e.g.* the obligation not to leave territorial limits determined by the judge; to present himself to authorities designated by the judge; to hand over his passport to the police, etc.). However, the investigating judge may issue a warrant for pre-trial detention where the accused has intentionally breached the conditions of the pre-trial supervision (article 141–2 *C.P.P.*).

Although the investigating judge is vested with wide-ranging powers, he will not always exercise them in person. Indeed, he is usually in charge of a number of cases at any one time and cannot take all the necessary measures himself. This is why he may delegate some of his powers, by means of *commissions rogatoires*, either to another judge (any judge of his court or any other investigating judge) or, more often, to a police officer (articles 151–155 *C.P.P.*).

As soon as the investigation appears to be complete, the investigating judge must inform the parties and their lawyers. These have then 20 days to request any further medical or

---

[78] Indeed, on January 1, 1992, 40 per cent of France's prison population was in pre-trial detention (see February 27, 1992: [1992] *Le Monde* 12).

Pre-trial detention has been the subject of a number of reforms since the adoption of the original *Code d'instruction criminelle*. Amongst the most recent ones, the 1984 and 1989 Acts have introduced new formal rules with the view to limiting its scope. Article 57 of the 1993 Reform Act further provided that the decision to place someone in detention or to extend the period of detention should be taken by a *chambre d'examen des mises en détentions provisoires* consisting of a judge from the *tribunal de grande instance* and two other judges (thus excluding the investigating judge) and to which the investigating judge had to refer every time he wished to order a detention or to extend an existing detention.

Under this Act, investigating judges had been deprived of some of these important powers. This led to a wave of discontent amongst them and some judges asked the Ministry of Justice to discharge them from the function of investigating judge. This movement which started in the court of Strasbourg (see January 10–11, 1993: [1993] *Le Monde* 9) extended to the judges of Paris (see January 13, 1993: [1993] *Le Monde* 13) and has affected 120 out of 550 judges (see January 26, 1993: [1993] *Le Monde* 1, 10).

Their powers were restored under the Act of August 24, 1993.

psychological tests or relevant measures (under article 81(9) C.P.P.), further investigation (under article 82(1) C.P.P.), other experts' opinion (under article 156(1) C.P.P.), or to challenge before the Indictment Division any act of procedure they deem to be invalid (under article 156(3) C.P.P.). At the end of this period of time the judge will issue an *ordonnance de soit-communiqué* by which he communicates the investigation file to the prosecutor (article 175 C.P.P. as amended by Act 93–1013 of August 24, 1993). The prosecutor must then reply — within one month if the accused is in detention or three months in other cases — with his *réquisitoire*. This may be either *supplétif* (a supplementary application) if he requests further investigation, or *définitif* (a final application), in which case he indicates what further action must be taken. The prosecutor's application is not binding on the judge who, after he has received it or after the time-limit has expired, will issue an *ordonnance de règlement* or *de clôture* (closing order), thus putting an end to his investigation. If the judge reckons that there are insufficient grounds for prosecution, he issues an *ordonnance de non-lieu* (discharge order)[79] in which case any accused person in pre-trial detention must be released (article 177 C.P.P.). If he decides that the facts constitute a minor or a major offence, he will refer the case to a competent court by means of an *ordonnance de renvoi* (committal for trial order). With respect to serious crimes, the case is transferred, by means of an *ordonnance de transmission* (file transfer order), without delay via the prosecutor to the Indictment Division of the Court of Appeal for further examination and final decision (article 181 C.P.P.) (see below).

From this description of the investigation procedure, the impression might be that, given the wide powers of the judge, it

---

[79] In order to avoid protracted and futile proceedings, the new art. 175–1 (added by art. 41 of the Reform Act) provides that any *personne mise en examen*, or civil party, may request the investigating judge to refer the case to a trial court or to drop the case one year after the commencement of the *mise en examen* or after the *constitution de partie civile*. The judge will then have one month in which to make a reasoned decision; if he fails to do so, the parties may then take the case to the Indictment Division directly which then has 20 days in which to make a decision.

It has to be noted that out of 73,649 *inculpations* in 1990, 7,762 (*i.e.* 11.12 per cent) were ended by a *non-lieu* (see December 23, 1992: [1992] *Le Monde* 10).

is more favourable to the prosecution than to the accused. However, appeals to the Indictment Division against most of the orders of the investigating judge[80] are available to the accused (article 186(1) *C.P.P.*). The civil party can also appeal against the judge's *ordonnance de non-informer* (order not to investigate) or against an *ordonnance de non-lieu* (article 186(2) *C.P.P.*). The scope of the prosecutor's appeal is the widest since he can challenge any orders which have been made (article 185 *C.P.P.*).[81]

Furthermore, under article 83(2) *C.P.P.* (as amended by article 19 of the Reform Act), when the case is deemed to be serious and complex the investigating judge may, following a decision of the President of the court, be joined by one or more investigating judges, either from the start of the investigation or, at his request, at any time during it.

The investigation by the *chambre d'accusation*

The role of the Indictment Division is not only to hear appeals against orders of the investigating judge or to examine the regularity of the proceedings before him but also to re-investigate cases concerning serious crimes, whether there is an appeal or not.

On appeal and annulment the Indictment Division has extensive powers and discretion since it may examine not only the specific issue submitted to it but the whole case. These powers include the following. First, it may decide to release the accused (article 201(2) *C.P.P.*). Secondly, it may order new investigations with respect to the principal or related offences which appear from the investigation file but have not been considered by the investigating judge (article 202 *C.P.P.*), and therefore extend the scope of the prosecution to these offences (article 204 *C.P.P.*). Thirdly, it may order any *acte d'information complémentaire* (supplementary investigative measure) that it deems useful and which the investigating judge refused to

---

[80] These are exhaustively listed in article 186 *C.P.P.* Appeals are available against orders relating to the judge's jurisdiction, admissibility of *constitution de partie civile*, pre-trial detention or judicial supervision.

[81] The appeal must be lodged by means of a declaration to the *greffe* of the court, within five (prosecutor's appeal) or 10 (other appeals) days of notification of the judge's order. The investigation file is then transmitted to the Principal Prosecutor of the Court of Appeal who will submit it to the Indictment Division.

order[82] (article 201(1) *C.P.P.*) or a *supplément d'information* (supplementary investigation)[83] (article 205 *C.P.P.*). Fourthly, it may reverse an order of the investigating judge against which an appeal lies, in which case it may either *évoquer le dossier, i.e.* keep the file and continue the investigation,[84] or remit it to the same or another investigating judge (article 207(2) *C.P.P.*). Fifthly, it can pronounce the nullity of all or part of the proceedings where these are tainted with irregularities, in which case it has the same choice as above to continue the investigation (article 206 *C.P.P.*). Finally, in cases where it hears appeals against a closing order or where it decides to continue the investigation, the Indictment Division must examine whether there are sufficient charges against the accused and then order the closure of the investigation.

Where a serious crime has been committed and the investigating judge is convinced that its perpetrator is guilty, the case must be referred to the Indictment Division by means of *ordonnance de transmission* (see above). The investigating judge cannot commit the accused for trial directly before the Court of Assize. Due to the gravity of such a decision, the case must be re-examined by a higher court. Only the Indictment Court, after completing its investigation, is competent to decide whether or not to commit the accused for trial. After examination of the case it will deliver one of the following decisions: an *arrêt de non-lieu* (discharge) if there are no grounds for a trial (article 212 *C.P.P.*); an *arrêt de renvoi* (committal for trial), by which it remits the case to the police court or the *tribunal correctionnel* if it considers that the facts constitute a minor or a major offence (article 215 *C.P.P.*); or an *arrêt de mise en accusation* (committal for trial on indictment), by which the accused[85] is committed for trial at the Court of Assize (article 215 *C.P.P.*). In addition to the latter decision, it

---

[82] For instance, it may require the investigating judge to order a *contre-expertise* (second expert's report verifying the first one).

[83] Such further investigation includes a number of different measures which are useful for establishing the truth. The investigation is conducted, in accordance with the same provisions as the prior investigation, either by a member of the Division or by an investigating judge who has been appointed for that purpose.

[84] However, this cannot be the case as regards pre-trial detention where the file must be returned, without delay, to the investigating judge (art. 207(1) *C.P.P.*).

[85] The *inculpé* (accused) (or the *personne mise en examen* in the new terminology) is then called *accusé* (accused).

may issue an *ordonnance de prise de corps* (arrest order) in order to ensure the appearance of the accused in court. This is used if the accused did not comply with the conditions of the judicial supervision or did not appear before the President of the Court of Assize for questioning prior to the hearing (article 215(2) *C.P.P.*).

Judgments of the Indictment Division may be challenged before the Court of Cassation although, under articles 574 & 575 *C.P.P.*, such appeals are limited to certain cases and subject to specific conditions.

(4) The trial

Whereas the police and the judicial investigations must be in some respects secret as they require discretion, once the criminal case is ready for trial the inquisitorial procedure gives way to the accusatorial one. Such was the intention of the draftsmen of the *Code d'instruction criminelle* as well as those of the *Code de procédure criminelle*. This accusatorial dimension was also particularly emphasised by the reformers of the Code of Criminal Procedure in 1992 when they reduced the inquisitorial role of the judge.[86]

Indeed, as mentioned above in the introduction to this chapter, the three characteristics of the accusatorial system can be found in the criminal trial phase: the procedure is oral,[87] public[88] and *contradictoire*.

---

[86] Notably, under article 83 of the 1993 Reform Act, which amended article 309 *C.P.P.*, the presiding judge no longer had the leading role in a trial and could be compared to an umpire of the Common Law model.

[87] The so-called *principle of oralité des débats* is strictly applied in the Court of Assize. The court makes a judgment on the basis of the evidence which has been produced. Article 331(3) *C.P.P.* provides that witnesses shall testify orally (the same rule applies to hearings in the Police Court and the *tribunal correctionnel* (arts. 452 & 536 *C.P.P.*)). Furthermore, article 347 *C.P.P.* provides that the case file shall not be produced in the deliberation room unless it is deemed necessary to re-examine parts of the proceedings, in which case it is re-opened in the presence of the prosecutor, the counsels of the accused and the civil party. However, with respect to the *tribunal correctionnel*, in practice it may make a decision mainly on the basis of documentary evidence.

[88] Criminal trials are open to the public unless *huis clos* has been ordered for reasons of public policy or public morality (art. 306 *C.P.P.*). Hearings may also, under certain conditions, be reported in the press (arts. 308 *C.P.P.* & 226 *C.P.P.*).

The trial at the Court of Assize

The President of the Court of Assize plays an important role during the trial since he is responsible for maintaining order in the Court and guaranteeing that nothing affects the dignity of the trial and he conducts the trial (article 309 *C.P.P.*). Furthermore, he is vested with discretionary powers which permit him to take any measure that he believes useful for the discovery of the truth (article 310 *C.P.P.*). [89]

The trial is divided into two stages: the *instruction définitive* (final investigation), and the *plaidoiries* (oral arguments) and the *réquisitoire* of the *ministère public* (address by the prosecutor to the court).

The trial begins with the *interrogatoire* (questioning) of the accused with regard to his identity (article 294 *C.P.P.*). [90] The President of the Court then ascertains that the parties concerned, the witnesses, [91] experts and interpreters are all present at the hearing. The hearing itself begins with the accused being questioned and heard by the President of the Court. The latter must not indicate his opinion as to the guilt or not of the accused (article 328 C.P.P). [92]

After the questioning of the accused, the witnesses testify, by means of *dépositions*, separately from each other in an order established by the President. Once the oath is taken, they must "speak without hatred and without fear, to tell the whole truth and nothing but the truth" [93] (article 331 *C.P.P.*). [94] In principle, *témoins à charge* (witnesses for the prosecution) are heard before *témoins à décharge* (witnesses for the defence). The President of the Court may question the witnesses after each

---

[89] Under this provision he may, in particular, hear all persons who are not listed as witnesses and whose statements are considered only to be general information, or he may have new evidence admitted.

[90] Under article 328 *C.P.P.* as amended by article 86 of the Reform Act, character could be the subject of this questionning only after the facts of the case with which the accused is charged. It was intended to avoid the statement of character influencing the assessment of guilt in relation to the facts. However this was abolished under the Act of August 24, 1993.

[91] Witnesses then withdraw into a separate room.

[92] The Reform Act provided that the accused could be questioned in turn by the prosecutor, the civil party's counsel and the defence counsel.

[93] *"de parler sans haine et sans crainte, de dire toute la vérité, rien que la vérité"*.

[94] Article 331(5) *C.P.P.* provided that the witnesses could testify only on either the facts charged against the accused or on his character and morals. This was abolished by article 87(III) of the Reform Act but re-established by the Act of August 24, 1993.

testimony (article 328(1) C.P.P.), as may, through the intermediary of the President, the public prosecutor, the defence counsel(s) and the counsel(s) of the civil party(ies), the accused and civil parties (article 328(2) C.P.P.). *Assesseurs* (the two judges other than the presiding one) and jurors must request permission from the President if they wish to question the witnesses or the accused (article 311 C.P.P.).[95]

Expert witnesses are also heard but unlike ordinary witnesses, they may consult written documents, *i.e.* their reports and annexes (article 168 C.P.P.).

This phase of investigation usually takes place over more than one hearing. When it is completed the civil party's counsel (when there is one) presents final arguments and the public prosecutor addresses the Court prior to the counsel for the defence being heard (articles 346(1) & (2) C.P.P.). The civil party is then permitted a *réplique* (reply) as is the prosecutor, but the accused or the defence counsel always has the last word (article 346(3)). The President then officially declares the hearing to be at an end (article 347 C.P.P.).[96] At this point, and prior to the Court and the jurors retiring to *déliberer*, *i.e.* discuss the case, the presiding judge orders the investigation file to be deposited with the *greffier* of the Court of Assize.[97] For the purpose of the *délibérations* however, he may retain the committal order delivered by the Indictment Division (article 347(3)). Finally, he reads out the questions — on guilt, the facts set out in the committal order and aggravating circumstances (article 349 C.P.P.) — to be answered by the Court and the jury (article 348 C.P.P.)[98] as well as the rule on *intime conviction* (inner

---

[95] Under the Reform Act a more accusatorial approach had been adopted but without introducing the techniques of examination (*interrogatoire en chef*) and cross-examination (*contre-interrogatoire*). The presiding judge lost his leading role in the questioning of the witnesses who could now be directly questioned in turn by the prosecutor, defence counsels and civil parties' counsels. It is regrettable that these amendments were repealed before they came into force by the Act of August 24, 1993.

[96] Unlike in the English criminal procedure, the presiding judge cannot sum up the arguments to the jury (art. 347(2) C.P.P.).

[97] If during the *délibérations* the presiding judge deems it necessary to re-examine one or more parts of the file, he may order it to be brought and re-open it in the presence of the parties' counsels and the public prosecutor (art. 347(4)).

[98] The presiding judge is under no obligation to read them out when they are stated in the committal order or when the accused or the defence counsel do not wish them to be read.

certainty) laid down in article 353 of the Code of Criminal Procedure.[99]

So far it has been assumed that the person being tried was present in court. However, it may happen that an accused does not surrender to law, in which case he is tried in the Court of Assize under the special procedure of *contumace* (articles 627–641 *C.P.P.*). The defaulting accused, called the *contumax*, is tried without a jury on the basis of documentary evidence alone. The accused has no right to legal representation. This procedure is therefore written and not *contradictoire*. If the accused is convicted, as is usually the case in practice, his goods are confiscated and secured (article 633 *C.P.P.*) and once the judgment of conviction is made public, the convicted person is subject to any deprivation of rights provided for by law (article 635 *C.P.P.*). The *contumax* cannot appeal by way of *cassation* (article 636 *C.P.P.*). If he surrenders or is arrested before the prescription of the sentence, the judgment of conviction is annulled and the case is tried according to the ordinary procedure. This procedure is called *purge par contumace* (article 639 *C.P.P.*).

The trial at the *tribunal correctionnel* and the *tribunal de police*

Before the *tribunal correctionnel* the trial is less formal and complex than before the Court of Assize. Once the President has established, under article 406 *C.P.P.*, the identity of the accused, checked that the parties concerned and the witnesses are present and informed the Court of the *acte saisissant le tribunal* (the issue before the court), evidence is produced and debated. As in the Court of Assize, the questioning of the accused, known as *prévenu*, is conducted by the presiding judge throughout the hearing (article 442 *C.P.P.*).[1] Official reports and experts' reports are read out, witnesses are heard and the *pièces à conviction* (objects produced in evidence) are produced. On rare occasions the court may even order *transport sur les lieux* (visit to the

---

[99] Under this rule, judges assess the evidence produced as their own conscience dictates. Their sentence will depend on whether they believe that the accused is guilty or not.

[1] Again, under article 94 of the 1993 Reform Act, this stage of the trial would have been conducted in a more accusatorial manner. This was repealed under the Act of August 24, 1993 (art. 28).

scene of the offence), expert reports or supplementary investigations (articles 434, 456, & 463 *C.P.P.*). At the end of this stage the civil party is heard, the prosecution addressed to the court and the defence presented, each party having the right to reply (article 460 *C.P.P.*). The judgment is then given either at the same or at a later hearing (article 462 *C.P.P.*).

The trial proceedings at the Police Court are quite similar to those described above but swifter. Furthermore, in order to deal with the increasing number of minor offences, the need for a judgment has been abolished in order to avoid the courts being overwhelmed. First, by means of the *procédure simplifiée* (simplified procedure), which applies to the majority of minor offences, the prosecutor may request the judge to deliver an *ordonnance pénale* (criminal order) without a prior hearing (articles 524 *et seq. C.P.P.*). In the case of conviction the accused will either serve the sentence or appeal against the order by means of *opposition* (see below). Secondly, the procedure of the *amende forfaitaire* (standard fine) is even more expeditious since it allows a swift payment of fines to the police, notably in cases of traffic offences, without the need for a judge to intervene (articles 529 *et seq. C.P.P.*).

(5) Judgments and sentences

Judgments

As in civil procedure, criminal judgments must of course be considered before they are delivered, whether the court consists of a single judge or a Bench of judges. In the Court of Assize *déliberations* start immediately after the closure of the hearing and are conducted without interruption until a decision is reached. In the Police Court and the *tribunal correctionnel*, these are not subject to a time-limit and may take place immediately after the hearing, in which case the decision is delivered *sur le siège, i.e.* during the sitting. In more complex cases however, the court retires to consider the case *en chambre du conseil* (in camera) in which case its President informs the parties of the date on which the judgment will be rendered. The case is then said to be *mis en délibéré* (reserved or adjourned for further consideration). Judgments must be given in open court even in cases where the trial took place *in camera*. Apart from those of the Court of Assize, which are based on a verdict, judgments must also, as with civil judgments, state the reasons on which they are based. The ruling must set out the offences which the person(s) mentioned are declared guilty of or liable for as well as the sentence and civil liability (article 485(3) C.P.P.).

French criminal trials end either in an acquittal or an exemption from punishment or, more often, in a conviction. An acquittal is called *"acquittement"* in the Court of Assize and *"relaxe"* in the other courts. In both cases, the prosecution is deemed to be ill-founded and dismissed. If the accused was in custody, release is immediately ordered (articles 367 & 471 C.P.P.). In the case of *acquittement*, the person acquitted may not be accused again on the same facts (article 368 C.P.P.) whereas a decision of *relaxe* may be reversed on appeal. Moreover, in the case of acquittal, the victim cannot, in principle, be awarded damages by the criminal court which is then deemed to be incompetent to decide on the *action civile*.[2]

The criminal court may decide on an *absolution*,[3] by which the accused is considered guilty but is exempted from punishment on statutory grounds (*excuses absolutoires*): for example, where a person convicted of acts of terrorism or conspiracy has prevented their commission (articles 101 & 463(1) C.P.P.). Furthermore, in the case of minor or major offences and if the penalty is imprisonment, the accused may benefit from a *dispense de peine* which is a judicial act of clemency where there is a finding of guilt but no punishment is imposed. Such a dispensation may be granted where the rehabilitation of the accused is accomplished, the harm caused is compensated and the trouble resulting from the offence has ceased (article 469(2) C.P.P.). Unlike the case of acquittal, the accused bears the costs of the trial and may be sentenced to pay damages to the civil party (articles 372 & 468 C.P.P.).

In most cases, there will be a decision of *condamnation* (conviction and sentence) by which the court establishes the guilt of the accused and determines the sentence to be served. Such a judgment enables the criminal court to award damages to the civil party (articles 371 & 464 C.P.P.).[4] The accused is no

---

[2] However, under article 372 C.P.P., the Court of Assize may award damages to the victim where the facts of the charge show that the accused was at fault. Alternatively, the accused may be awarded damages against the civil party (arts. 371 & 472 C.P.P.).

[3] Or an *exemption de peine* according to the new terminology introduced under the Act of December 16, 1992.

[4] In the Court of Assize the jury does not participate in the ruling on damages.

longer sentenced to pay the costs of the case to the State (articles 366(3) & 473 *C.P.P.* as amended by articles 126 & 128 of the 1993 Reform Act), but he will be sentenced to pay the costs of the civil party where these are not covered by the State (articles 375 & 475 as amended by articles 127 & 129 of the 1993 Act). However, the court must determine these costs fairly and take into account the economic situation of the accused (*ibid.*).

Sentences

Apart from the case of absolution and *dispense de peine*, a *condamnation* entails a *peine* (sentence, penalty or punishment). This *peine* will be either a *peine criminelle*, a *peine correctionnelle* or a *peine de police*, according to the category of offence committed. These different sentences may themselves be subdivided into the following categories.

First, an offence always entails a *peine principale* (principal penalty) which is automatically accompanied by a *peine accessoire* (ancillary penalty). The latter need not be mentioned expressly in the sentence and its purpose is mainly to ensure the efficacy of the former. A *peine complémentaire* (additional penalty), either mandatory or optional, may also be imposed but in express terms only.[5] Secondly, the *peines criminelles* are divided into *peines afflictives et infamantes* and *peines infamantes*. While the former have both physical (*afflictif*) and dishonouring (*infamant*) effects on the person, the latter is a dishonouring penalty only. Thirdly, penalties for crimes may also be either *perpétuelles* (for life) or *temporaires* (for a fixed term).

However, these classifications do not cover all sentences and it is more convenient to distinguish between those sentences which have physical effects on a person and those which affect his rights. Apart from the death penalty, which was abolished by the Act of October 9, 1981, the first category includes the *peines privatives de liberté* (custodial sentences) and the *peines restrictives de liberté* (penalties restricting liberty). Custodial sentences for serious crimes are the *réclusion criminelle* — which is either *à perpétuité* (life imprisonment) or *à temps* (fixed-term imprisonment) (article 7 *C.P.P.*) — and the *détention criminelle à perpétuité* (life detention) or *à temps*

---

[5] Therefore, if the judge neglects to mention it in the sentence, unlike the *peine accessoire*, the *peine complémentaire obligatoire* will not be enforceable.

(fixed-term detention) — which is a political sentence[6] with the same legal effects as the *réclusion*. The sentence punishing major crimes is called *emprisonnement correctionnel* — which is, in principle, for up to ten years.[7] In the case of a *peine restrictive de liberté*, the convicted person is not kept in custody but forbidden to reside in certain areas (*interdiction de séjour*).[8]

The second category includes *peines privatives de droits* (sentences entailing loss of rights) such as the *interdiction légale* (where the convict may only exercise his property rights through a guardian),[9] and the *dégradation civique* (loss of civic rights).[10] Also included in this category are *peines pécuniaires* (pecuniary sentences) which affect property either by means of an *amende* (fine) or a *jour-amende*[11] or by means of *confiscation* (confiscation).

When fixing sentences the French judge, like his English counterpart, may of course take into account any *circonstances aggravantes* (aggravating circumstances) which are all defined by statute; or any *excuses atténuantes* (statutorily defined mitigating factors) as well as any *circonstances atténuantes* (extenuating circumstances) which are discretionnarily defined by the court.

As in English law, sentences may be wholly or partly suspended by means of *sursis*. This may be a *sursis simple* or a *sursis avec mise à l'épreuve*. The *sursis simple* is applicable to sentences of imprisonment or fines for serious crimes or major offences, as well as for most serious minor offences (*contraventions de 5ème classe*). It may be granted provided that during

---

[6] As opposed to non-political sentences called *peines de droit commun*.

[7] However, since 1975, non-custodial sentences called *peines de substitution* may be imposed instead of imprisonment. These can consist either of a fine, or in the withdrawal of driving and other licences, or in the disqualification from certain professional activities, or in the seizure of a car, etc.; and since 1983, in the *travail d'intérêt général* (community service).

[8] *Bannissement, i.e.* the prohibition of a French criminal from residing in France, is no longer imposed. Such a sentence would violate article 3 of the fourth protocol of the European Convention on Human Rights.

[9] This is an ancillary penalty for non-political, serious crimes.

[10] This expression must not be confused with the *interdiction de certain droits civiques* which is a *peine correctionnelle* and not a *peine criminelle*. Furthermore, in the case of *interdiction civique*, the convict is deprived of all his civil rights and not of only some of them.

[11] Created in 1983 on the German and Austrian models this fine, the amount of which may never be above FF 2,000, is to be paid daily for up to 360 days. Failure to pay entails imprisonment for half the number of unpaid fine-days.

the five years preceding the matter the offender has not been convicted of a non-political serious crime or a major offence. The *sursis avec mise à l'épreuve* (also called *probation*) is a conditional suspension of the sentence by which the offender is subject, for not less than six months and not more than three years, to certain obligations, to supervision and social control. Such suspension may only be granted in the case of prison sentences for non-political, serious crimes or major offences. This *sursis* is closely related to the English law idea of probation, although it only applies as a means of suspending other sentences and not as a way of replacing them.

(6) *Voies de recours*

Apart from the *tierce opposition* criminal appeals are similar to civil appeals. Therefore, it is only necessary to stress the particularities inherent to criminal law.

The *appel*

An *appel* may be lodged with the *chambre des appels correctionnels* of the Court of Appeal against judgments of the *tribunal correctionnel* and those of the Police Court by the prosecutor, the accused, the civil party, or the Principal Public Prosecutor of the Court of Appeal (articles 496 & 546 *C.P.P.*).[12] On the other hand, judgments of the Court of Assize are not appealable.

The *opposition*

Where a default judgment has been passed, the accused or the civil party may challenge it by means of *opposition*. This appeal is only available against judgments of the *tribunal correctionnel* and the Police Court. With respect to those of the Court of Assize, another different procedure, the *purge de contumace* (see above) is used. As a result of the *opposition*, the enforcement of the challenged judgment is suspended (*effet suspensif*). Furthermore, *opposition* may entail the annulment of the judgment challenged (*effet extinctif*), the case being re-examined by the same court as that which delivered the first decision. This court may either confirm its first decision or amend it by reducing or increasing the sentence.

---

[12] Appeals must be lodged within 10 days (art. 498 *C.P.P.*). By way of exception, the Principal Public Prosecutor has two months to do so (art. 505 *C.P.P.*).

Opposition must be lodged within 10 days if the accused lives in France — or within two months if he lives abroad — from where the judgment is served on him (article 491 *C.P.P.*).

The *pourvoi en cassation*

Any party who has an interest has the right to lodge a *pourvoi en cassation* in order to challenge any procedural irregularities carried out by the criminal court (for example the court's lack of competence, *ultra vires*, wrong application of the criminal law, etc.). Appeals by way of *cassation* are only available against judgments delivered *en dernier ressort*, *i.e.* those which are not challengeable before a Court of Appeal, and — under complex conditions laid down in articles 574 & 575 *C.P.P.* — against the decisions of the Indictment Division.[13]

There are two other cases in which a *pourvoi en cassation* may be lodged. In the interest of the administration of justice the *procureur général*, attached to the Court of Cassation, may challenge a criminal decision of a lower court where it is manifestly in contradiction with the case-law of the Court of Cassation, provided that the decision concerned has not been previously challenged within the time-limit of an appeal in cassation, or is not challengeable in the Court of Cassation (article 621 *C.P.P.*). Similarly he may, on the orders of the Minister of Justice, challenge decisions as well as non-judicial acts of the courts — such as the irregular composition of the jury — with a view to obtaining their annulment.

The *pourvoi en révision*

Through the *pourvoi en révision*,[14] a criminal case may be re-examined and re-tried for the benefit of the convicted person in the event of judicial mistake. Article 622 *C.P.P.* provides four situations in which such a request may be made:

— when, after a conviction for homicide, evidence appears that indicates that the supposed victim is still alive; or
— when, after conviction for a serious crime or major offence, another accused has been convicted of the same act and

---

[13] A *pourvoi en cassation* must be lodged within five days and, according to the various situations provided for by article 568 *C.P.P.*, either from the date of the judgment or after it has been served or from the day where an appeal by way of *opposition* is no longer available.

[14] This is a similar application to the *recours en révision* in civil procedure (see above).

where the two convictions are irreconcilable, their contradiction is proof of the innocence of one or other of the convicted persons; or

— when, after conviction, one of the witnesses has been prosecuted and convicted for false testimony against the accused; or

— when, after conviction, new facts or evidence unknown at the time of the trial is produced or revealed so as to create doubt about the guilt of the accused.

The *révision* may be initiated at the request of the Minister of Justice, the convict or his legal representative, and, after his death, his wife, children, relatives and legatees. The request is lodged with a commission of five judges of the Court of Cassation which acts as an investigating body (article 623 *C.P.P.*). It may at any time order the enforcement of the conviction judgment to be suspended. If the request appears to be admissible, the commission transfers it to the Criminal Division of the Court of Cassation. This Division, which sits as a *cour de révision*, will annul the conviction judgment if it declares the request admissible and consider whether it is possible to proceed to a new trial, in which event the case is remitted to another court of the same rank as the one which delivered the annulled judgment (article 625 *C.P.P.*). Apart from annulling the conviction, the ruling by which the innocence of the convicted person is established, may include an award of damages for the prejudice caused by the conviction (article 626 *C.P.P.*).

6. ADMINISTRATIVE PROCEDURE

(A) DEFINITION OF ADMINISTRATIVE PROCEDURE

Administrative procedure or *contentieux administratif* includes those rules applicable to litigation which involve the administration and are brought for settlement before administrative courts. In this respect, litigation dealt with by ordinary courts is not covered by rules of administrative procedure.[15]

---

[15] Part of the activities of the administration fall within the jurisdiction of ordinary courts (*e.g.* public services governed by private law, protection of individual rights and freedoms and express legislative provisions).

Being a branch of general administrative law, the *contentieux administratif* deals only with the rules governing the organisation of administrative courts and their operation. Having already examined the courts' structure in Chapter Three, the emphasis here will be placed on the internal working of the courts.

(B) GENERAL FEATURES OF ADMINISTRATIVE PROCEDURE

As has been mentioned previously, unlike civil and criminal procedures, administrative procedure is predominantly inquisitorial, thus vesting administrative judges with wide powers to conduct the proceedings. [16]

Administrative procedure is also mainly written. The parties' arguments are first expressed in writing by means of *mémoires*. Even during the hearings the parties may only raise arguments which have been previously mentioned in their *mémoires*. As a result of the written character of the procedure judges make their judgments on the basis of documents contained in the file. These documents must be in French.

Modelled on the operation of the French administration, administrative proceedings are mostly characterised by secrecy. The investigation phase is not public and only the persons concerned may have access to the file. Hearings of administrative courts are only held in public where legal texts expressly provide so.

However, administrative justice has the advantage of being less expensive than civil and criminal justice. Legal assistance and representation are not mandatory in a number of actions, notably in the most important one, *i.e.* the *recours pour excès de pouvoir* (judicial review of administrative action) (see below) although, in practice, the complexity of administrative law makes it indispensable. Moreover, costs of administrative justice have always been less than those of ordinary justice.

(C) SOURCES OF ADMINISTRATIVE PROCEDURE

Whereas the rules of civil and criminal procedure were codified early on, those governing administrative procedure are

---

[16] For instance, the judge fixes the length of the investigation phase; he sets out the time-limits within which written arguments have to be submitted and he may order the administration to disclose evidence, etc.

found in diverse and scattered texts which were collated in an artificial *Code administratif* in the twentieth century. However these texts govern only part of administrative procedure and, quite often, they simply establish rules originating from the decisions of the courts.

Since 1958, Parliament has had no specific powers to create rules of administrative procedure. As a result of the distribution of legislative powers between Parliament and the Government, as provided for by articles 34 and 37 of the 1958 Constitution (see Chapter Two, above), the main reforms of administrative procedure have been enacted under the *pouvoir réglementaire*.[17]

Another source of law is to be found in the general rules of procedure established by case-law where texts were non-existent. Some of these have been ranked as *principes généraux du droit* (see Chapter Two, above) — which may be amended only by an Act of Parliament[18] — but the majority of them are *règles supplétives* (see Chapter One, above). By contrast, these may be amended or abolished by means of *règlements*.

(D) ADMINISTRATIVE COURSES OF ACTION

Administrative courses of action are more limited than those of civil procedure. The plaintiff may bring an action to court within a pre-existing and strict framework only. This may explain why their classification is more formal in administrative procedural law than in civil law.

Administrative courses of action may be classified according to the powers of the judge or the nature of the issue in question. The first classification[19] distinguishes between the following four types of actions:

— the *recours* (or *contentieux*) *de pleine juridiction* for which the court has full jurisdiction. This means that it may not

---

[17] This is the case, for instance, with the status of the *conseillers d'Etat*, the rules on time-limits, appeals, etc. However, new courts may be created only by an Act of Parliament (*e.g.* the administrative Courts of Appeal were created by the 1987 Act).

[18] For instance, the right to bring an application for judicial review of administrative action or under the protection of *droits de la défense* (rights of the defence or — for the purists — natural justice or due process of law) belong to this category of rules.

[19] Established by L. Aucoc (1878) and E. Lafferrière (1896).

only annul but also amend administrative acts and above all award damages. Actions for damages, actions in contractual matters, actions in fiscal matters and actions to have an election declared invalid, fall under this heading.

— the *recours* (or *contentieux*) *en annulation*, the only example[20] of which is the *recours pour excès de pouvoir*, by which the plaintiff seeks the annulment of an administrative act on the grounds of illegality. The powers of the court are then limited to the annulment of the act challenged.

— the *recours* (or *contentieux*) *en interprétation et appréciation de légalité* (action for interpretation and review of legality) by which an ordinary court requests, by means of a *question préjudicielle* (preliminary reference), the administrative judge to interpret an administrative act in order to explain its legal meaning and significance, or to rule on its validity.[21]

— the *contentieux de la répression* for which the administrative court has criminal jurisdiction and may, at the request of the administration, impose a fine on an individual citizen in relation to any damage caused to public roads, railways and inland waterways, such offence being known as *contravention de grande voirie*.

Following criticism of this classification on the ground that it was unscientific, L. Duguit (1911), G. Jèze (1909) and M. Waline (1935) advocated a classification based on the nature of the issue in question, thus making a distinction between:

— the *recours* (or *contentieux*) *objectif* (also called *contentieux de la légalité*) where the issue in question is the violation of a rule of law of general application (*droit objectif*). The best examples of this category are the *recours pour excès de pouvoir* and the *recours en appréciation de légalité*.

— and the *recours* (or *contentieux*) *subjectif* where the issue in question is the violation of a specific right of the plaintiff (*droit subjectif*). Actions for damages and actions in

---

[20] The *recours en cassation* — which is usually included in this category — is in reality an appeal against an administrative court's decision and not an action against an administrative act.

[21] It may be noted that such a course of action is very similar to the reference for preliminary ruling under article 177 of the Treaty of Rome.

contractual matters are typical examples of this second category.

Although both classifications are useful, their role should not be overestimated, the main distinction being that between the *recours pour excès de pouvoir* and other actions.

The *recours pour excès de pouvoir* is certainly the most familiar, the most important and the most original course of action under French administrative law. It was also essentially the creation of the *Conseil d'Etat* before being enshrined in legislation. For all these reasons, particular attention will be given to this action.

The *recours pour excès de pouvoir*

As mentioned above, this is an action by which an individual citizen requests the administrative judge to examine whether an administrative act complies with rules and laws of general application and, in the event that it does not, to declare it null and void. This principle applies to all administrative measures, whether they apply unilaterally to individuals or are administrative contracts or regulatory measures. The *recours pour excès de pouvoir* is therefore founded on the violation of the fundamental *principe de légalité* according to which the administration must be subject to the *loi* or *légalité* in the English sense of Rule of Law.[22]

It constitutes the most efficient protection for individual citizens against unlawful administrative acts and is a *recours de droit commun* in the sense that it is always available even if no text provides so.[23]

However, assuming that the litigation concerned falls within the jurisdiction of the administrative court, a number of *conditions de recevabilité* (conditions for admissibility) must be met before the judge may proceed with an examination of the grounds of the action.

---

[22] Such a definition based on the broad sense of the word *"légalité"* (see Chap. Two, above) has been criticised by Ch. Eisenmann who considered that, under this principle, the administration was subject to *lois* understood in the narrow sense as Acts of Parliaments; see *Le droit administratif et le principe de légalité*: [1957] E.D.C.E. 25.

[23] In its decision *Dame Lamotte* of February 17, 1950: [1957] Rec. Lebon 110, the *Conseil d'Etat* ruled that this action for annulment may be excluded only by express provision of an Act of Parliament.

Conditions for admissibility

Conditions for admissibility relate to the nature of reviewable acts, to the *locus standi* of the plaintiff, to the absence of any *action parallèle* (parallel action) and to time-limits.

Administrative courts' powers of judicial review require the existence of an *"acte administratif faisant grief"* (an administrative act causing prejudice), *i.e.* administrative measures which emanate from administrative authorities — including central government authorities and even the Head of State — and which impose a change of legal situation on a citizen. Such a notion covers not only measures of general application — the so-called *actes réglementaires* — but also those which apply to a single individual citizen, known as *actes individuels*, or to a group of individuals, known as *actes collectifs*. Moreover, case-law has extended this notion to include silence on the part of the administration in the face of a citizen's request, which constitutes, after four months, an implied rejection of that request. Judicial review is also admissible against decisions emanating from private bodies in charge of the administration of a public service. However, not all administrative actions are open to judicial review. Acts emanating from foreign authorities or from judicial authorities, and all parliamentary action — notably statutes — may not be subject to judicial review. Similarly, administrative courts have no jurisdiction to review the so-called *actes de gouvernement* (acts of State) which are acts regarding international relations or the relations between the Government and Parliament. Also, administrative measures solely concerning the internal organisation of the administration, known as *mesures d'ordre intérieur*, are regarded as non-reviewable. Finally, because reviewable acts are *actes unilatéraux*, in that they impose obligations upon citizens without their consent, administrative contracts are also excluded from this category.[24]

As a general principle of French procedural law, the plaintiff must demonstrate that the measure challenged has caused him a prejudice, in other words that he has some personal interest in the proceedings. Although reluctant to admit an *actio popularis*, which would allow every citizen to challenge any administrative measure and would lead to abuse, the *Conseil d'Etat* has adopted

---

[24] The annulment of an administrative contract may therefore be obtained only by means of a *recours de pleine juridiction*. However, according to the doctrine of the *acte détachable*, any act or measure which can be separated from the contract may be subject to judicial review.

a liberal approach with respect to the notion of *"intérêt à agir"*. This interest may be of a purely "moral" nature, as in the decision *Société des amis de l'Ecole Polytechnique* (C.E., July 13, 1948: [1948] Rec. Lebon 330) in which *alumni* students were held to be entitled to challenge appointment decisions which were likely to affect the prestige of their former school. This interest must also be "personal" in the sense that the plaintiff must be individually and directly concerned by the decision challenged. For instance, a citizen may attack a decision refusing planning permission to himself. However, the notion of individual concern has been widely interpreted by administrative courts. Users of a public service, as in *Syndicat du quartier Croix de Seguey-Tivoli*[25] or local taxpayers, as in *Casanova*,[26] are entitled to bring an action for annulment against decisions affecting the operation of the service, or decisions having repercussions on the finances of a local authority.[27] Similarly, a voter may challenge a measure relating to elections, such as that modifying electoral constituencies as in *Chabot*.[28] However, a "collective" interest will also suffice, thus allowing a "legal" person (such as a trade union, an association, etc.) to bring an action for annulment either against a measure of general application or a decision applying to a single individual affecting the general interests of the group.

As with any administrative litigious action, judicial review is available only within a set time-limit, known as *délai de recours*, at the expiry of which the action is no longer admissible. The plaintiff must take action within two months from the date when the challenged decision is either published (in the case of a decision of general application or applying to a group of individuals), or notified to the plaintiff (in the case of a decision applying to a single individual). In the absence of an express decision, this period of two months runs after four months of silence by the administration.

Where another course of action is as effective and satisfactory as the *recours pour excès de pouvoir*, the latter will be declared inadmissible. This negative requirement, which applies only to

---

[25] (C.E.), December 21, 1906: [1906] Rec. Lebon 962.
[26] (C.E.), March 29, 1901: [1901] Rec. Lebon 333.
[27] However, in *Dufour* (C.E.), February 13, 1930: [1930] Rec. Lebon 176, the *Conseil d'Etat* dismissed an application made by a taxpayer against a national tax decision. Indeed, this would have led to an *actio popularis*.
[28] (C.E.), August 7, 1903: [1903] Rec. Lebon 619.

proceedings to annul, is known as *"exception de recours parallel"* (absence of a parallel action). Such a parallel action must be a *recours juridictionnel* (action in court) — as opposed to a *recours administratif* (action brought to the administration itself) — and must enable the plaintiff to seek annulment of the measure challenged. Consequently, in principle, a *recours de pleine juridiction* makes the action for annulment inadmissible.[29] Similarly, an action brought before a specialised administrative court would rule out the action for annulment brought before a court of general jurisdiction.[30] However, the *recours pour excès de pouvoir* remains available if annulment cannot be obtained by means of a parallel action, in which case the principle of the *acte détachable* (see footnote 124) applies.

Grounds for annulment

Called *"cas d'ouverture"* or *"moyens d'annulation"*, there are four grounds for annulment: *incompétence* (lack of competence), *vice de forme* (procedural irregularity or impropriety), *détournement de pouvoir* (misuse of powers) and *violation de la loi* (infringement of the law).[31]

Historically, these grounds for annulment have not developed simultaneously but successively. Originally, the action for annulment was admissible only on the basis of lack of competence. This was actually designated by the Act of October 7–13, 1790 as a *"réclamation[32] d'incompétence"* which could

---

[29] In the *Lafage* decision (C.E.), March 8, 1912: [1912] Rec. Lebon 348 however, the *Conseil d'Etat* declared admissible an action for annulment brought by a civil servant — in lieu of an action for damages — against the refusal by the administration to pay him a sum of money which he pretended to be entitled to by virtue of a regulation. Although an action for damages would have been the relevant action to take, the action for annulment was declared admissible since the plaintiff opted exclusively for the annulment of the administration's refusal as being in contradiction with the regulation. Had the financial benefit been the object of a contract — for instance between the administration and a temporary agent — an action for annulment would have been declared inadmissible, as in *Boyer* (C.E.), May 14, 1937: [1932] Rec. Lebon 500 and *Lozachmeur* ((C.E.), February 1, 1946: [1946] Rec. Lebon 32).

[30] For instance, see the decision in *Dame Martin* (C.E.), December 12, 1952 [1951] Rec. Lebon 570, where a parallel action brought before a Social Security Court made the action for annulment inadmissible.

[31] It should be noted that the grounds for annulment provided for by article 173 of the Treaty of Rome have been drawn directly from French administrative law.

[32] The term *"réclamation"* has the more usual meaning of "protest" or "complaint", rather than the legal meaning of "action" or "claim."

only be brought before the "King, head of the general Administration". *Incompétence* is equivalent to the English doctrine of substantive *ultra vires*. Where an administrative authority has adopted a measure, despite lacking the legal authority to do so, the measure in question will be annulled on the ground of lack of competence. This is the most serious ground for annulment since the notion of competence lies at the heart of public law. Indeed, the powers of administrative authorities are strictly defined by law. Consequently, this ground for annulment may be raised by the judge on his own motion.[33] Lack of competence may be *"ratione materiae"* (lack of competence regarding the subject-matter), *"ratione loci"* (an administrative authority taking a measure outside its territorial jurisdiction), or *"ratione temporis"* (lack of competence regarding the time when the measure was taken).

Vice de forme, which corresponds to the English notion of procedural *ultra vires*, emerged as a ground for annulment soon after that of lack of competence. Any administrative authority, when taking administrative measures, must comply with formal rules and follow the correct procedures. These formal and procedural requirements constitute protection for citizens' rights, but their observance should not lead to some formalism which would paralyse administrative action. This is why the *Conseil d'Etat* has elaborated a body of case-law distinguishing between *formalités substantielles*, the infringement of which entails annulment of an administrative measure, and *formalités accessoires* which have no impact on the measure itself.

Détournement de pouvoir was made available to citizens in 1840. As with article 173 of the Treaty of Rome, this means the use of a power by an administrative authority for purposes other than those for which it was originally granted by law. This challenge enables the administrative judge to examine the content of the administrative measure itself and, in particular, the subjective motives and intentions which prompted the administrative agent to take this measure. There is misuse of powers where, for instance, the administrative measure in question has not been taken in the general interest,[34] or where a measure has been taken for a purpose other than that stipulated

---

[33] See *Couvenhes* (C.E.), July 16, 1955: [1955] Rec. Lebon 239.
[34] See *Dlle Rault* (C.E.), March 14, 1934: [1934] Rec. Lebon 337, where regulations issued by the mayor of a town prohibited the holding of balls in all establishments but appeared not to apply to his own inn.

by a statute.[35] The misuse of an administrative procedure, the so-called *détournement de procédure*, also constitutes a misuse of power in the sense that an administrative authority uses an unsuitable but more convenient legal procedure to achieve a specific objective.[36]

Finally, while simplifying the *recours pour excès de pouvoir*, the *décret* of November 2, 1864 created a new ground for annulment, the *violation de la loi*. This is a complementary ground for annulment as it covers illegalities which cannot be sanctioned under one of the previous grounds. Indeed, the term "*loi*" must be understood here in its wide sense (see Chapter Two, above), thus making this ground for annulment the most effective protection of the *principe de légalité*. Furthermore, as the texts are imprecise, administrative judges have extended the applicable scope of this ground, thus permitting the sanction not only of mere infringements of the law but also *erreurs de droit et de fait* (legal and factual errors) made by the administration. The action of the administration may constitute a direct infringement of the law, as in the case of a *préfet* who dismissed a temporary nurse from a medical institution while she was pregnant, thus violating the general principle of law for the protection of pregnant women — as provided for in article L 122–25–2 *C.Trav.* — *Dame Peynet.*[37] In practice, such infringements of the law cover a variety of situations, including a breach of a constitutional provision, *G.I.S.T.I.*,[38] or even a breach of an international treaty, as in *C.G.T.*;[39] or a refusal by the administration to apply the law *Sociéte immobilière d'économie mixte de la ville de Paris.*[40] All these cases are examples of a direct infringement of the law where

---

[35] See *Beaugé* (C.E.), July 4, 1924: [1924] Rec. Lebon 641, where a mayor misused his police powers; *i.e.* rather than using his authority to maintain order, he used them to increase the financial resources of his town, by making an order prohibiting dressing and undressing on the beach and thus compelling bathers to pay for the use of the municipal changing rooms installed on the beach.

[36] See *Société Frampar* (C.E.), June 24, 1960: [1960] Rec. Lebon 412, where the *Conseil d'Etat* ruled that a *préfet*, who, for reasons of public order wanted to prevent, by means of seizure, the distribution of a newspaper, could not use the procedure of seizure provided for in article 10 of the *Code d'instruction criminelle*, the purpose of which was to repress criminal offences against national security.

[37] (C.E.), June 8, 1973; [1973] Rec. Lebon 406.

[38] (C.E.), December 8, 1978: [1978] Rec. Lebon 493.

[39] (C.E.), November 24, 1978: [1978] Rec. Lebon 461.

[40] (C.E.), July 1, 1988: [1988] Rec. Lebon 274.

the object of the administrative measure was scrutinised by the judge. However, the judge may also examine the legal and factual motives underlying the measure in question, rather than its content, and examine whether or not the administration has made an *erreur de droit* by applying the law wrongly or has made an *erreur de fait* by applying the law to wrong or inaccurate facts. An *erreur de droit* is mostly the result of a misinterpretation of the law[41] but may also arise where a measure is based on a provision which is not applicable to the situation in question.[42]

For a long time, the *Conseil d'Etat* considered that it was only competent to examine legal issues and not factual errors of the administration. However, a wrong appreciation of the facts leads inevitably to a wrong application of the law. It was only at the turn of this century that the *Conseil d'Etat* admitted that it was competent to examine the *exactitude matérielle des faits* (accuracy of the facts) upon which the administrative measure is based.[43] For instance, in its decision *Trépont*,[44] the *Conseil d'Etat* declared null and void the decision to dismiss a *préfet* allegedly "at his own request", where the person concerned had made no such request. In this case, although the Government had discretionary powers to take such a decision, it could not base it on facts which were non-existent. Furthermore, the *Conseil d'Etat* ruled in *Gomel*[45] that it was competent to examine the so-called *qualification juridique des faits* (legal classification of facts) according to which an administrative judge examines whether the facts, which actually occurred, justify the decision taken. In the *Gomel* case the *préfet de la Seine* refused to grant planning permission on Beauvau Square on the grounds that the project in question would affect the monumental character of this square. The issue was not whether the square existed or not (*matérialité des faits*) but rather, whether

---

[41] See *Ministre des affaires sociales v. Hess* (C.E.), May 27, 1988: [1988] Rec. Lebon 212, where a pharmacist was compelled by a ministerial decision to cease the works for the improvement of his practice. This decision was taken on the incorrect grounds that the authorisation for such works was subject to an amendment of his licence to practice.

[42] See *S.C.I. Résidence Neptune* (C.E), February 19, 1975: [1975] Rec. Lebon 131, where the administration's refusal to extend planning permission was based on a *plan d'ocupation des sols* (planning programme) which had not yet been published.

[43] See notably *Camino* (C.E.), January 14, 1916: [1916] Rec. Lebon 15.

[44] (C.E.), January 20, 1922: [1922] Rec. Lebon 65.

[45] (C.E.), April 4, 1914: [1914] Rec. Lebon 488.

it could be regarded as having the character of monument within the meaning of the law relating to town-planning (*qualification juridique des faits*).

(E) ADMINISTRATIVE PROCEEDINGS

(1) The rule of the *décision préalable*

Generally, in civil proceedings and, in certain cases, in criminal proceedings, a plaintiff may summon the defendant to appear in court without having previously informed him of his intentions.

However, as a result of the principle of *décision préalable*, any proceedings before an administrative court must be brought against a decision which has already been taken by the administration.

This rule applies automatically in an action for annulment but has more significance in a *recours de pleine juridiction*. In the latter court action, the plaintiff may institute proceedings in court only after his request to the administrative authority has been rejected. For instance, before bringing an action for damages in court the plaintiff must obtain from the administration a decision either refusing to pay damages or awarding damages which he deems to be inadequate. Because the cause of the prejudice is a material fact and not a legal act, the claim for damages must take the form of a complaint directed against this administrative decision.

The requirement of a *décision préalable* is laid down in article 40 of the *ordonnance* of July 31, 1945 — relating to the *Conseil d'Etat* — and in article 1 of the *décret* of January 11, 1965[46] — relating to time-limits in administrative proceedings. It originates from the doctrine of the last century of the *"ministre-juge"*, according to which actions by an aggrieved citizen had to be brought first to the relevant minister and then, on appeal against the minister's decision, to the *Conseil d'Etat*. It was only in 1889 in the *Cadot* decision, that the *Conseil d'Etat* ruled that administrative proceedings could be directly instituted before it, thus making itself *juge de droit commun* in lieu of the minister.

---

[46] "*Sauf en matière de travaux publics, la juridiction administrative ne peut être saisie que par voie de recours formé contre une décision, ...*" ("Except in matters relating to public works, action may be brought to administrative courts only by way of proceedings instituted against a decision, ...").

Nowadays, this rule is justified on the grounds that it gives the administration the opportunity to explain its position in the absence of an express decision and may facilitate conciliation between the administration and the citizen, thus leading to a swift settlement and preventing a court action.

(2) Commencement of the proceedings

Administrative proceedings are initiated by the plaintiff's *requête* (application) lodged with the court in a written form.[47] The document in question is called a *"mémoire introductif d'instance"*.

In order to be admissible, the application must be drafted in French.[48] In his application, having indicated the names and domicile of the parties, the plaintiff must present the facts of the case, his legal arguments and his final submissions. In general, the plaintiff may lodge a summary application and then a more detailed presentation of his arguments. Finally, the application must be signed by the appointed lawyer where legal representation is mandatory, or by the applicant himself where it is not.[49] The application must also be accompanied by the decision challenged (or proof of the implied decision) in accordance with the principle of *décision préalable* discussed above (article 4 of the *ord.* of 1945 cited above).

The application must be lodged within two months of the publication of the decision if it is a *règlement*, or of the notification to the plaintiff, in the case of decisions addressed to individuals. In the case of an implied decision, the time-limit runs from the end of the four month silence by the administration.[50]

Applications brought before the *Conseil d'Etat* must be deposited at its *greffe (secrétariat du Contentieux, Conseil*

---

[47] Oral applications or applications by telephone are not admissible. However, the latter may be declared admissible provided they are confirmed in writing and that they contain all the necessary elements.

[48] See *Quillevère* (C.E. Sect.), November 22, 1985: [1985] Rec. Lebon 333, which confirms this general principle of procedure laid down by King François I in the 1539 *Ordonnance de Villers-Cotterêt*.

[49] Until 1977, all applications were subject to a *droit de timbre* (stamp duty) which, until 1968 was a condition for admissibility. This was finally abolished by the Act of December 30, 1977 which laid down the principle of gratuitous justice.

[50] There are a few exceptional time-limits: *e.g.* one year to challenge the changing of a name, four months to challenge the creation of a trade union, five days to challenge the elections of local councillors, etc.

d'Etat, Place du Palais Royal, Paris). Applications relating to direct taxes, elections and *contraventions de grande voirie* (see above), can be sent to the *préfecture* or *sous-préfecture* of the plaintiff's domicile. With respect to applications lodged with a *tribunal administratif,* they must be deposited at the *greffe* of the court or one of its subsidiary offices.

Representation by a lawyer is the normal rule. In the *Conseil d'Etat,* this lawyer is an *avocat au Conseil d'Etat.* In the *tribunaux administratifs* and the *cours administratives d'appel,* the parties may be represented by an *avocat au Conseil d'Etat,* an *avocat,* or an *avoué près les cours d'appel* (see Chapter Four, above). However, in order to reduce the legal costs, legal representation has been made optional in a number of cases, notably in a *recours pour excès de pouvoir.*

(3) Measures prior to the preparation of a case

The *sursis à exécution*

In principle, proceedings instituted in an administrative court have no suspensive effect. Indeed the administrative decision remains enforceable. This avoids administrative action being paralysed by ill-founded actions. However, such a prerogative in the hands of the administration could lead to serious consequences which the court might no longer be able to remedy.

The purpose of the *sursis à exécution* (stay of execution) is precisely to prevent such an event from occurring. The plaintiff affected by a decision may request the administrative judge to order the administration to refrain from implementing the decision in question until the court has made a ruling.

Although the *Conseil d'Etat* was vested with such a power by article 48 of the *décret* of July 21, 1945, very strict conditions were imposed. This procedure is only allowed where the decision challenged has caused serious harm which would prove difficult to remedy (such as in *Mouvement social français des Croix de feu.*[51]) Moreover, the *Conseil d'Etat* will only grant a stay of execution if the arguments of the plaintiff appear to be well founded; *Chambre syndicale des constructeurs de moteurs d'avions.*[52]

The *décret* of September 30, 1953 prohibited the *tribunaux administratifs* from granting a stay of execution of decisions concerning public policy. Therefore, a stay of execution had to

---

[51] (C.E.), November 27, 1936: [1936] Rec. Lebon 1039.
[52] (C.E.), November 12, 1938: [1938] Rec. Lebon 840.

be requested from the *Conseil d'Etat* even if the case fell within the competence of a *tribunal administratif* (for example *Ferrandiz Gil Ortega*.[53] However, the *tribunaux administratifs* were eventually authorised to grant stays of execution, first by a *décret* of 1980, against decisions of public policy in connection with entry and residence of foreign nationals in France, and then by a *décret* of 1983, against all decisions of public policy.

The *référé administratif*

For a long time the procedure of *référé*, available in civil procedure (as seen above), was unknown in administrative procedure. It was only in 1945 that the President of the *Section du contentieux* (Judicial Division) of the *Conseil d'Etat*, and in 1955 the *tribunaux administratifs* were permitted to use this procedure.

By this special procedure, on application by the plaintiff, the administrative judge may order the appointment of an expert or take any "useful measure" for the investigation, *i.e.* in order to ascertain the facts in dispute. In these two cases the plaintiff need not prove urgency but simply the usefulness of the requested judicial measure. On the other hand, where the judge is requested to order provisional remedies, urgency must be established. In such a case it is sufficient to demonstrate that the distortion or disappearance of facts which have caused the harm may result in the impossibility of remedying it. For instance, in the *Bourma* case,[54] the court considered that it was urgent to establish the condition of perishable goods retained by customs officers.

Furthermore, the administrative judge may use the procedure of *référé-provision* which was introduced into administrative procedure by the *décret* of September 2, 1988. In this case he may, like judges of civil courts, grant a creditor who is involved in proceedings before the court, a provision, *i.e.* amount provisionally allocated (such as damages in a case of liability or payment of salary in a case of redundancy) when the obligation of the other party is indisputable.

The *constat d'urgence*

This is a procedure whereby the judge, at the request of the plaintiff and in the case of urgency, may order measures to be taken to determine and ascertain the facts of the case which are likely to disappear before the investigation is initiated.

---

[53] (C.E. Ass.), July 23, 1974: [1974] Rec. Lebon 447.
[54] (T.A. Algier), March 26, 1957: [1957] Rec. Lebon 739.

(4) Preparation of the case: the *instruction*

Once the application is received by the court it is numbered and, in the *Conseil d'Etat*, allocated by the President of the Judicial Division to one of the *sous-sections* (sections). A *juge rapporteur* and a *commissaire du gouvernement* (see Chapter Three, above) are then appointed from amongst the members of the section.

The task of the *rapporteur* is to examine the application, to organise the instruction of the case, *i.e.* to decide what measures of investigation to take, and to order the disclosure of documents. In this respect his role is very similar to that of the *juge de la mise en état* in civil procedure (see above).

The application is served on the defendant who presents his observations in a *mémoire* which will be made available to the plaintiff for examination. The latter may then reply to the observations of the defendant in a *mémoire en réplique* (reply). The exchange of arguments usually ends when the administration rejoins with further comments in a *mémoire en duplique*.

These submissions must be deposited at the court within the time-limits fixed by the judge. Failure by the parties to submit their arguments within these time-limits does not normally result in nullity unless a *mise en demeure* (injunction) is sent to the defaulting party or the instruction has been closed. If the *mise en demeure* has no effect, the judge draws the conclusion that the defaulting plaintiff has withdrawn or that the defaulting defendant has agreed with the facts presented in the application, and may make his decision accordingly. However the procedure of *mise en demeure* is only used by the judge in cases where the bad faith of the parties is clear. More usually, the judge uses his power to condemn dilatory manoeuvres — such as in the *Ledoux* case where the plaintiff requested legal aid and representation, which he was entitled to, only after he was informed of the date of the hearing (C.E., July 13, 1968).

By fixing time-limits within which the parties must submit their observations and comment upon those of the opponent, the judge has the power to regulate the pace of the instruction.

When the *juge rapporteur* believes that the case is ready for trial he proceeds to re-examine the file and draft a report in which he sets out the facts, summarises the arguments of the parties and suggests a solution in the light of the relevant law. Finally, he draws up a *projet d'arrêt* (draft judgment). Once completed, the report is transmitted to the President of the section in charge of the case and together with the draft judgment, examined and discussed by the section in a session called the *"séance d'instruction"*. When the discussion is concluded, the section will either accept the *rapporteur*'s opinion or, more rarely in practice, ask him to revise his report. If the report is accepted it is handed over to the member of the section acting as *commissaire du gouvernement*.

(5) The trial phase

Once the case is put on the list for the *séance de jugement* (trial) — either by the President of the *tribunal administratif*, or the *cour administrative d'appel*, or the section of the *Conseil d'Etat* — the parties are informed of the date of the hearing.

Hearings of the *Conseil d'Etat* and other administrative courts are in principle open to the public except in fiscal and disciplinary matters.

After a case is called to the court[55] the *rapporteur* reads his report. The lawyers of the parties may present oral arguments provided that they add nothing to their written submissions. Except in the *Conseil d'Etat*, the parties themselves may submit observations.

However, the reading of his opinion by the *commissaire du gouvernment* is the most important moment of the hearing. His role is to propose to the court a completely independent solution to the case in the light of the law. Opinions of the *commissaire du gouvernement* enjoy great authority and have often influenced the courts. The most important are published and facilitate an understanding of the significance of judgments.

After the reading of the opinion of the *commissaire du gouvernement*, the case is remitted for *déliberation* and the next case is called.

(6) Judgments

The making of judgments
After the conclusion of the hearing, the court sits *en délibéré* (or *en audience privée*) in order to discuss the case. Sometimes, the *déliberations* may take place *"sur le siège"*, *i.e. sotto voce*

---

[55] More than one case is usually called during the same *séance de jugement* and these are heard successively until the case list is concluded.

during the sitting. They always take place in private and all members of the court may take part in them. The *commissaire du gouverment* may not take part in the vote, although he is present during the discussion. The decision of the court is then drafted by the *rapporteur* and read publicly at a subsequent hearing.

The judgment — which is called *arrêt* when given by the *Conseil d'Etat* and a *cour administrative d'appel*, or *jugement* when delivered by a *tribunal administratif* — is in a very bald and concise form. It uniformly consists of: the *visas* ("*vu*") — in which the court refers to the documents underlying its decision; the *motifs* or *considérants* ("*considérant*"), *i.e.* the grounds for the decision; the *dispositif* ([the court] "*décide*") — which contains the solution to the case; and finally, the *formule exécutoire* (executory formula), whereby the court designates the public authorities responsible for the enforcement of the judgment.

Enforcement of judgments

The enforcement of judgments depends very much on the goodwill of the administration since there is no coercive means of obliging the administration to comply with a decision of an administrative court. Judicial decisions are usually obeyed by the administration. However, there have been cases where the administration refused to comply with a judgment — in particular in proceedings for annulment, thus forcing the original plaintiff to seek damages.

A series of reforms initiated in 1963 attempted to remedy this problem. First, the minister concerned may ask the *Conseil d'Etat* to explain the implications of the decision and how it should be enforced. Secondly, the *Conseil d'Etat* may draw the attention of the administration to the implications of the decision. Thirdly, the plaintiff may himself, within three months following the judgment, report to the *section des rapports et des études* (Report and Research Division) of the *Conseil* any difficulty of enforcement. Furthermore, the Act of July 16, 1980, supplemented by the *décret* of May 12, 1981, introduced two important means of enforcing judgments against the administration. Where the administration has been declared liable to pay damages, payment must be made within four months. Furthermore the *Conseil d'Etat* may, by means of an *astreinte*, order the administration to pay a certain sum of money for each day of non-compliance with the original judgment. Such a remedy is used to ensure the enforcement of judgments awarding damages as well as judgments repealing illegal administrative decisions following an action for annulment. The *astreinte* may be requested by the original plaintiff only after six months of non-compliance, or immediately if the court has ordered an emergency measure, notably a stay of execution. The introduction of this remedy constitutes an important innovation in administrative procedure although the *Conseil d'Etat* has used it with moderation within the last 10 years.

(7)   *Voies de recours*

As in civil and criminal procedures (see above), a distinction in appeals is made between the *voies de réformation,* such as the *appel* and the *recours en cassation,* and the *voies de rétractation* namely the *opposition,* the *tierce opposition,* the *recours en révision,* and the *recours en rectification d'erreur matérielle.*

The *appel*
All decisions of the *tribunaux administratifs* may be challenged by means of an *appel* before either the *Conseil d'Etat* or, since the 1987 Act, the *cours administratives d'appel.* This appeal is only available to the parties within a time-limit of two months from the day the judgment was served. Unlike the *appel* in civil procedure, the administrative *appel* has no suspensive effect unless the court has ordered a stay of execution of the judgment.

Because the *appel* has an *effet dévolutif,* the appeal judge has the same powers as the judge of first instance and may re-examine the case.

If the *tribunal administratif* has not ruled on the merits of the case, because of its incompetence to do so, the appeal judge may do so, having repealed the decision of lack of competence, provided the consent of the appellant is given and the case is ready for trial. This is the power of *évocation* of the appeal judge. By this procedure the case is tried only once and more swiftly than if it was remitted to a *tribunal administratif.*

The *recours en cassation*
As in civil or criminal procedures, a *recours en cassation* is available. This may be lodged with the *Conseil d'Etat* against the

judgment of a lower administrative court[56] on the grounds that the judgment does not comply with the law.

Only judgments given *en dernier ressort* may be subject to an appeal by way of *cassation*. Therefore, where an *appel* is still available, or where a party negligently fails to use it within the time-limit, the *recours en cassation* is deemed to be inadmissible. Moreover, default judgments, which are subject to an appeal by means of *opposition*, may be brought in *cassation* only after the expiry of the time-limit for the *opposition*.

The *recours en cassation* may be lodged by either party within a period of two months after the judgment passed *en dernier ressort*. Legal representation by an *avocat au Conseil* has been mandatory since 1953.

In order to prevent an undue increase in the number of appeals by way of *cassation* which would delay the proceedings, article 11 of the 1987 Act created a filtering procedure for admissibility called *"procédure préalable d'admission"*. For this purpose a *commission d'admission des pourvois en cassation*, created within the *Conseil d'Etat*, may reject any appeal which is deemed to be inadmissible or which is not founded on serious grounds. Its decisions may be challenged only by means of a *recours en révision* or a *recours en rectification d'erreur matérielle*.

In principle the appeal in *cassation* has no suspensive effect unless a stay of execution of the challenged judgment has been granted by the *Conseil d'Etat*.

The *juge de cassation* only examines issues of law, and only those which have been brought to the attention of the judge of the lower court. Therefore, new arguments put forward by the parties have always been declared inadmissible[57] unless they are based on the irregularity of the decision challenged or on *moyens d'ordre public* (grounds of public policy).

Except for misuse of powers, all the grounds of a *recours en cassation* are identical to those of the *recours pour excès de*

---

[56] The *recours en cassation* lies against judicial decisions only and not against decisions made by non-judicial administrative bodies although this distinction is sometimes difficult to make. For instance, in *L'Etang* July 12, 1969: [1969] Rec. Lebon 388, the *Conseil d'Etat* ruled that the decisions of the *Conseil supérieure de la Magistrature* sitting as a disciplinary body may be subject to a *recours en cassation*. Moreover, the Act of December 31, 1987 has extended the scope of application of the appeal by way of *cassation* to judgments of the *cours administratives d'appel*.

[57] See *Viallat et fils* (C.E.), June 27, 1919: [1919] Rec. Lebon 561.

pouvoir, namely lack of competence of the lower court, procedural irregularities and infringement of the law.

Where the appeal has passed through the procedure of admissibility the *Conseil d'Etat* may either reject it and declare that the judgment challenged complies with the law or, after considering it to be well-founded, quash the judgment. In the latter case, the *Conseil d'Etat* will remit the case to a competent lower court but it may also decide the case itself if the case is *"en état"*, *i.e.* ready to be examined on the merits.

The *opposition*

The procedure of *opposition* (an application to set aside a decision) has been available in the *Conseil d'Etat* since 1806 and was established through a constant line of decisions in the old *conseils de préfecture* although no text provided for this. Furthermore, the *Conseil d'Etat* ruled in its decisions *Caubet*[58] and *Desseaux*[59] that *opposition* was a general rule of procedure applicable in all courts even if there was no text to this effect. However, an appeal by means of *opposition* is only available against a default judgment when no legal provision expressly excludes it, as in the case of default judgments of the *tribunaux administratifs* since 1959.[60] On the other hand, default judgments of the *cours administratives d'appel* may be subject to *opposition* (article 31 of *décret* of May 9, 1988).

Such an appeal must be lodged within two months from notification of the default judgment.

The *tierce opposition*

The *tierce opposition* is intended to protect third parties from the effects of a judgment which they have not been party to or represented in, and which have effectively caused them prejudice.

The *Conseil d'Etat* has always regarded this appeal as being available even if this is not expressly provided,[61] notably, as in its

---

[58] (C.E. Ass.), June 9, 1939: [1939] Rec. Lebon 382.
[59] (C.E. Sect.), October 12, 1956: [1956] Rec. Lebon 364.
[60] Article 2 of the *décret* of April 10, 1959, incorporated in article R 223 of the *Code des tribunaux administratifs et cours administratives d'appel* (*C.T.A.*), provides that "judgments of the *tribunaux administratifs* may not be challenged by means of *opposition*" ("*Les jugements des tribunaux administratifs ne sont pas susceptibles d'opposition*").
[61] See *Franc* (C.E.), November 20, 1931: [1932], S. March 21.

decision in *Ruez*,[62] by referring directly to article 474 (now 585) of the Code of Civil Procedure. However, *tierce opposition* is made expressly available by articles R. 225 to 227 *C.T.A.* against judgments of the *tribunaux administratifs* and the *cours administratives d'appel*.

Tierce opposition is admissible against judgments following a *recours de pleine juridiction*[63] or a *recours pour excès de pouvoir*. With respect to the latter, the *Conseil d'Etat* ruled in *Boussage*[64] that the *tierce opposition* is admissible against judgments of annulment although an action for annulment is not, strictly speaking, a dispute between two parties.

Tierce opposition is not subject to any time-limit except in the case of judgments of *tribunaux administratifs* and *cours administratives d'appel*, where such an appeal must be lodged within two months from the day when the judgment was served on the parties.

If the *tierce opposition* is declared admissible the court will not re-examine the case in its entirety but only within the limits of the arguments of the new plaintiff. The challenged judgment is either confirmed or those parts of it which have caused prejudice to the plaintiff are set aside.

The *recours en révision*

This appeal, which resembles and has the same purpose as the *recours en révision* in civil procedure, is only available against decisions of the *Conseil d'Etat*.

The grounds of the *révision* are strictly defined in the *ordonnance* of July 31, 1945 (articles 75–77). Indeed, a *révision* may be lodged only in the following cases:

— where a decision has been made on the basis of false documents; or
— where a party has lost a case because he was unable to produce an essential document which has been retained by the opponent; or
— where the procedure followed was tainted with irregularities (*e.g.* irregular composition of the court, infringement of the rules concerning the publicity of the hearings, the parties were unable to present oral arguments, the *commissaire du gouvernement* failed to submit his opinion, etc.).

---

[62] (C.E. Sect.), June 2, 1933: [1933] Rec. Lebon 605.
[63] Except in electoral or income tax litigation.
[64] (C.E.), November 29, [1912] Rec. Lebon 1128.

The *recours en révision* is only available to those parties against whom the challenged judgment is made. It must be lodged via a lawyer within two months from the judgment.

The *recours en rectification d'erreur matérielle*

Because the *recours en révision* may only be instituted in limited cases, the administrative courts were encouraged to create on an ad hoc basis another *voie de rétractation*. A party to a judgment may apply for a *recours en rectification d'erreur matérielle* where he can demonstrate that an error of fact has had a prejudicial effect on the judgment, provided that this error has not been made by the applicant himself.

This appeal may only be lodged against judgments passed *en dernier ressort*. It is therefore unavailable in the *tribunaux administratifs* but can be applied for in the *cours administratives d'appel* (article 33 of the *décret* of May 9, 1988) and, of course, before the *Conseil d'Etat* (article 78 *Ord.* of July 31, 1945). However, it may not be lodged where the same remedy can be provided by a *recours en cassation*, such as in the case of a material error made by the judge himself.

Index

[All references are to page number]